Strange Days

Strange Days

The Adventures of a Grumpy Rock 'N' Roll Journalist in Los Angeles

Dean Goodman

OUTPOST BOOKS
MUNICH LOS ANGELES

Copyright © 2014 by Dean Goodman

All rights reserved, including the right to reproduce this book or portions thereof in any form whatsoever.
First printing
Manufactured in the United States of America

Cover photo courtesy of Sonja Quintero

Library of Congress Control Number 2014904518
ISBN 978-0-9894420-0-8
ISBN 978-0-9894420-1-5 (ebook)

Outpost Books
P.O. Box 6752
Burbank, CA 91510-6752

To those about to rock

and to the memory of Ray Manzarek, Davy Jones, Donald "Duck" Dunn, and Lou Reed, who were all alive when I started this book

*Don't be surprised if, right before your eyes,
you see someone you might know*

*More famous people stay right here in L.A.
than anywhere else in the world*

—Barry White, "L.A. My Kinda Place"

CONTENTS

Introduction	1
At Home with Johnny and June Carter Cash	15
In Defense of Mike Love	31
David Bowie: The Golden Years	57
Steve Cropper: Soul Sideman	75
Garth Brooks, Chris Gaines, & The Air Headed Reporter	87
Guns N' Roses: In Bed with Steven Adler	91
Ice-T Fought the Law	99
Phil Collins: No More Mr. Nice Guy	111
Queen: The Show Must Go On	121
Gene Simmons: Kiss My Ass	131
Strange Days Dog the Doors	147
Aerosmith: Wings Clipped	161
Ray Charles: Best Funeral Ever	175
Isaac Hayes: Bald and Beautiful	181
INXS: Flesh and Blood	189
Billy Idol: Internet Icon	203
Putting the "Sex" in Sex Pistols	211
John Cale, Doug Yule: Velvets Underground	215
Dancing with Iggy Pop	229

Sporty Spice: My Big Scoop	241
Some Kind of Conspiracy: The Ballad of Artimus Pyle	247
Michael Nesmith: Mystery Monkee	265
Permission Credits	281
Acknowledgements and Sourcing	283

INTRODUCTION

Kids from all over the world come to Los Angeles dreaming of stardom. I was one of them, but my expectations were modest since I am inherently lazy. After watching Oliver Stone's *Doors* movie four times, I quit my job in 1992 and flew out from New Zealand to Jim Morrison's old haunt of Venice Beach. The bohemian lifestyle grew old after a few weeks when I remembered that I'm not much of a beach person and am immensely bothered by sand. Nor am I able to sing, write music, or look like a Rock God.

Fortunately I already had four years under my belt as a financial journalist at Reuters, where I also covered politics, sport, and, occasionally, a mass murder or porn star. The company's Los Angeles outpost hired me part-time to help out on business news, and gratefully accepted my offer to write about pop music because no one else was doing it seriously. A veteran reporter usually covered the biggest event on the music calendar, the Grammy Awards, by watching the tape-delayed broadcast at home. He dined out for years on his infamous reference to the female pop trio Wilson Phillips as "he."

I had to explain to the wary record labels both who I was and what Reuters was. Peasants in Kazakhstan know the global news agency and its humble start delivering European stock quotes via carrier pigeon during the 1850s. But Americans were oblivious, and no one could say the name properly. Somebody once asked me if the company was named after the 1940 Edward G. Robinson movie *A Dispatch from Reuters*. Reuters (pronounced Roy-ters, not Rooters) was dwarfed in America by the Associated Press, the giant newspaper cooperative. Over and over I told the labels that my reports would reach thousands of media outlets around the world, a very efficient way for them to get publicity for their stars. "We're like AP," I said, "but better."

My first few stories—a reunion by the soporific rock band Foreigner, a book by Janis Joplin's sister, the grunge music fad—were hardly groundbreaking. But three helium-voiced rodents came to my rescue. The Chipmunks had also "reunited," for a country album with A-list country stars such as Garth Brooks and Billy Ray Cyrus. I interviewed their wranglers, Ross Bagdasarian Jr. and his wife Janice, and my story ran in the *Los Angeles Times* during the traditional post-Christmas lull when the short-staffed paper resorted to running wire copy from AP and Reuters. Everyone in town saw it, and I officially became a member of the Los Angeles rock 'n' roll media cognoscenti.

I still had to hustle, but the interviews, parties, rubber-chicken dinners, concerts, and movie premieres piled up. Less than a year earlier, I had been covering corporate takeovers, cricket, and central bank monetary policy in an obscure South Pacific nation. Now I was watching Keith Richards in concert, interviewing David Bowie, and attending a Rock and Roll Hall of Fame induction. The 1990s were the last hurrah of the music industry before Napster & Co. destroyed it, and I was lucky to feast on the scraps that fell from the table.

I made the best out of my clichéd fish-out-of-water existence in a city still shaken by the Rodney King riots that preceded my arrival by three months. The local economy was already reeling from the aerospace and real estate busts, and worse was to come with mudslides, fires, and the Northridge earthquake. My adopted hometown was considered the armpit of America, vividly summarized in the David Rieff book *Los Angeles: Capital of the Third World*.

As one of the few white people in Los Angeles without a car, I braved the rudimentary bus network alongside pensioners, bums, and the odd confused tourist. Friends were shocked that I took public transport. "How do you survive?" they asked, like I was some brave adventurer. Easy, I was just a 24-year-old kid doing what was necessary to live out my rock 'n' roll dreams and meet boldfaced names with whom I never thought I'd get to share a continent.

Black-tie events could be a hassle, though. Who wants to ride on the bus dressed like a penguin? One of those sartorial trips was to the Rock and Roll Hall of Fame dinner in 1993. Back when the annual event still had some prestige, despite the prescient tut-tutting of some of us, the New York–based jamboree ventured to Los Angeles for a night of firsts. The Doors were inducted, and the three surviving members played publicly for the first time in two decades as a relatively unknown Eddie Vedder stood in for Jim Morrison. The power rock trio Cream played for the first time since 1968. I stood on a table in the ballroom to watch Eric Clapton, Jack Bruce, and Ginger Baker banging out "Sunshine of Your Love."

Creedence Clearwater Revival, another defunct holdover from the '60s, was also honored. But singer/songwriter John Fogerty refused to share the stage with his long-estranged rhythm section. Instead, Stu Cook and Doug Clifford walked out of the ballroom while Fogerty awkwardly played his old hits with ringers Bruce Springsteen and Robbie Robertson. I saw one of the guys nursing his sorrows at the bar, and went up to offer a sympathetic ear while he gave me some incendiary quotes. But I wasn't sure if it was Stu or Doug, and I couldn't compound the indignity by asking which one he was. So I asked for his autograph, and Doug "Cosmo" Clifford signed my souvenir program, helping me out of a jam and maybe restoring his spirits a little.

I long considered Fogerty a schmuck for not burying the hatchet for just one night. But then I got to interview him a few times and concluded he was a decent chap, if somewhat beholden to his wife. As with any relationship, bands have unique dynamics that are incomprehensible to outsiders.

Over the years I interviewed pretty much every rock star I dug as a youngster. I also spoke to plenty of people whose music I didn't care for, various rappers, pop starlets, and members of 'N Sync. I tried to avoid actors and the rigid studio publicity regimen that accompanied them, but I did run into a few at the odd Hollywood event. Yes, they're always smaller in real life and they don't have a lot to say unless there's a script written for them.

I hate to dispel any myths, but many rock stars are terrifyingly smart. Mick Jones from the Clash would be a great "lifeline" on *Who Wants to Be a Millionaire*, and I wrote that Motörhead frontman Lemmy's decision to become a rock star was academia's loss. Wild men like Iggy Pop and Marilyn Manson were quietly profound.

Similarly stimulating were behind-the-scenes guys—low-key producers and songwriters including Motown hitmakers Holland-Dozier-Holland, who asked if they could give me a personalized signed photo, fellow soul legends Gamble & Huff, Lady Gaga's Moroccan producer RedOne, and Franke Previte, the struggling musician who won the lottery by co-writing the *Dirty Dancing* anthem "(I've Had) The Time of My Life." Moguls such as *Rolling Stone* publisher Jann Wenner, Atlantic Records co-founder Ahmet Ertegun, and Hugh Hefner were fascinating. "Hef" hosted me at the Playboy Mansion, and his parting comment—"good interview"—still gives me warm fuzzies.

At the other end of the age spectrum, I interviewed the three Hanson brothers before they became teen idols with "MmmBop," one of the deepest pop songs ever written. I semi-seriously vowed that if I ever had to interview *their* kids then I should get out of the business. Sixteen years later, they're all married with children. The eldest of their 10 kids is aged 11, so the timing of my enforced exit (keep reading!) was good.

The hot new flavors of the month were generally more difficult to get interviews with. They were run off their feet and surrounded by a flotilla of anxious publicists. Alanis Morissette's people frequently turned me down when she was selling millions of albums. Years later, when her use-by date had passed and interview opportunities were offered, I turned the tables on them. Backstage at a recent awards show, Lady Gaga's handlers decreed that she would answer questions only from four preapproved reporters. I look forward to the day when she has to beg for media attention.

My interviews were an equal mix of "phoners" and "in-persons." As long as my interviewee was focused on me and not multitasking—Peter Gabriel called me while he was giving his baby a bath—I did not mind how we did it. The in-persons were usually at the office of the record label or publicist. Others were in hotel rooms, recording studios, concert venues, bars, and restaurants. Sometimes the musicians were rehearsing, and I was treated to private shows by Rod Stewart, Ringo Starr, and Billy Idol. I also made house calls. Glen Campbell, a Southern Baptist, had a thing for Jewish memorabilia. John Lee Hooker's spartan living room contained a couch and a big-screen TV showing Mariah Carey videos. Ice-T played me a porn clip. Solomon Burke sat on a throne. Lindsey Buckingham noodled on a guitar.

I prepared diligently because I did not want to insult the stars with the same old questions or bore my readers with a bunch of stale answers. If possible, I listened to the artist's new music on advance cassettes or CDs sent by the label, and perused my personal archive of newspaper clippings, press releases, books, and carefully catalogued magazines. For a 30- or 40-minute interview, this level of research was probably overkill.

I treated the interviews as conversations, trying to ensure that the mood was relaxed. Even jaded rock stars can be nervous. Or maybe they've already done 10 interviews that day. Maybe we're both hungover. Most were at least on their best behavior. They were selling themselves, after all.

Carly Simon, Christine McVie, and Robbie Robertson were so disarming that I worried I was letting them off easy. Mark Knopfler and John Mellencamp asked almost as many questions as I asked them. Mick Jagger is one of the most focused people I ever met, and Michael Stipe one of the politest. Keith Richards asked me to send him a memo with set list requests. Chrissie Hynde and Joan Armatrading, weary of the rock-star charade, were tough nuts to crack. A few, quite simply, were boring. Lenny Kravitz seemed as dull as his insipid lyrics. I couldn't get any straight answers from Stevie Wonder or Prince, and I swear I nearly nodded off while talking to Steve Winwood on the phone.

Then there was Phil Collins, who is famous for being one of the cheeriest guys in the business. Alas, he could not have been glummer when we chatted in 1993, and my obnoxious questions did not help. It was like a bad date, but one where I'm labeled an "arsehole" and worse before the menu has arrived. Years later, we had a second date and were both our usual charming selves.

Because of my nosiness and business background, I often asked about money. Roger Daltrey admitted he was a lousy investor. Ice-T vowed to save more aggressively. Jeff Beck blew his cash on hot rods, but wouldn't say which one was best for romancing his wife. Cream's Jack Bruce owned homes around the world. Yusuf Islam, a.k.a. Cat Stevens, occasionally indulged in Persian carpets and expensive sushi.

Their health and romantic histories were always of interest. Duff McKagan of Guns N' Roses and Ozzy Osbourne opened up about their battles with drugs. Chris Cornell and John Hiatt both quit addictions without the aid of 12-step programs. Robin Gibb of the Bee Gees talked about his wife's breakup with her girlfriend. Iggy Pop recalled picking up a lesbian drug dealer. But Chrissie Hynde coyly noted that it would be very difficult to get laid if she kissed and told.

Religious talk bored me, even if Eddie Van Halen or Smokey Robinson were trying to save my soul. Difficult questions—Why is your career in the toilet? Why did that album suck?—were best asked when a level of trust had been established, and certainly could not be phrased that way. Most artists blamed their labels. Keith Richards and Mick Jagger blamed each other. David Bowie simply said of some unloved '80s albums, "I don't know what happened there!"

The interview process could be intense especially if I was forging a bond, turning the meeting into a therapy session and maybe even achieving some sort of breakthrough. Neil Diamond said he would have to discuss with his shrink some of the issues raised in our chat. Bowie's eyes welled up when he mentioned his dead half-brother. Tom Petty talked about his depression and how his meds had not dampened his sex life.

My head would spin in multiple directions as I processed their answers. Is that the million-dollar quote I can build the story around? Is that a glib sound bite he gives everyone? Do I have enough time to ask a follow-up question? Do I pretend to know what she's talking about? How do I get him back on track? Is my tape recorder working? What the hell am I doing here? Is that a lie? Journalists and cops have one thing in common. We are lied to—or at least "spun"—as a matter of course. If we're often bitter and jaded, that's why.

I felt a sense of professional satisfaction after a successful interview, newly armed with juicy gossip, pearls of wisdom, and poignant quotes. And, let's be honest, I'd just had quality one-on-one time with someone whom most people would only hear on the radio or see from afar at a concert. I was privileged, no doubt.

Hopefully my enthusiasm is not mistaken for the giddiness displayed by sports reporters in the presence of star athletes or by journalists at the indecorous White House Correspondents' Dinner. If anything, I developed a mild case of "paradise syndrome" after a couple of years: Life is so wonderful that it's making me grumpy. David Stewart of the Eurythmics coined the term to much guffawing, and later told me he had been joking. It seemed real for me, though, possibly caused by wild swings between inspirational rock-star encounters and quotidian reality. Or maybe it was anxiety about becoming a virtual publicist—a small cog in the labels' marketing machines.

Symptoms included entrenched cynicism and sporadic outbreaks of entitlement, envy, and spite. I was annoyed if my free concert ticket was not close enough to the stage or if rival scribes had better seats. I sometimes reveled in a musician's commercial failures, ignoring any artistic virtues. A cash bar or other slight could influence the tone of my story. Sad but true.

While I never sold myself out for "access," I might have been open to offers. Alas, Mötley Crüe and Van Halen never invited me to any bacchanals, nor did Lemmy ask me to his place to see his collection of World War II memorabilia. No female rockers ever succumbed to my charms. The luckiest I got was accidentally grabbing Courtney Love's bare breast when she stage dived on top of me at the Hollywood Palladium. An ungainly rival claimed he turned down an unidentified rock chick's advances, which annoyed me on multiple levels.

People often ask if I got backstage passes. Yes, sometimes. But if they were giving passes to me they were giving them to everyone, and we were usually herded into a sub-VIP area featuring warm domestic "beer" and carrot sticks. A radio DJ might be the closest thing to a celebrity in our midst.

The only thing better than interviewing a real live celebrity was writing about a freshly deceased one. Obituaries were my chance to stick it to someone one last time or to cover an underappreciated person in glory. In the former category, I delighted in pointing out that Linda McCartney could not sing. I tried to do a revisionist piece on Jerry Garcia of the Grateful Dead, whose music I deplore, but it was a "too soon" moment for the expert Dead detractors I called. Subjects in the latter category included reggae pioneer Desmond Dekker, Delta bluesman R. L. Burnside, Motown songwriter/producer Norman Whitfield, folklorist Alan Lomax, and Mick Jagger's dad. My boss did not consider the death of Len Lesser (*Seinfeld*'s Uncle Leo) to be newsworthy, but I went ahead and wrote an obituary that circulated widely. I got the scoop on Dennis Hopper's death, and was all over big departures, like those of George Harrison, Kurt Cobain, Barry White, and Isaac Hayes. On a slow news day, I spent way too much time on an obituary for Gidget the "Yo Quiero Taco Bell" Chihuahua, who suffered a stroke while watching television.

I was on vacation when Johnny Cash died, but I had already written his obituary. Most news organizations have a "morgue" containing pre-written obituaries that can be published as soon as a death is confirmed. Preparation is key in this profession. Sometimes the subjects outlive their profilers, as was the case with Elizabeth Taylor and her obituarist at *The New York Times*, and will probably be the case with Charlie Sheen and me. Pre-writing obituaries became a hobby, making me some sort of journalistic Grim Reaper. I compiled lists of people who could—or really ought to—die soon. Among them was Aaron Spelling, whom I saw in a wheelchair at a charity event in 2005. He was dead a year later. By that time I had already dug into my personal archive to write a nice tribute to the television mogul.

If obituaries were the best part of my job, the worst part was transcribing interviews. Both the task itself and the dread beforehand deepened my grumpiness. But I made it worse for myself by obsessively typing up every word in my spare time. It was arguably pointless since there was space for only three or four quotes. I convinced myself that the complete transcripts would come in handy at obituary time, no matter how young the subject.

Writing an article of 700 words or so was easy once I had worked out the general thrust. With a little luck, that had come to me during the interview. All I needed was a succinct "lede," or opening sentence, and a sexy quote high up. Things flowed from there. The challenge was balancing news with background—important at Reuters, where the target audience was patronizingly referred to as the "Kansas City milkman," i.e., an ignoramus. I wrote for the 14-year-old kid who had scraped together enough pocket money to buy one album. She could go either way—the new Black Eyed Peas record or a Stooges reissue. Hopefully she could make an informed decision after reading my story on the latter, and I had changed her life in a small way.

Although Reuters was terrified of anything that smacked of an opinion, and its core business as a financial-news operation encouraged a dull writing style, I invariably injected some edge into my copy to the amusement of my colleagues. But the tight word count prevented me from stretching out and getting too artistic. I was envious of newspaper and magazine writers who made names for themselves by spending extended periods of time with their subjects and writing lengthy color pieces.

On the other hand, the restrictions suited my superficial personality. Reuters also gave me complete creative control. No one ordered me to do anything, and the editors rarely tinkered with my prose, not that I paid much attention after submitting it. I had moved on to the next story.

Covering awards shows like the Grammys and Oscars could also make me grumpy. They allow rich and famous people to become even richer and more famous, and I was part of the problem. I understand some of the psychology behind stars making a big deal out of getting cheap tchotchkes, corporate "attaboys." They overcame the odds to achieve their fleeting fame, after all. But they're also millionaires with fancy cars, big homes, and jet-setting lifestyles. Isn't that reward enough? And, not to sound too idealistic, but why are we treating artistic endeavors as if they were the Olympics? It's remarkable how a serious performer's cynicism toward awards shows melts when he gets a prize.

I can't decide if it's good or bad that awards shows have been reduced to fashion shows. The talk of the 2000 Grammys was not Santana's sweep of the top prizes but Jennifer Lopez's plunging Versace dress, which incidentally is stored at the Grammy Museum in Los Angeles.

None of the on-camera glamour is evident in the cramped and distant press rooms. Maybe if the organizers had plied the media with alcohol and a buffet, I would have been more enthused. We struggled to follow the developments on TV monitors that were periodically silenced when trophy-toting celebs graced us with their presence. Among them was Elton John, proudly bearing a Grammy "Legend" honor. But we were so busy writing our stories that we didn't notice him. Ignored for perhaps the first time in his life, the sensitive artiste stormed off the podium after a few awkward moments.

Maybe it was for the best. The investigative reporters from *People* and *Us Weekly* would have pounced on him with deep questions like,

Who are you wearing? What are you doing for Thanksgiving (in nine months' time)? Do you have favorite school moments? The Academy Awards are actually worse. "Could you two be any more adorable?" someone asked an Oscar-winning couple in 2014.

Sometimes I enlivened things to stave off boredom. Citing a 1994 news report that Whitney Houston's cover of "I Will Always Love You" was the most requested song at British crematorium funerals, I asked the pop diva backstage at the American Music Awards if she planned to have the song played at her own funeral. She glared at me, and then-husband Bobby Brown looked as if he might pounce. Well, we eventually found out the obvious answer.

The American Music Awards are a low-rent version of the Grammys. For many years, the big AMA winners did not even turn up. Those who did pretended to be ecstatic to add a pointed acrylic statuette to their collection of junk. The performances were lip-synched, which never bothered the excitable civilians dressed to the nines in the cheap seats.

The Grammys, for some unjustifiable reason given their appalling track record of tone-deaf choices, brought out my obsessive competitiveness and some good old-fashioned professional pride. I covered them singlehandedly, crushing AP's large crew. A week or two beforehand, I prewrote stories, gathered statistics and fun facts, and color-coded artists' names in the weighty list of nominations. With 100-plus categories to keep tabs on, a lot of math was involved and the organizers were too inept to provide tallies or historical data. Nowhere on the Grammys website can you find a list of the most-honored artists in Grammy history. I have that list. Every year I prepared a story in case Neil Young won the first Grammy of his 40-year career. Finally he won in 2010, and my exhaustive piece went worldwide within minutes of his name being called out.

I was genuinely pleased for underdog or surprise Grammy winners, especially if I had interviewed them. But it was a slippery slope. Why did I care that Carlos Santana or Justin Timberlake or Jay-Z had been judged to be the "best" in their musical genres? Did I really gasp when Maroon 5 was named best new artist? Or when

Eminem got beaten for album of the year a couple of times? I should have taken a page from his rule book. He doesn't seem to give a crap about awards. He did not even show up to the Academy Awards to collect his songwriting Oscar for *8 Mile*.

I was a no-show sometimes, too. Like my infamous "Wilson Phillips" colleague, I monitored some events on television. Once I watched Miss USA on one channel and the Daytime Emmy Awards on another, writing my stories simultaneously on a split laptop screen. I never missed the Spirit Awards, though. The art house version of the Oscars was a boozy midday gathering underneath a marquee on Santa Monica beach, and I composed some of my best literature while loaded on gin and tonics.

The other big Hollywood events—the Oscars, Golden Globes, Primetime Emmys—were team efforts under others' control. Some of my colleagues lobbied furiously to attend these shows, desperate to be a tiny part of the tightly policed glamour. I preferred to review them from the relative calm of the office, where pizza was ordered in—or from home, where I didn't have to bother getting dressed. Far from the madding crowd, I carved out a niche as Mr. Negative, writing about the "losers"—the films and TV shows that were snubbed.

I probably should have been embarrassed to attend awards shows once I reached the wrong side of 40. The last one I attended was the MTV Movie Awards in 2011. I surveyed my fellow two dozen scribes. They were mostly eager young women who knew the names of all the reality-show B-listers on hand. The old-timers with whom I had covered these things a decade or two earlier had grown up, moved to proper jobs, died, or been laid off.

Among the celebs I did recognize was Blake Lively. This was shortly after some nude pictures of the pretty *Gossip Girls* starlet had hit the Web. We had been told she would pose for the photographers who shared the tent with us, but would not take any questions. Undaunted, I yelled out to her: "Blake, do you plan to pose for any more nude photos?" She either ignored or didn't hear me. Her publicist shot me a venomous glance, and an MTV stooge reprimanded me: "No questions!"

* * *

Given my disdain for awards shows, it's poetic that I got fired for writing about one. The BET Awards, which honor black entertainers, are a joke. Denzel Washington was once given an honorary prize for his humanitarian works and didn't show up to collect it. Each year the organizers were so afraid that thuggish Death Row Records founder Marion "Suge" Knight and his entourage would tear up the place that they gave him tickets as guests of billionaire BET founder Bob Johnson so that it was easier to keep them corralled.

Anyway, I watched the 2011 version unfold on a television in the bureau on a Sunday afternoon. Chris Brown and Lil Wayne were picking up a bunch of prizes, and I also noticed that Michael Vick was named best sportsman. I don't follow American sports but I knew that Vick did prison time for abusing dogs and was briefly the most hated man in America until Bernie Madoff or Jesse James or Dominique Strauss-Kahn stole the crown. Chris Brown beat up his girlfriend, and Lil Wayne spent much of 2010 in jail on drugs charges. That was the angle: The BET Awards honor winners with criminal pasts.

I kept the story very matter-of-fact and included lots of background on their transgressions. There was a secondary angle when a fan was brought onstage to announce a winner, but the organizers screwed up by giving the poor girl the wrong information to read. I also noted that rapper Rick Ross had man boobs, and recounted a presenter's joke that the former prison guard should wear a sports bra. Funny piece overall, certainly not one of my worst. An editor signed off on it, and I went home.

But about ten days later a newly appointed editorial executive, fresh from a stint in PR, informed me via teleconference from the East Coast that I was to be terminated immediately because I had contravened a company policy pertaining to "integrity, independence, and freedom from bias." And thus ended my 23 years at Reuters: escorted out of the building by a security guard, and a year's worth of fruitful litigation ahead of me. The offending article was not corrected—there was nothing wrong with it—and it remains on the company's website as my epitaph.

* * *

I was burned out anyway, more interested in writing about new retro albums by Steve Cropper and Jeff Beck than in pursuing the latest musical trends. I got old and stopped caring. I had no desire to interview Rihanna or Mumford & Sons or Skrillex. I'm not among the 1.9 billion people who clicked on the "Gangnam Style" video. Journalism in general had lost its appeal. We get too wrapped up in the lives of others, not unlike Stasi eavesdroppers. Time to live my own life.

Most of the interviews in this book come from the 1990s. I'm doing my bit to foment nostalgia for a time when my second coming-of-age coincided with the waning glory days of the music business. If only the British music lobbyist who proclaimed in 1995 that "the Internet has a very long way to go before it has an impact like that of CD" had been right. Unfortunately, fans took to heart the inherent rebelliousness of pop music and stole their music over the Web. Clueless label bosses responded by filing lawsuits and axing artists and employees. When I got to L.A. there were six major labels; now there are three—France's Universal Music, Japan's Sony Music, and Warner Music, which is owned by a Ukrainian-born oligarch.

The freebies have dried up. Promotional CDs have given way to temporary MP3 files that I listen to on my tinny laptop speakers. I'm not sure that's the delivery method audiophiles like Neil Young and Roger Waters had in mind when they went to the trouble of creating their music. My wistfulness for an underappreciated decade will doubtless seem tragically comical to the music and media veterans who drank, snorted, and sleazed their way through the '60s, '70s, and '80s. But that's the way it was for me.

AT HOME WITH JOHNNY AND JUNE CARTER CASH

"Dean, would you like a tour of the house?" I did not want to impose on June Carter Cash, but I wasn't completely insane, either. Of course I wanted to see where she and Johnny Cash hung their hats.

It was May 1999, and June and Johnny were hosting several hundred people at their home in Hendersonville, Tenn. We were celebrating the release of *Press On*, a remarkable acoustic album June had recorded in a log cabin on the property with family and friends. A big tent was set up on the tennis court, and nothing stronger than apple cider and Coca-Cola was on offer. Fellow country music survivor George Jones popped in briefly, three days after pleading guilty to drunk-driving charges stemming from a near-fatal car wreck. I chased after him as he returned to his limo and breathlessly congratulated him on surviving his latest crash. He said it was a close call and graciously signed my official program.

On that sweltering Saturday afternoon, a perspiring Johnny, in his usual black garb, was surrounded by well-wishers. He looked bad. He sported a pair of hearing aids, and his hair was surprisingly thin.

Still, he was a huge presence in the tent. I kept my distance. What on earth could I say to him that he hadn't heard before? Instead, I contented myself to let a cute young blonde rub my bald head for luck.

June was sitting by herself at one of the tables, reading a folder of press clippings. I had interviewed her on the phone two weeks earlier, so that was my "in" to sidle up to her, introduce myself, and tell her that my article was probably there somewhere. June introduced me to family friend Jane Seymour and her husband. Then came the invitation to tour the house. I faked reluctance, but she insisted and said she would show me around afterward.

A little later, Johnny took the stage to introduce his wife before she played a few songs. "Her time is now," he told us. "I've encouraged it all these years, to let people know what she has to offer . . . Now you know." When Johnny joined her on the Terry Smith gospel standard "Far-Side Banks of Jordan," a paean to eternal love, country star Naomi Judd started crying and retreated to the house.

Afterward, June and I walked arm in arm back to the sprawling wooden abode, where I was formally introduced to Naomi. I told her she was even more beautiful in real life (as her husband looked on). It's a pity her actress daughter Ashley Judd wasn't there; my charm needle was at 11 that night. Also on hand were the actress Diane Ladd, who was delightfully nutty and kissed me on the cheek, and her husband Robert, whom I accidentally called Bruce (the name of her first husband). June asked one of her assistants, Ramona, to take Diane, Robert, and me on the tour. Actually, "lady-in-waiting" is probably a better term for Ramona. She was one of a coterie of middle-aged ladies hanging around the house, not really doing much.

"My mother, she was the dominant personality in the household. There's no doubt," John Carter Cash, the couple's only child together, explained to me a few years later. "She liked having a lot of people around her to help her and to support her. She had a lot of employees. It was just their way of existence. I didn't always feel totally comfortable there after a while, y'know?"

The lakefront house seemed quite feminized with rooms full of tables and cabinets groaning under the weight of untold dinner services. Piles of plates, bowls, crystal, cutlery, and related artifacts gave it the unfortunate appearance of a junk store. The furniture was heavy on floral upholstery. Every nook and cranny was crammed with mementos. I joked that June and my grandmother should get together to discuss their aggressive acquisition habits. (Less impressed with the Cashes' tastes was Billy Bob Thornton, who has a phobia about antiques and allegedly had a meltdown when he visited their place.)

Johnny Cash, one of the greatest American men ever, had been assigned a small upstairs den, where his Grammys and other trophies were displayed in an open cabinet. A small daybed ran alongside one of the walls. Clearly, this was June's house, and Johnny was merely a guest.

The tour probably took me past a bronze version of the ancient Greek discus thrower. The statuette ended up at my house in 2004, adding to my own growing piles of consumerist junk, after Sotheby's held an estate sale to help the family pay off death taxes. John Carter later told me that Johnny had bought the piece himself and always admired it. It cost me a modest $1,080. For $1,200, I also ended up with one of June's passports.

A group of us gathered in the kitchen/living room area. Jane Seymour took up residence on a couch. June touched my forearm for effect whenever she told a joke and gave me an autographed copy of her CD. But she also shot me a steely stare while I was talking to Johnny's niece, Kelly. Perhaps a little too excitedly, I remembered that Kelly's parents and Johnny had been sued by the U.S. government for accidentally causing a California forest fire in 1965. The incident bolstered Johnny's badass credentials, but June did not need another reminder. Johnny was not part of the post-party festivities. He was resting in the master bedroom, not feeling great.

Four years later to the day, in 2003, June died after heart surgery. Johnny followed her four months later. His death, at the age of 71, was not exactly a shock to me. He had been in and out of hospitals for years, and I had prewritten an obituary that was ready to be dusted off at a moment's notice. Unfortunately, I was on vacation in Belfast when I learned about his death the old-fashioned away, from a big front-page headline in the local newspaper. So someone else in the office did the dusting off and added pertinent details.

His grim video for "Hurt," released the year before, was clearly a farewell missive. "Everyone I know goes away in the end," he sang shakily as footage from his past decadence alternated with scenes showing his present decay. I assumed that the surprise passing of June, who appears in the video casting an anxious gaze at her frail lover, was the final blow.

But Rick Rubin, the producer and confidant who launched Cash's comeback in 1994 with a series of largely acoustic albums, recalled that he was shocked to get the death call. "From the last six months of his life he went from being almost blind and in a wheelchair to being able to see better, being able to read again, and he could walk again," Rubin told me in 2010. "Had he lived, we would have continued recording and there'd be more."

Cash was in better form when I encountered him for the first time at the 1994 South by Southwest Music Festival in Austin, Texas, as the promotional campaign kicked into full gear for his first collaboration with Rubin, *American Recordings*.

He delivered the keynote address to a hall full of hipsters who showered his brief remarks and acoustic set with standing ovations. He spoke to a few press types afterward. "It's very stimulating for me as an artist and a songwriter to be in a place like Austin, with all that's going on right now," he said, referring to the backlash against the polished Nashville sound that had relegated old-timers like Cash to also-ran status. "I'm excited about rediscovering my music."

That night, he took to the stage at Emo's, a grungy dive bar, for the hot-ticket show of the festival. Battling laryngitis, he started out with a solo acoustic set of most of the songs from the upcoming album, including the first single "Delia's Gone" (the one with the video in which he buries Kate Moss) and tunes written by the likes of heavy metaler Glenn Danzig, Tom Waits, and Leonard Cohen. Then he brought out his old band the Tennessee Three for the usual favorites, including "Get Rhythm," "Ring of Fire," "I Walk the Line," "Folsom Prison Blues," and "A Boy Named Sue," with the customized, crowd-pleasing punch line, "And if I ever have a son, I'm going to name him—Emo!"

"I got a lot of great reaction to it," Cash told me on the phone a few weeks after the Texas foray, still battling laryngitis and doubtless other ailments. "It's the kind of thing that's my cup of tea if I feel good, in good voice. I love to do the old stuff with my rhythm section, but it felt good to do the songs from the album too. It would have felt better if I'd been in good voice."

A month later, *American Recordings* debuted at No. 110 on the U.S. pop chart, Cash's first entry in almost 20 years. But I'd naively thought it would do much better. The PR machine was on full bore—magazine cover stories were everywhere—playing up the lovefest between Cash and Gen X. Older acts like Tony Bennett and Frank Sinatra had already been courting the marginalized demographic. Sinatra released a *Duets* album in 1993 and an inevitable sequel the following year. His partners included Bono and Chrissie Hynde. Bennett, ably managed by his son, opened for Porno for Pyros, and won the top Grammy in 1995 for an *MTV Unplugged* album. Such outreach efforts to the cool cats did not always work. Remember Pat Boone's heavy metal album in 1997?

There was no doubt about the integrity of Cash's new project. He was certainly a White House–approved "establishment," but he was also a battle-scarred rebel. And no one could deny his credentials as a prototypical punk rocker alongside Sun Records labelmates Elvis Presley and Jerry Lee Lewis. In the summer of 1994 Cash performed at Britain's premier festival, Glastonbury, on a bill that included the Beastie Boys, Bjork, and Beck. It was all organic, nothing forced.

"I'm very fortunate and blessed to have another shot at it," he told me. "It's a real challenge because I know how old I am [62 at the time, seemingly ancient but the same age as Sting at time of writing].

I know my audience. Being in this business and making records, you try to make them for human beings, for people, regardless of the age. There are some things I do that I think the younger generation will like . . . I don't have much to lose except some time."

Cash had already scored a demographic bull's-eye in the late 1960s, thanks to his hit prison albums from Folsom and San Quentin, a couple of hit singles, including Shel Silverstein's novelty tune "A Boy Named Sue," and a TV variety show that showcased edgy acts such as Bob Dylan, Joni Mitchell, and Pete Seeger. He and June played for the troops in Vietnam, and he managed a tricky balancing act by proclaiming himself a "dove with claws." (Noted Kris Kristofferson, whom Cash rescued from obscurity by covering his tune "Sunday Morning Coming Down," "I remember Shel Silverstein said, 'What the hell is that?!'")

Cash remained a popular touring act through the '70s and '80s, but his recordings met with increasing commercial indifference. Columbia Records shocked Nashville by dropping Cash in 1986. But he bore no grudge, telling me he understood its decision and was still friends with the executive who axed him. He recorded a few solid albums for Mercury Records, but claimed his efforts were hampered by a meager promotion budget. "There was just a lot of apathy because there were younger hot artists that had 'em really excited and that's where their money went. So I just kinda went my own way and there wasn't a year went by that I couldn't find work. I was busier than I wanted to be every year really."

John Carter Cash had a different take on it, recalling that the '80s were lean years financially. "My parents were making their living on the road, but their stage show—by the time they supported the tour and had their hotel expenses and tour buses and airplanes and everything else—they were just little over breaking even. The cycle just never really got 'em anywhere back in the '80s. They just kept touring, just barely breaking even. You could look at their income statements and they were pretty good, making lots of money. But they were also spending audaciously high amounts of money just in the process of having the traveling road show."

June sold her jewelry to help make ends meet, her son recounted in his 2007 memoir, *Anchored in Love: The Life and Legacy of June Carter Cash*. But it wasn't quite as bad as it sounded, he told me. "[B]ack in the '70s, that was part of their plan: 'OK, let me buy so much jewelry and do this and let's make investments, and if on down the line we aren't doing so well then we can sell this stuff.'"

Rick Rubin entered the picture in the spring of 1993. At 30, he was half Cash's age. The hirsute producer behind the Beastie Boys, Slayer, and the Red Hot Chili Peppers checked out a few of Cash's shows in Southern California. "Two or three times he came, and each time he came I more and more liked the way he talked," Cash said. "He let me know he wanted to get the best out of me for whatever that was. He said he didn't care about anything I'd ever recorded; he didn't want to think about it. He wanted to hear me with my guitar singing the songs I wanted to sing, and that's the approach we took."

For his part, Cash told Rubin up front "that if I did record for him—or whoever I recorded for—that I would do it the way I felt it or I wouldn't record, that I would take time to make records the way they felt right."

In fact, Cash had signaled a year before meeting Rubin that he was planning a musical makeover. His Mercury swan song, 1991's *The Mystery of Life*, was a tentative first step, tipping its hat to Sun Records' legendary lo-fi sound. It was even produced by Jack Clement, the songwriter/producer who played an important role in Cash's early career. Alongside solid redos of "Hey Porter" and "Wanted Man" were rockin' tunes like "Goin' by the Book" and the gospel "The Greatest Cowboy of Them All." The reissue features "The Wanderer," a tune Cash recorded with U2 for their 1993 album *Zooropa*.

Nobody bought *The Mystery of Life*, but Cash was undaunted. "We're going a little bit more heavy on the old boom-chicka-boom on my next album," he told Jim Washburn of the *Los Angeles Times* in August 1992. "It'll be the Sun sound a la 1992."

Without naming names, Cash admitted in the *Times* interview that he had been badly produced over the years, "but I'm not going to work that way anymore. The last album is indicative of more simplification to follow. I think I'm going to be a little more bare even than that, and a little more stark."

American Recordings sounded like a lot of rough demos, which is basically what it was. Cash and Rubin recorded over a hundred songs, all the while turning each other on to new material. Most of the recordings featured nothing more than Cash and his guitar. They realized the demos were fine, and that's how the album ended up sounding so unadorned. "It's just a whole lot of Johnny Cash coming right in your face," Cash told me.

Perhaps the most personal song was "The Beast in Me," written with Cash in mind by former stepson-in-law Nick Lowe during the late 1970s. (Lowe's version was later used over the closing credits of the *Sopranos* pilot episode.) "I became a Christian when I was 12 and I kinda went northwest several times, off track," Cash explained. "But just like my mother said, you bring up a child the way he should go and he'll always come back. Maybe that's what I do. The older I get the more determined I'm not to stray too far. It's a constant battle with me as it is with anybody. Well, maybe more so with me, I dunno. I had so many devils yapping at my heels for so many years with all of the drugs and everything, life on the road and whatever. I'm very aware and conscious every day of the fight that is within me and of making my commitment to God to try to overcome the destructive forces in my life."

Predictably ignored by the new Nashville mainstream (it reached No. 23 on the country chart), *American Recordings* won the Grammy for best contemporary folk album. I liked Cash's 1996 follow-up better. *Unchained* was more of a band effort, thanks to the recruitment of Tom Petty and the Heartbreakers. Among the tracks was a new arrangement of Soundgarden's speed-metal song "Rusty Cage," which paved the way for his reworking of Nine Inch Nails' "Hurt" in 2002. "The very first time I heard it, it was strange," Soundgarden frontman Chris Cornell, the song's writer, told me. "And then after that I liked it. It just felt strange, and I don't know if it's because being the person that wrote the song, hearing it done so completely differently, and then also being a fan of Johnny Cash since I was a little kid, it felt uncomfortable in a way. But I like it a lot. It's very much a different song, obviously, and musically the references to the original are vague."

Bizarrely, *Unchained* stalled at No. 170 on the pop chart (No. 26 on the country chart). But after it won the Grammy for best country album, Rubin took out a full-page *Billboard* ad sarcastically thanking country music radio for its support. It was a reproduction of the famous Jim Marshall photo of a meth-addled Cash hoisting his middle finger at the camera lens while rehearsing for his San Quentin gig in 1969. (It's not known what Cash's mother-in-law thought about being in the background of the shot.) Some in Nashville were scandalized by the ad. "Johnny Cash can stand there and flip the bird to country radio all he wants, but the album wasn't even serviced to country radio, and there was certainly never a single worked to country radio," radio station consultant Bob Moody told *Billboard*, inadvertently outing radio programmers as a bunch of lazy morons. "To criticize country radio for not playing something they weren't sent is hypocritical."

As Cash's health deteriorated, his sales improved. He stopped touring in 1997 when he was misdiagnosed with a neurological disease and given a year to live. Double pneumonia almost killed him in early 1998. His third album with Rubin, *Solitary Man* (featuring the Neil Diamond title track), reached No. 88 (No. 11 country) in 2000. *The Man Comes Around* hit No. 22 (No. 2 country) in 2002. Thanks to the "Hurt" cover—and despite the appalling Grammy-nominated duet on "Bridge Over Troubled Water" with Fiona Apple—it became the biggest seller of the series. After Cash died, Rubin released the *Unearthed* boxed set in 2003 and *A Hundred Highways* in 2006. The latter album went to No. 1 at pop and country. The series ended in 2010 with *Ain't No Grave*, a top-three entry on both charts.

Like everyone else, I got caught up in the moment and spent a decade writing about Cash's breathtaking series of comeback albums. But I never played them much after the initial burst. They were dreary, no fun. Listen to a similar concept from the '70s—Muddy Waters' comeback at the age of 63 under the guidance of Johnny Winter in *Hard Again*—and you immediately know that everyone is having a good time. Cash, on the other hand, seems to be calling in from death row.

In 2009 Bob Dylan told *Rolling Stone* that he considered the series to be "notorious low-grade stuff," and the only way to appreciate Cash was to listen to the Sun recordings from the dawn of his career in the '50s. "Interesting. I had not seen that," Rubin told me when I sought his reaction. "Wow, interesting!"

I joked that Rubin—now Dylan's nominal boss as co-chairman of Columbia Records—would have to fire Dylan. "No, it's all good. We love Bob. His manager said he wanted to get together because he liked the songs on *American Recordings*, and we should talk about 'em. Funny."

Another contrarian commentary came from Julian Raymond, who produced a 2008 Glen Campbell acoustic album that featured Green Day, U2, and Foo Fighters covers. "Even though I love the work that he [Rubin] did with Johnny Cash I don't think those records were anything like Johnny Cash," Raymond said. "Johnny was a pretty upbeat guy. I produced [Cash's eldest daughter] Rosanne Cash, so I got the inside scoop on what goes on with him and what his life was about as well. But he was a happy guy. He had his demons, of course, but those records are really dark records and the song selections are really dark. I don't think Johnny's traditional stuff that he did back in the day was like that at all. His subject matter was a little weird at times, but for the most part he was a cool rock 'n' roll and country kinda guy. I think he [Rubin] reinvented him to have this gothic kinda darker image. Certainly, the videos and a lot of the songs that made it to the mainstream are that way."

Responded Rubin when I ran that by him, "Yeah. I could see that. I would say he was more rounded than those records show. I would say that. A lot of it had to do with songs that I would suggest. More than half the songs were picked by him and not me, and all the songs were chosen by him ultimately because I pitched loads of songs to him. But I tended to pick more serious songs just because I always thought of what suits the Man in Black, and I really thought of him more as a mythological figure than as the flesh-and-blood funny guy."

So you wanted to perpetuate the mythology? "That's what I wanted to hear," Rubin said. "When I think of Johnny Cash that's what I think of and I wanted to hear music that supported that. That was my taste. . . . At one point he did do some songs like 'The Chicken in Black.' I think we remember him more for 'I shot a man in Reno just to watch him die . . .' [from "Folsom Prison Blues] than for some of the more comedic songs."

Cash wasn't keen on pushing the stern Man in Black mythology all the time. During our 1994 phone chat he told me he owned all sorts of colored shirts, and one of his favorites was a red Bugs Bunny number. Still, our conversation was rather weighty, for which he blamed me. "You've been asking me about a lot of serious things," he said.

I noted that the song "Drive On" was inspired by several books he'd read about Vietnam, and he patiently explained that he wore black and wrote "Man in Black" in part as a symbol of mourning for the "hundred fine young men" that were dying every week over in Vietnam.

"Actually, I went there in 1969 to sing for them, to entertain the troops that were there because they're ours, you know? They're our brothers and our sons. I just felt like I wanted to go, and June and I went and it was after the Tet Offensive, and they wouldn't let us leave Long Binh Air Force Base, so we sang in the hospitals for the wounded and we talked to them. Sometimes we'd do a little show for one or two people. And June took names and addresses of these guys, the wounded. We got back to Okinawa. She spent three days on the phone calling mothers and relatives back in the States, telling them that we saw your son or your husband, and try to give hope to the people back home. That was our involvement in the Vietnam War."

Fast-forward to the 1990s and he was hardly enthused about the state of things. "I think the government needs to take the AIDS crisis a lot more seriously than they do. I think the budget for that should be as big as the defense budget. Of course that'll never happen. I've got problems with the way this country treats the elderly and education and the care of the mentally retarded and the autistic. They got no money, no program for them. I'm very close to two retarded people and an autistic person and so we know that problem there. There are a lot of issues. Why should I speak out on them? It's not what I do. I'm trying to make music again. But I'm a member of this society and I have my likes and dislikes and resentments and appreciations."

He was also keenly aware of the failings of the penal system, having had a few overrated brushes with the law himself, and having made millions with his prison albums. "The majority of them are in there because of drugs or alcohol, and I can certainly relate to that. But for the grace of God there I'd be. I think that's the shame of the prisons, all the nonviolent offenders that are in there with the violent. That's one of the shames."

Like Rick Rubin, I got off on strolling through the dark side with Johnny. But we never spoke again. He did plenty of interviews right to the end and I probably should have been more aggressive about getting back on the phone with him, if only to get more material for the obituary. But I felt he didn't need to waste his valuable time talking to me.

In 1999, his touring days over, Cash gladly stepped back from the spotlight as June put out one of the best records of the decade. *Press On* was a folksy album recorded in a few days during a sing-along session at the Cash compound. "My mother always said you should just do an album of your own," she told me on the phone two weeks before the bash at her place. "I was so busy doing other things. I didn't really have time to concentrate about what I was going to do."

By no means much of a singer or even much of a musician, June spent her entire life in showbiz, mostly in supporting roles to terrifyingly vast talents. As a youngster, she performed and toured with her mother, Maybelle Carter of the Carter Family, and sisters Helen and Anita. Among the millions who tuned in to their regular radio broadcasts from just across the Mexican border was a young Johnny Cash, who dreamed that he would one day marry June. Helen Carter, the eldest sister, was an ace guitarist like her mother; Anita, the youngest, had the most beautiful voice in country music with looks to match. That left June as the family livewire, winning over audiences with her cheesy jokes, autoharp riffs, and intriguing syntax.

"I'm a little crazy at times," she told me. "Sometimes on the stage, people don't know whether I'm going to be real serious or whether I'm gonna get a little crazy on people. I don't mean by 'crazy' actually crazy, but I used to do comedy years ago and whatever I feel like that I'm liable to do."

After her first marriage dissolved, she studied acting in New York with Elia Kazan and Lee Strasberg, and hung out with James Dean. Years later, another former classmate, Robert Duvall, hired June to play his frail mother (!) in *The Apostle*. Cash recruited the Carter women for his traveling road show in 1962. He became June's third husband six years later after she made the hell-raiser clean up his act, temporarily.

June earned her place in the annals by writing "Ring of Fire," a song partly inspired by her forbidden love for Johnny Cash, when both were married to other people at the time. Officially, June co-wrote the song in 1963 with her manager, Merle Kilgore. But I managed to pry out of her the real story about the song's authorship. "He [Kilgore] was very encouraging to me, and let's just leave it that way. His name is on it and that's the way I want it," she said.

But I couldn't leave it that way. It was essentially her song and she added his name to the credits out of the goodness of her heart, June admitted. "But don't say that, please. He'll feel really bad if he hears it. It annoys Johnny Cash sometimes. He said, 'You shouldn't have done it, you shouldn't have given it to him.' And I said, 'Why? I would have never been this kind of a writer.' But I don't want Kilgore to ever feel bad. And that's why I'm the co-writer. Still, I won't lie about it. You seemed to ask some kind of question about it that caught me because I seldom tell people. I don't want Kilgore to ever feel bad." (Kilgore died in 2005.)

June recalled that she and Johnny were driving to a show one night and heard Kilgore tell a radio interviewer how he had written "Ring of Fire." He did not mention June, and Johnny got mad. At June's request he sent a telegram to the radio station. It read: "Be advised that June Carter and Merle Kilgore wrote 'Ring of Fire.' Please read this on your program. Johnny Cash." Continued June, "And Kilgore had to sit there and listen while they read that from John. I think that was bad enough. He deserved it."

Her request of me? "Mention that I co-wrote it . . . put my name first." (Kilgore's name appears first on the original version, sung by Anita Carter, and on Ray Charles' sibilant 1970 cover.) "It must have been recorded a hundred times, more than that," June continued. Ray Charles called the Cash household "out of the clear blue sky" to say it's his "favorite song of all time," she said. She liked Bob Dylan's version—presumably the unreleased duet he did with Johnny in 1969. Her album, naturally, featured a new version of the song. "I could live very comfortably, I think, for the rest of my life. It's become a classic, I think."

Alas, the woman who had the first bite at the song was dying as we spoke. Anita Carter's version, titled *Love's Ring of Fire*, clocked in at a mere 1:57, her angelic voice complemented by banjo, lute, and a harp. No one took any notice of the recording, and Johnny did his version with mariachi horns a few months later. It became the biggest hit of his career. Anita should have been a superstar but never particularly cared for the business even after signing multiple label deals. She died just three months after June's party following a 15-year battle with rheumatoid arthritis. She was 66. Helen had died a year earlier, aged 70.

Press On marked June's follow-up to an album released in 1975, *Appalachian Pride*. She claimed Columbia pressed only 20,000 copies of the earlier disc. "It sold out so fast and I wish they would have made some more of it. You can't find 'em anywhere." Neither of the albums charted. In 1967 she recorded a hit duets album with Johnny. *Carryin' on with Johnny Cash and June Carter* reached No. 5 on the country chart. They also won Grammys for their covers of "Jackson" and "If I Were a Carpenter." (Those statuettes sold for $15,600 and $22,800, respectively, at Sotheby's, quickly blowing my bids out of the water.)

But June seemed happiest supporting her husband, albeit on her own neo-feminist terms. "I've been walking just far enough behind John for him to think that he was way out in front! Women, if they've got any sense, will do that. They walk just far enough behind. That's where they stay."

She recorded *Press On* at the behest of two other former sons-in-law, Rodney Crowell and Marty Stuart. The whole process took about three or four days. June had a cold and assumed she would do overdubs later. Her son told her the original vocals were fine.

"We were all in front of the fireplace and we would just sit back in our little chairs," June said. "I sang everything by heart. It wasn't something I was sticking the music up in front of me. We were just having fun."

For a no-budget recording released on a tiny label, a lot of effort and expenditure was put into the artwork. "It was like they let me write a book," she said. "People are going to know me better." I spent hours perusing the Carter/Cash family photos and reading the exhaustive liner notes. But being a glass-half-empty guy, my joy when *Press On* won a Grammy for traditional folk album was tempered by disappointment that it failed to garner nominations for packaging or liner notes.

Johnny appears on the album, dueting on "Far-Side Banks of Jordan." (He was also sitting next to June during our phone conversation, and she occasionally deferred to him for help with some answers.) I had plenty of questions to ask about him, but wanted to keep the focus on June and her album. Still, I had been intrigued by references in Nicholas Dawidoff's book *In the Country of Country* to Cash allegedly selling out to religion. Moreover, it was claimed, Johnny tried to be so pure around June that he lost his rugged identity.

"Johnny Cash can do anything he chooses to do," June said. "He's a good man. He's the best man I know. And in the '60s I think we helped each other with life along there. I couldn't take any kind of credit for having straightened him out. The man has to straighten himself out no matter who he is, or he doesn't have the grit to do it in the first place. I think we loved each other and we wanted to have a good life together, and I think we've both just worked at it. So I couldn't take all that credit. I just am so glad that he chose to have a better life."

Setting the scene for the steely glare I'd get in person a few weeks later, I asked how she felt about people who get their kicks out of Johnny's bad-boy exploits. She was a southern diplomat. "I always have tried to say thank you with whatever kind of a situation we were up against, because you never know the good if you don't know the bad. You never know the top of the mountain if you've not been in the valley. I still try to thank God in all things, and that's how I recognize the good things."

June underwent heart surgery in Nashville in May 2003, shortly after completing work on her third album, *Wildwood Flower*, and died eight days later. Her stanza from "Far-Side Banks of Jordan" proved prophetic:

> *If it proves to be His will that I am first to cross—*
> *And somehow I've a feeling it will be—*
> *When it comes your time to travel likewise, don't feel lost,*
> *For I will be the first one that you'll see.*

IN DEFENSE OF MIKE LOVE

This book was originally going to be called *In Defense of Mike Love*, followed by a helpful subtitle. I figured it would be weird and contrarian because the Beach Boys singer has a reputation as one of the most-loathed people in the music business. But my focus group, i.e., my wife, did not know who Mike Love was and why he needed to be defended. So out it went. First rule of journalism: Don't confuse your readers.

This interview from Halloween 1992 evokes special memories for me, especially the bit where I swallowed a fly. Love had a good laugh at my expense, kept talking while I choked, and reluctantly let me drink some of his Snapple to wash it down. He was one of my first major interviews after I got to America that summer. My boss had suggested doing a Beach Boys story because the entity that was once America's greatest rock 'n' roll band was somehow still around. Their '60s anthems such as "Surfin' USA," "Little Deuce Coupe," and "California Girls" helped perpetuate the California myth of sun, surf, cars, and girls.

But any talk of the Beach Boys by the '90s centered not on their soaring vocal harmonies but on the soap opera involving Brian Wilson, the band's primary songwriter. Wilson, who was also Love's first cousin, was lucky to be alive after spending much of his life beholden to drugs, pills, junk food, and various manipulators.

According to legend, he met two young girls backstage at a concert in the '70s. He introduced himself by saying, "I'm Brian." "We know," one replied. "We're your children."

Brian's 1991 memoir *Wouldn't It Be Nice: My Own Story* featured terrifying stories about the childhood abuse that he and younger brothers Dennis and Carl suffered at the hands of their father. Murry Wilson once forced Brian to empty his bowels on a newspaper laid out on the kitchen floor as his lush of a mother silently looked on ("he . . . raped me," Brian wrote).

Murry went on to guide his sons' professional lives after they formed the Beach Boys with Love and their pal Al Jardine in 1961. Brian stopped touring after suffering a breakdown in 1964, turning his talents toward masterminding such projects as the Beach Boys' 1966 opus *Pet Sounds* and the discarded follow-up *Smile*. Fans loved the troubled genius. In their eyes Wilson was both a victim (bingo!) and a survivor (ditto).

Whereas Wilson was shy and socially awkward, Love was ambitious and extroverted. The lead singer on "California Girls," "I Get Around," "Surfin' Safari," and, ahem, "Kokomo" gravitated to—some might say "hogged"—the spotlight. Wilson, 15 months his junior, recounted in *Wouldn't It Be Nice* that he "both envied and felt intimidated by" Love when they were boys. "Tall and blond, he exuded confidence and swagger. He had a big ego. He wasn't especially nice."

Love says what's on his mind, even if it's not very nice. In 1988, the Beach Boys, the Beatles, and Bob Dylan were among the inductees at the third annual Rock and Roll Hall of Fame ceremony. Paul McCartney boycotted the event citing "business differences" with his former bandmates and Yoko Ono. Diana Ross was also a no-show for the Supremes' induction. In his acceptance speech, Love said it was a "bummer" that McCartney and Ross were absent. The applause from the $1,000-per-ticket black-tie crowd sent him off on a tangent. Love challenged A-listers like Bruce Springsteen and Billy Joel to get on stage and play. He accused Mick Jagger of cowardice, claiming that the Rolling Stones frontman opted to stay in

England rather than attend the event. "He's always been too chickenshit to get on a stage with the Beach Boys!" (Jagger was seated about 20 feet away in the audience.) The applause turned into widespread booing, and Dylan got the biggest laugh of the night after he thanked Love "for not mentioning *me*."

Ten days before our interview, Love sued Wilson for slander and libel. The suit claimed Wilson's memoir downplayed Love's songwriting abilities and his contributions to the group ("if not for me, he'd still be pumping gas," went one passage in the book). To Love's annoyance, Wilson claimed full credit for writing songs like "I Get Around," "All Summer Long," and "Good Vibrations." Love was indirectly quoted in the book as calling the latter masterpiece "more avant-garde crap and too long." Love also took offense at depictions of him as being more interested in money than music ("Mike was the least musical of anyone in the band and the most commercially inclined"), although he copped to that charge in our interview. More favorably, Wilson wrote that Love produced the world's biggest turd, 14 inches, in an Australian toilet.

Also named in the suit were credited ghostwriter Todd Gold, publisher HarperCollins, and Wilson's controversial, all-powerful psychologist Eugene Landy, who was assumed to have written much of the book. Landy was the other villain in the Beach Boys drama, crossing the ethical line between therapist and business associate in a partly successful, if unorthodox, quest to save Wilson during the 1980s. He was eventually forced to give up his license, and died in obscurity in 2006.

The suit was settled in 1994 when insurers paid Love $1.5 million. He said in a statement at the time, "In my heart, I knew that Brian never said those things about me and the band, and he has my continued love and support." Later that year, Wilson's mother, Audree, and Carl Wilson decided they had also been defamed in the book. They sued Landy and HarperCollins for more than $15 million. A federal judge ruled against Audree in 1997 and limited the scope of Carl's claim. Within seven months, both plaintiffs were dead. Brian outlived his parents and siblings (Murry died in 1973 and Dennis in 1983).

The songwriting dispute was a separate legal matter. Murry Wilson had sold the Beach Boys' lucrative copyrights for a mere $700,000 (about $4 million in today's money) to a music publishing firm in 1969, and kept the money. In 1989 Wilson sued the publishing firm, Almo/Irving, and the lawyers who handled the sale of the 75-song catalog. He received a $10 million settlement in June 1992. The following month, Love filed his own lawsuit against his cousin and the aforementioned defendants. His case against Wilson went to trial in 1994 after he received a $1.6 million settlement from Almo/Irving and the lawyers. A jury agreed that Love should receive full co-writing credit and one-third of Wilson's $10 million settlement. Wilson generously testified on Love's behalf.

When Love and I spoke, as all that litigation was raging, the Beach Boys had just self-released their first album of new material since 1985 and their first without any involvement from Brian. *Summer in Paradise* included a remake of their debut single "Surfin'," a cover of Sly and the Family Stone's "Hot Fun in the Summertime," and an update of "Under the Boardwalk" with some fresh lyrics from Love. Critics hated the album—*Blender* magazine later described it as a "train wreck"—and it failed to chart. (Now out of print, it is a costly item on Amazon.com.)

The poor reaction didn't matter too much because the Beach Boys were doing well on the golden-oldies touring circuit, buoyed by their 1988 chart-topper "Kokomo" (which frequently pops up in various "worst song" lists). The night before our interview, the Beach Boys played the Greek Theatre, although I saw U2 at Dodger Stadium instead. As I noted in my resulting story—headlined "The Sun Sets on the Beach Boys"—the *Chicago Tribune* had recently suggested that if the Beatles had stopped recording just before *Sgt. Pepper's* and kept touring to this day with early hits "She Loves You" and "I Want to Hold Your Hand" as the centerpieces, that would approximate what the Beach Boys were doing.

The formula still worked in 2012 when Brian reunited with the Beach Boys for a 50th anniversary world tour. The trek, accompanied by a brand-new hit album, was rapturously received by fans and critics. But just when Brian was looking forward to more touring and recording, Love cut him loose and hit the road with his own version of the Beach Boys.

Love, 51 at the time of our interview, and his fifth wife were staying at a friend's Benedict Canyon home, not far from the Sharon Tate murder house. We chatted for 90 minutes in the garden high above Los Angeles, sitting in the shade where some pesky flies were hovering. Sporting his trademark baseball cap, he patiently gave lengthy answers to my impertinent questions and never displayed any discomfort as we ripped the scabs off old wounds. Sure, Love was a tad kooky. But it wasn't hard to muster up some sympathy for the old devil. He had been swindled by his own family and his integrity had been impugned. All the while, he had tried to keep his band together and entertain fans around the world.

What's the motivation to keep getting out there? Did you do this album because you were sick of doing the classic songs and you wanted to expand the repertoire?
No. Some people get sick of their songs, but maybe they're sick of their own life or something. Maybe some period of time has a negative connotation to them. If you take yourself very seriously, sometimes that can enter into the picture. But we don't have any problem with doing the older songs at all. In fact, it's kind of an art to do them really well. We try to do them as well as we did in the '60s, to re-create them. It is a form of re-creation. It's also an artistic achievement to be able to sing all those harmonies in the same keys that you sang in 20, 30 years ago.

It's nature that leads you to want to do what you like to do. In other words, we started out to become a singing group not because there was a precedent for the type of group we'd become and the type of industry it has become. The only people that we heard on the radio that we liked were the doo-wop groups of the time in the '50s, Little Richard, Chuck Berry, and the Everly Brothers. Those were the early influences of the Beach Boys. There were no Rolling Stones, no Beatles, no Beach Boys and all that. So the rock industry became an industry, rock music became a growth industry in the '60s with the advent of the Beach Boys and the Beatles and the Rolling Stones. And all the rest, the Who and so on, came along after that. It's like the "begats" in the Bible, I guess. At any rate I think it's our own nature, what we started out to do—not because we got paid for it a lot, not because we were trying to be like somebody, not because we were driven to be stars. If we had been driven to be stars, we would have probably done things a lot differently. We'd have tried to make a television show or more movies and such. But we never even tried to do that stuff. We just made music, and people liked it, and we continued to make music and tour and so on.

And even when cousin Brian got self-destructive through drugs and so on—he was the main musical force of the Beach Boys, and I contributed lyrics and concepts. . . . There was a good merger there. But when he started to self-destruct with the drugs—and I say "self-destruct," he didn't destroy himself like Dennis did, but he did a pretty good job on his psyche with acid and other excesses—it was like the engine falling out of your car that's going a hundred miles an hour. The car continues with that momentum as long as you're going on a flat surface.

I don't want to say downhill, do I?!

It can be downhill. It was downhill creatively from where it was in 1966 with "Good Vibrations." 1969, '70, '71, that was not a peak time by any stretch of the imagination. But it was mainly due to Brian's incapacitation. At that time of our career I decided to go into meditation whereas Brian went into drugs, and Dennis went into drugs and alcohol. We met Maharishi in December of '67. I learned TM from that time on. I didn't drink anything. I didn't take any drugs or anything. I was very happy with meditating twice a day.

Before the meditation were you into drugs and alcohol perhaps more than was healthy?

No. I drank alcohol for relaxation.

But the whole summer of love thing bypassed you totally?

No, I wasn't into that at all. That wasn't a factor. Well, that was more Northern California, Haight-Asbury and stuff. It didn't resonate with me. Personally, you're talking to somebody who doesn't really need to get in a large group of people and say how great this pot is or how great this sex is or how great anything is. Astrologically speaking, I'm Mercury in Aquarius, which means my mind is Aquarius—humanitarian, futuristic, free-thinking—and I don't really care what other people think of me if it's from the standpoint of negativity out of ignorance. I don't mind if somebody knows of what they speak and then determines that they don't particularly like that. That's their choice. But when people make assumptions based on lack of knowledge, then to me their opinions are irrelevant: people thinking that maybe the Beach Boys weren't happening simply because we didn't take acid or weren't doing so much drugs.

Plenty of us in the group were doing things such as that, but I was seeing too many people be destroyed by it or acting crazy or weird or just not functioning. And that just wasn't my cup of tea, nor was it Al Jardine's or [Wilson's touring replacement] Bruce Johnston's. And Carl had his escapades, but by and large over the years he's been very stalwart and very productive and dependable and stuff. It's hard to do shows when people are all messed up. That was a bone of contention there with Dennis Wilson at times. He would be drunk. When you have a drummer who's drunk, it completely ruins the performance. So we would have to throw him out of the group, and he would be violent and vitriolic, and we'd say, "Well, sorry, but this is not working out!"

Did he ever go through rehab?

Yeah, he would go in for a day, and get right out.

Do you take any personal blame and say, I wish we'd done things a bit better as far as he was concerned?

Oh yeah. People in families often don't know how to cope with someone who's a serious addict, of either drugs or alcohol. And that's why they have professional people that deal with those kinds of things, that people ask into the situation. And we tried to do what we could do with Dennis to discourage his bad behavior and encourage good behavior, but obviously we weren't competent to deal with his problem to the degree that he had it. He just appeared to be very self-destructive.

You were all so young at the time. You're looking back on it now with the wisdom of being 50.

Right. Hindsight. 20/20. Obviously. In fact that's one of the reasons why we were so concerned about Brian in the early 1980s. Very concerned. He was up over 300 pounds. Brian's an excessive personality. If he's excessively into music that's fabulous, but if he's excessively into food. . . . He was 312 or -14 pounds when we checked him into a hospital.

But he was always quite big, though?

Not 300 pounds, 190 maybe. He had a tendency towards weight but it wasn't helped by drinking too much or eating too much. If he took drugs, he'd take way more drugs than anybody's supposed to take, or anybody's heard of taking! In fact, Terry Melcher, who produced "Kokomo" and was a buddy of mine back in those days, has seen Brian take more drugs than anybody ever saw. Other than John Phillips [of the Mamas and Papas, who died in 2001]. It's a miracle that he's alive. But we did take him—because of Dennis' passing away, and we all felt collectively like we could have or should have done more to avoid that or avert that had we acted in a more concerted, dynamic fashion, not just let him live his life type-thing. But with Brian, that scared us enough to wake everybody up to want to deal with Brian's condition.

And of course Dr. Eugene Landy, who was Brian's nefarious, notorious psychotherapist, came in the picture and did well for him in the first few years. He did very well for him, physically and I'm sure mentally as well. What with the 24-hour therapy that he designed, which is kinda like a velvet prison [laughs], Brian relearned how to be responsible for himself and learned a bit of discipline and so on, some very healthy things. Unfortunately, we were told that it would be necessary to have this type of therapy for a year to a year and a half, and it went on as recently as a year ago before a conservator was appointed to take care of Brian's affairs, because Landy became a little overzealous in the control department.

Is Landy totally out of the picture now?

Brian surrendered to a conservatorship and part of the agreement was that Landy would be out of his life.

What does a conservatorship do for him?

It just makes sure that everything that Brian does financially is reviewed by the conservator who makes sure that he's not being abused or ripped off or spending his money on things that he's not supposed to. And then to try to make sure that Brian has the right mental therapy and right physical circumstances that are right for him.

Will he always require special treatment?

Yeah, he'll always require special treatment. He could be much more balanced and much better were he to get into the right regimen of therapies and so on. I happen to practice some health therapies, it's called Ayurveda—"ayu" means life in Sanskrit and "veda" means knowledge, and there's a whole complete compendium of techniques and technologies, everything from aromatherapy to something called marmotherapy, which is the original blueprint for acupressure, acupuncture, and all that. These Ayurvedic texts go back about 5,000 years. Everything is natural. There's a herbal pharmacopeia there, a complete knowledge of herbs so that one can bring back balance between the mind, body, and the environment; purification techniques, where one can reverse the aging process, and so on. It's quite fascinating, really. I'm hoping that someday soon we can get to the point where Brian can take advantage of some of these treatments in the context of some group creative process or project.

What's the extent of his contact with the members of the band now?

Well, not that much.

Is he still a Beach Boy?

Yeah. Well, he's still a member of what we call Brother Records, which is our corporation, and he still votes on issues that need to be decided. He was asked to participate on the *Summer in Paradise* album, but he chose not to. He is paranoid schizophrenic, [which] is one of the things that's wrong with him. "Paranoia" meaning fear and "schizophrenia" meaning your view of the world is not really reality. It's filtered through his own particular psychoses. There was so much divisiveness created by Landy that divided Brian from his mother, his daughters, the group. All with the idea, I believe, that Landy could control Brian and he could be Brian's co-writer, co-producer, partner in acquisition of properties, and so on. He took total advantage of the fiduciary relationship between a therapist and a client, completely abused that whole relationship.

They were calling each other "Brian Landy" and "Eugene Wilson" at some stage.

That's right, all that kind of stuff. It takes a while for someone who's been in a mind-control situation like Brian has been through for eight or nine years, it takes a while for that to unravel. So we can't push that. We can only encourage that he does the things that relieve him of his paranoia and create a space in which he feels safe and secure, and so he can be once again productive. I know Brian's innate nature, I've known him for so many years—he's one year younger than I am—I'm his older cousin. I've known him for so long, that I know he's innately gifted musically, and if he has the right environment, the right moment, and the right concept, I could get with him today, tomorrow, a week from now, a year from now and create—I believe—hit songs with him. I don't think he can create it on his own, because he's just not very with it. His verbal communication skills—he could sit down and talk to you, and then go off into his own world or some kind of strange rap or something. He does suffer delusions sometimes, and hears inner voices and all that sort of thing. But his innate musical nature is incredible, he's unbelievably gifted. So it's a question of creating an environment with enough balance, enough harmony, enough support along with a lot of positivity, and then there's no problem—just give him a keyboard!

What did you think of his solo record (*Brian Wilson*) a few years ago?

Didn't like it.

Why?

I'm sure there are some people that liked it because they're quote-unquote "Brian Wilson fans," and they'll like anything that he does, and that's fair. That's fine enough. But it wasn't a success in terms of commercial success [peaking at No. 54]. And I am guilty, as stated in Brian's book that he supposedly authored, of being the most commercial-minded fellow of the Beach Boys. I am, because I think the challenge is to make artistry enjoyable. Do not sacrifice artistry for commerciality, but do make your artistic achievements commercially practical. Otherwise you're just doing simply a self-indulgent exercise in creating things just for your own enjoyment. [Love's 1981 solo album, *Looking Back With Love*, failed to chart.]

How commercial is the new Beach Boys album?

It remains to be seen. If there are a couple of singles on the album, which we hope there are. . . . We're working on a single version of a song on the album called "Island Fever," doing a special version for a single recording. If we come up with something we're happy with, it'll probably be released in January. And we're planning on putting out "Under the Boardwalk" for next summer. [Neither song was released as a single, although the "Island Fever" update appeared on the U.K. version of the album that was released in May 1993.]

I understand there's a wee bit of litigation between you and Brian?

Oh, a fair amount!

What's the update on that?

The update is that in the '60s my cousin Brian and his father Murry Wilson were responsible for filing the copyrights and licenses for the songs we wrote and recorded, and Brian disincluded me on "California Girls." I wrote every word of "California Girls," every verse of "Little Saint Nick," the same with "Catch a Wave" and "Hawaii," and wrote significant parts of "I Get Around"—I wrote the part "'Round, 'Round Get Around, I Get Around," the musical part as well, as the words of several of the verses. I contributed to "Help Me Rhonda," "Be True to Your School," all of which I was disincluded from the co-authorship. I was told at the time that it was an oversight, and this and that, and they just kept saying they'd take care of it, they'd take care of it. Then Brian went into a period.

The publishing company was sold, and I really had nothing in writing. It was [only the word of] my uncle and my cousin. The publishing was sold and at the time Brian was completely nuts because his father forced him to sign over his publishing. Brian was forced to give his publishing rights to Murry who then in turn sold them to Almo/Irving, which is a publishing company run by A&M Records [founders] Herb Alpert and Jerry Moss. So he was completely—in addition to taking drugs and being paranoid schizophrenic and having an abusive father—he was completely destroyed at that period of time. That practically killed him because it was like having his babies sold. Now he wasn't completely on the up-and-up because he had not credited me for my contributions. My uncle Murry had up until 1969 always said that he was going to sell the publishing back to his boys, the group, and so on, and he double-crossed us and he sold it to somebody else.

He got the proceeds from that sale?

Oh yeah, all of it, Uncle Murry took all of the money. It was an awful abuse. I didn't have anything in writing and I wasn't advised by an attorney other than the one that was attorney for the group, Abe Somer was his name. And we come to find out later that he was the attorney for the publishing company that acquired it. So it was a conflict of interest. [Somer, who has been practicing law in California for 50 years, had a history of sexual harassment complaints at the firm, according to a *Los Angeles Times* report in 1991, but the State Bar of California has no public record of discipline or administrative actions against him.] I felt sorry for Brian basically because he was so messed up emotionally, and this only exacerbated that. So up until the time he sold it, I was told we were going to work it out, between Brian and myself. It was a family affair. But then after that, the publishing was sold, and I was told that I had no recourse.

So you haven't received a cent for any of those songs?

No, zero. And just recently Brian got a huge settlement from his lawsuit that he brought against Almo/Irving and Mitchell Silberberg & Knupp, the law firm at which Abe Somer worked. So he got this enormous settlement, and he didn't call me. Nobody from his side, even though they knew and Brian admits I'm owed for songwriters' royalties, if not publishing revenues. Nobody called me.

How much are you after?

Well, I would like to get the copyrights to the songs back. I would like to overturn the sale. My lawsuit is against Brian Wilson, Mitchell Silberberg & Knupp, and Almo/Irving. I would like to get the publishing rights back. I think we were defrauded. I think we were misrepresented. I know we were, and I know I haven't been paid by Brian or anybody for the songs I did. And he admits that I wrote them and he even called me about a month ago and said, "Mike, you were right to sue me. It's been a long time coming. I wanna get together with you and your attorneys and work this out."

What was his settlement from the law firm?

Ten million dollars. Plus he's made all this money all this time on "California Girls" and all these songs I mentioned. The broadcast rights—BMI, it's called [Broadcast Music Inc., a royalties collection firm]—because every time a song's played on the radio [the songwriter and copyright owner each receive a small royalty, even for cover versions] . . . "California Girls" has been played on radio stations a lot and so have many of those other songs I mentioned. That is the highest-paying song of the catalog, of the records we made, "Good Vibrations" being the second. And I wrote all the words of "Good Vibrations," and I came up with [the chorus] "I'm pickin' up good vibrations, she's giving me the excitations." I came up with the musical part as well as the words. I was credited for doing that but was given a disproportionate share. I come to find out, even as cheated as I was, my uncle still underpaid me!

Why don't you sue the estate of Murry Wilson?

Because that would involve Audree Wilson, who is my aunt Audree, who is a sweet lady, and she had no more control over Murry's activities, I think, than did Brian. That would harm her and I don't really wish to do it. It wasn't her doing that caused all this. It was Murry and it was Mitchell Silberberg & Knupp. Almo/Irving bought stolen property.

So Almo/Irving owns the Beach Boys catalog?

Yes, they own the Sea of Tunes catalog. Every song written up until 1969.

That's like the Beatles and the Rolling Stones getting ripped off by [former manager] Allen Klein.

Quite a bit. We were before Allen Klein, but it's true, it's quite a bit like that. It's funny, isn't it? There are so many awful things. You think the music business: oh, beautiful, music, Venus the goddess of music, art, whatever. And there are such terrible things done.

Have you read [the music industry exposé] *Hit Men* by Fredric Dannen?

Oh, sure.

It's a pretty disgraceful book!

Yes, well. I once made a few remarks to the Rock and Roll Hall of Fame, which I prefer to call the Rock and Roll Hall of Shame, because of some of the things you read in *Hit Men*. Every record company president presides over a company that inherently has a built-in bias against the artist because the artist is an expense. So they inadvertently steal from the artist. One way or another, they'll steal from you. They do funny little calculations with the royalties. Maybe the royalties came in, but they don't pay you those royalties for six months or a year. So they have the use of the interest. Just any way they can. That's the subtlest and nicest form of thievery. There are nice personalities and nice people that we have met through the years and we liked through the years in the industry, but the industry itself is fraught with tons of problems.

It's almost as if it would be a good industry if it weren't for the musicians—

Necessary evil.

Was that the same speech where you called Mick Jagger "chickenshit"—

—To get on stage with the Beach Boys. That just came because nobody wants to go on after the Beach Boys. In the old days, in the early '60s, you'd have battles of the bands. But once you get into geriatric rock, people are very nervous about their franchise. . . . I just think that the ego part of it and hiding behind your agent, hiding behind your manager, hiding behind your attorney. . . . Attorneys cause such divisiveness, the Beatles being the biggest and best example of it.

When Paul McCartney refused to come to the Rock and Roll Hall of Fame that night to be with his mates who he started out with years ago, that, to me, was nauseating, because he's the richest one of all of us. Why didn't he come? Why? Because he had business differences with the other guys. What was it revolving about? Who knows? But you can be sure that his attorney and their attorneys are making a fortune by sustaining that antipathy. They're not into compromising. They're not into being creative and healing. They're into divisiveness and billing. And so I know that, so I don't particularly have any love for the attorneys in the music industry, except for the occasional decent person.

And I don't particularly have any fondness for the whole way that the music industry's set up. The artist is an expense and they'll screw you any way they can. And all the record company presidents know that, and the artists when they start out, maybe they know it, maybe they don't. But it's kind of pitiful when a person gives everything they can creatively from their heart, and it just gets slaughtered by these psychopaths, these thieves that are the music industry mavens. That's why I was a bad boy and I spoke out of turn at the Rock and Roll Hall of Shame. I'm so embarrassed! [laughs sarcastically]

Anyway, my ultimate point was that rather than have all this divisiveness, rather than have all this chicanery and thievery going on, wouldn't it be nice—to quote a song!—if the Rock and Roll Hall of Fame and the entire music industry could stand for something more than just an egotistic, self-indulgent pit of thieves. . . . I'd like to see a Mick Jagger and a Mike Love and a Bruce Springsteen do something that is real, to fix something, rather than just a photo opportunity like Live Aid, which has no design to change anything. It was a great press opportunity, and maybe they shipped a few million dollars' worth of something to the docks to be stolen by the people in Ethiopia.

So you old farts get together and do a song, what happens after that?

Nothing, usually, because it's a nice emotional moment.

But you're promoting this concept of you and Jagger and Springsteen getting together?

I said "what if" it were done in the context of something that would really do anything. Instead of just doing a photo opportunity, doing something good because your press agent says it's a good thing to do.

Those black-tie rock 'n' roll events seem very fake.

It is fake because they don't think any further than the footlights. And I don't like that, I'm not into that. I think black-tie benefits are great, but when they start losing money for the cause or they don't address the issues with dynamic enough results, then it's like a Pyrrhic thing. It doesn't mean anything. So I have to do things with my life that mean something ultimately. And I'm not saying that we've all done that, we've been able to achieve that, but I'm just decrying the malaise of the planet, I guess. It's symptomatic in our industry of what it is everywhere, I guess, about the planet that I really don't like so much.

One of my goals is to create a film company called Philanthropic Films, where the entire proceeds of that film and the soundtrack go to an endowment fund to put enormous amounts of money into things like education and health, human care and kindness and the environment. It used to be that wealthy people endowed the arts, the Medicis and so on, and the Sistine Chapel and so on. Now it's time for the arts and the wealthy people to get together and endow society, instead of just trying to make that money and put it in that pension plan or put it in the Swiss bank account or whatever. There has to be a transformation in the way our society runs itself—not only environmentally speaking, but in a humanitarian sense. There has to be a new paradigm of how and why people engage in creative things or engage in business. That's a more evolved state, so that's where I want to lend my energies when I'm not doing Beach Boys music.

To what extent have you put your money where your mouth is?

Well, I created a thing called the Love Foundation several years ago and we created something called StarServe, which is one tiny step in the direction I'm speaking of. StarServe is an acronym for Students

Taking Action and Responsibility in Service. It's something that we mailed out a couple of years in a row, we're going on three years now, to a hundred thousand public, private, and parochial schools across America, encouraging students to get more involved in community service in whatever way they are able or find is relevant in their community. So that's one thing.

Can I just get back to Brian Wilson? I understand you're also suing him for slander and libel? Brian and Todd Gold?

And Landy.

So I was surprised that despite this lawsuit, he rang you up and said you were right to sue him over the royalties. So there's not a bad feeling between you two, is there?

I'm not sure. I'm not sure what goes on in Brian's mind, but I'll find out.

Are you serious about suing Brian when maybe it should be Landy and Gold?

Oh, I'm serious about suing Brian. If Brian says that he didn't say this, didn't say that, Landy made that up and Todd Gold made that up, that's fine. Then I'll just keep suing them, and maybe Brian's out of that position, and I keep going after Landy and Gold and the publisher.

Don't you think that Brian's in such a fragile state of mind that he can do without this aggravation?

I've felt that way for about 25 years, but it hasn't gotten me anywhere. Brian said some outright lies in that book, and I want him to either retract them or substantiate them. And that's going to be good for him, because he is paranoid. He thinks that Mike is going to hit him or Mike is going to kill him, because I [i.e., Brian] didn't credit him for writing "California Girls," let's say, which he said to a number of people because he's paranoid. It triggers fear. If we can resolve those issues, if he can be absolved of the guilt, it won't trigger his paranoia like it has been. Right now he has a continuing open wound psychically with those unresolved issues borne of guilt that in his delicate paranoid schizophrenic psyche lead to delusions, lead to all kinds of things that go on. Now if we can get rid of those then that would be grounds for improvement in his health and his welfare and well-being. So although it sounds like it's a merciless thing for me to do on one level, on another level it's an extremely necessary thing to be done.

He said that if it wasn't for him, you'd be pumping gas.

The fact is we've supported Brian with touring revenues since 1965 . . . and for him to say disparaging things about myself or anybody else in the group, then fine. Give us all that money back and we'll just call it quits. We'll call it a day. I think that he was made to say some things, and if he really believes those things, then fine. There is no love lost, because there wasn't any love there. But if he didn't mean those things or was caused to say some things—words were put into his mouth, or something—then he can retract them or he can identify the culprit and then we'll go on from there. Or he can apologize. Things like that.

You'd be quite happy to settle for an apology?

No. Not until everything is worked out. I want to see everything resolved so that we can go forward positively. Or else, don't steal any more of my money. Start paying me.

Do you think he'll ever play again with the Beach Boys on tour?

That's up to him.

There is room for him?

Of course. Yeah. I don't mind. I can have differences with people, even altercations with people, arguments and so on, and still go on with life. It's called being married or being in a family! But with Brian it's different because he has this paranoid schizophrenia to deal with. So it's important that we deal with those issues. It's important that I get credit for what I did. It's important to me that I get money. I don't think I'll ever get as much money as I should have gotten, and I think I've been harmed for enough years. There's a legal term called lulled. I've been lulled for so many years on this. We tried to resolve this writing issue with John Mason, who was Brian's attorney for several years during the '80s. Then Mason was fired. Basically Landy made Brian fire Mason just a couple of years ago. So that all went to naught. It was said by Mason that Landy tore up the songwriter agreement between Brian and I that had been prepared. Tore it up. The reason why is Landy had himself in for a percentage of whatever Brian was to recover in his lawsuit. And if they gave some money to me that would impact upon what Landy would have gotten. So pretty interesting stuff, I come to find out!

Why are the Beach Boys such a big part of Americana? You tied your colors so firmly to a fad—surfing music—and yet you're still here.

Hmmmm. Well, the funny thing about surfing music is that songs about surfing, it's kind of extraordinary. We were No. 1 in Sweden and Holland, South Africa and the Philippines.

Well, they surf in South Africa. There are some lovely beaches there.

They do. I'm well aware of that. But also not everybody speaks our dialect, West Coast American. And England. There's not much surfing going on in England. It's quite incredible. First of all I think that the warmth of the harmony comes through. It creates a mood with people of happiness, love, and warmth. So there's an intangible, but yet emotional thing that happens with our music to some listeners, those who like our stuff. And the subject matter deals in a lot of very California surfing subculture, sort of all-American vignettes, encapsulated little vignettes that go on every day in middle-class American life.

Do you think America would be the same without the Beach Boys?

Well, that's a strange question. I don't know how to answer that! Without the Beach Boys.

You've made such a big impact, not only on the charts but on popular culture.

You mean, had there never been a Beach Boys? I think the body of American music would be lacking some positivity had the Beach Boys never existed. Or maybe it might be supplied by somebody else. At least in the '60s, the greatest things were going on musically. It was the richest period of time. Motown was around, the British musical influences also very dynamic. It was a body of music which was kinda innocent, and kinda positive and fun for the most part.

What are the relationships like among the band members? Do you hang out together?

We hang out about a hundred days a year together, touring and performing. So we get plenty of time together. In our free time we have families who we generally gravitate towards, as one would, and so that's basically it. It's more of a professional relationship, but it's one that just in the last year or so has been improved. We've actually sat down with a psychiatrist, Dr. Harold Bloomfield, who is a very well-known author and psychiatrist, who's a friend of mine for many years. He's also a practitioner of TM, the TM-Sidhi program, which is the advanced program. In fact I met him on this course. I went to a six-month-long training course to learn what they call the TM-Sidhi program. So we were there for six months together and we got to be pretty good friends. . . . At any rate, we sat down with Harold—Carl and Al and myself and even Bruce has joined the group—and we've been able to sort through some things that might have happened years ago that one might have harbored or had some misunderstanding about this other person. And we've been able to go through all these things, and I think it's been very healthy and kind of resolved some residual things that had been hanging around the atmosphere. As a result, as a consequence of these meetings—we've had several meetings, one in Rio, one in England when we went over to see the George Harrison concert for the Natural Law Party [in 1992], we met in Santa Barbara, San Diego, L.A., and all over the place—

What do you do? Sit in a circle, close your eyes, and hold hands?

We meditate together for a few minutes and then we talk.

Give me an example of one or two of these hang-ups.

I don't know, just things that happened a long time ago with respect to incidents. I dunno. It's kinda like unresolved issues. I don't want to really get specific about them, because they're private meetings. We agreed not to discuss the content of the meetings outside the group.

Is Bruce a full member of the Beach Boys?
He's not a member of the corporation, but he's definitely a full member of the Beach Boys when we record and perform. He's extremely conscientious and very positive and is always ready to drive. He's spent hours and days and weeks and months of otherwise time he could spend with the family to devote to, for instance, the *Summer in Paradise* project. He spends a lot of time just being there, helping Terry with something . . . structuring harmonies. He's a very good songwriter. I'm trying to get him to write more than he has so far with the group anyway. He wrote the [Barry Manilow] song "I Write the Songs," which is an enormous, huge hit. It's up there with "Yesterday" in terms of performances.

What's the future for the Beach Boys? Will you break up at some stage?
We might, as the Beach Boys, cease to tour. I don't know if we'd call it breaking up or something. Or we might limit it to a month a year, or something like that. But there are several things that we might do. One is a symphonic album, and tour with a symphony orchestra. I think the Moody Blues did that recently.

So in conclusion, there's this dichotomy between the Beach Boys who make the great music and then there's this seamy undercurrent with all the shit that's been going on for 20 or 30 years.
Well you see—
Ugh. I think I just swallowed a fly!
—the problems—
I swallowed a fly!
Oh, no. Serves you right for trying all that yellow journalism trash.
Do you have a cup of water?
I'll tell you what. We have a Snapple here. [I turned the tape recorder off and Mike continued talking while I choked] . . . I was discredited, disenfranchised. On an economic level there was a serious disenfranchisement of me. But on a perception level, in terms of the creative process of what led to the success of the Beach Boys, Brian almost made it look in his book like it was a one-man show and the

rest of us didn't have much to do with anything creatively, and that was not true. If you subtracted all the words to the Beach Boys songs, how many of them would be on the radio? And if Brian Wilson was successful with me at that time and he was totally unsuccessful since that time in a commercially creative sense, and had two solo album opportunities, one which [1990's *Sweet Insanity*] was rejected because of the lyrics, primarily, and another which didn't fare so well because of the concept and the lyrics, then I would say it's fair to say that Mike Love's importance in the creative process of the Beach Boys was quite critical. It was dramatic. And his book, which was rather defamatory of me, avoided saying what I contributed to the musical performances, and if anything made it look like my contribution was just next to nothing or meaningless or very either nominal or almost—not superfluous, but—silly. If it was all those things then why was "Good Vibrations" No. 1? Why is "California Girls" such a big hit? Why was "I Get Around" No. 1? Why was "Surfin' USA" No. 1? I wrote all the words to "Surfin' USA," and he studiously avoided giving me credit for that. It's fair for me to tell my side of what happened.

Why don't you put a book out?

Because I'm too much of an environmentalist. I don't want to kill a bunch of more trees to satisfy my ego! Maybe I'll put a DAT out on it!

You've got this band at the peak of their careers and you've got this undercurrent as well.

Yeah, there was an abusive father, a paranoid schizophrenic cousin, and we were young, like I pointed out earlier. I didn't even know what publishing was when I started. I did not know what publishing was. I knew that you copyrighted a song to let people know that you wrote the song and kept it from being stolen, but I didn't know what that implied in terms of its value. My uncle Murry did, and he usurped the publishing rights of the Beach Boys songs. And I never had an attorney. I didn't think you needed an attorney in dealing with your cousin and your uncle. It just never occurred to me.

Next time around, I suppose. In another life.

I guess. Exactly!

Does TM involve reincarnation as well?

No, TM is Transcendental Meditation. It's just a mental technique. . . . I've never heard Maharishi talk much about reincarnation. He talks about Jhotish Astrology. That's a Vedic astrology. It's a very scientific way of determining influences on either your health or your business or your personal relationships based on your own nature, and the influence that nature has upon you. And it's quite interesting. There's been a lot of actual courses that one can take on Jhotish Astrology offered by Maharishi at Vedic University. I haven't heard him talk about reincarnation. I think that's too bizarre for most Western minds. But a few years ago astrology was too bizarre, so who knows?

But anyway, we do practice a form of levitation. There are sutras involved. They're mantras that you learn. When you learn TM you're given a mantra, which is a word or sound that has this effect of quieting the mind and the nervous system, and then you transcend. You go beyond thinking the source of thought, and that gives you this incredible tranquility. And when your mind goes to these final levels of thought, your body correspondingly sinks into this deep level of rest. So TM gives you that deep relaxation, deep level of rest. Now, once you've done some TM, you learn this advanced program, the TM-Sidhi program. They give you these sutras, which are things that you focus on to develop specific attributes of the mind or the body or the mind-body.

There is a sutra for vision that you can cultivate. The human capacity for vision is virtually unlimited. The only limit is our physical ability to see how many miles or how close up or. . . . How acute your vision is is a relative matter, but the quality of vision is not necessarily limited to that. In other words, you could put your awareness on something and see it. If you have the technique to evolve your capacity for vision to its ultimate supreme value, you're clairvoyant. There are sutras developed—clairvoyance, clairaudience, different faculties of the mind, of the body—one of them being the ability to master gravity, to make the body lighter and disappear. There are all these different phenomenal things that one can do if one masters the mind. As they say we only use a few percent of our conscious mind. So there's a whole blueprint to mastery of the conscious mind.

Would you be interested in trying to master levitation and disappearing?

You're given all these different sutras, one of which is levitation.

And you've done it?

Oh yeah, I've been practicing it for years.

Rising off the ground?

Ahem, yeah. See, it takes supreme coordination. *Refinement* is a better word, the refinement of your mind and body. Your whole nervous system has to be so refined and so precisely balanced, and the atmosphere and the environment, the inner self, everything has to be right in order to master creation and to be able to levitate. In our DNA we have the capacity for immortality, but because of circumstances emotionally and physically, being born in this society with the kind of food we eat, the kind of stresses we have on us, the kind of education we have or don't have, the ultimate reality of life is lived by very few people. So the idea is you can begin to progressively grow and evolve and make refinements to whatever your situation is, whether it be the quality of your nervous system, your mind, or body. At this point in time you can always improve on it, and that is the blueprint for the path that Maharishi has laid out through the organization that he's created over the last 30-plus years.

To me that's a very interesting thing. Rather than just accepting the norm of aging, deterioration, disease, and death ultimately, with Ayurveda, which I mentioned earlier, you can reverse the aging process and live a longer life and perfect health in the direction of immortality. The idea is that two generations from now people may be living for 150, 200 years. In fact I read in the paper the other day that scientists have determined that there are people on the Earth now who will live to be a couple of hundred years old—people alive right this minute—because of science. But this is ancient science, this is Vedic science. And all the knowledge for this quality of life is available. It's been brought out from ancient scriptures by Maharishi.

It originally started with just TM—meditate twice a day, you'll feel better in your work or school, and it's good for your health. As it turns out, healthcare utilization costs for people who practice TM in the over-40 category are 70 percent less than the norm, and heart disease is almost 90 percent less. It's just simple relaxation, twice a day. Less wear and tear.

Interesting stuff.

Yeah, it is. It's fascinating. There's a whole range of knowledge there that we don't ordinarily know of in our Western societies.

DAVID BOWIE: THE GOLDEN YEARS

I was on a shaky first date when David Bowie came up. In conversation, not in person. It's a solid move when such encounters are not going well. After all, I'm a music journalist and people are music fans. I casually mentioned that I had hung out with Bowie and my date was suddenly all ears. As I launched into some well-rehearsed tidbits, my penny stock soared. The time I made him cry, the time he forecast a race war in America, the time we chatted at a party.

Then she asked what my favorite Bowie record is. Without thinking, I told her it was *Let's Dance*. Crickets. Her pretty face turned sour. I tried to explain, desperately. Obviously it's not his best album, but it was a coming-of-age talisman for a schoolboy imprisoned in a boarding school. It represented an '80s comeback for Bowie, overdue financial recognition, a big world tour, a *Time* magazine cover. But I was drowning, and she was rowing away.

I dissected the exchange in my mind for years to come, grimaced every time the title track or "Modern Love" came on the radio. I crossed the street to avoid men with bottle-blonde hair or women wearing red shoes. It was traumatic. She had destroyed my guilty pleasure. If only I'd answered *Low* or *Ziggy Stardust*, or even that weird Christmas record with Bing Crosby. Maybe I could have confounded her with my other guilty pleasure, Tin Machine, and recounted how Bowie and I competed with each other to pour praise on his underappreciated hard-rock band. Maybe I should've just dated David Bowie.

My love for *Let's Dance* has returned, and my passion for Tin Machine's debut album just gets stronger. People like to ridicule Bowie's '80s output, but it was a tough decade for many '60s holdovers. The Rolling Stones and the Who broke up. Bob Dylan sang on "We Are the World." Paul McCartney dueted with Michael Jackson. Neil Young got sued by his label for not sounding like himself.

For Bowie personally, the sun finally started shining in the '80s. He'd spent the previous decade on a coke-and-pill bender, and now he sported a healthy tan while miming for the "Let's Dance" video in a dusty Australian outback bar. "I was a casualty for many years all through the '70s, right through to the very end," Bowie told me in 1993, when we met to discuss his first solo album in six years, *Black Tie White Noise*. "I think I really started to get a glimmer of what life could be like in the early '80s."

By then, he was single again. His decadelong marriage to Angela Bowie officially ended in 1980, and he got off very lightly. Alimony totaled about $980,000 in today's terms, according to some signed divorce documents I bought at a memorabilia auction. He also allowed Angela to take random contents from their home in the Swiss countryside, like a waste paper basket in the master bathroom, a cracked art deco vase from the ground floor hallway, and assorted fashion magazines from the basement.

He then focused on raising their young son, Joe, just like John Lennon was doing in New York. That partly explains the relatively long interregnum between that year's *Scary Monsters* and *Let's Dance*. "My son has helped me grow up an incredible amount," Bowie told *Entertainment Tonight* in 1987. "What he teaches me is an abundance of enthusiasm for everything that he approaches. That is great, when you're that age, that the world is so big and the horizon is so massive and everything's possible. It's a rejuvenating kind of thing. And for him, I think he kinda finds it fun that I like the Sex Pistols more than he does!" (Joe, now known as Duncan Jones, is a promising movie director who claims to be disinterested in his father's music.)

The '90s were also good to Bowie. He married mononymous Somali supermodel Iman in 1992, instantly becoming a stepdad and eventually a dad again. "Let me assure you that my life is wonderful," he told me in late 1999. "Really, I'm at probably the apex of my existence in some ways. The last 10 to 12 years have been just extraordinary, a virtual lesson in how to enjoy life."

It's easy to understand, in hindsight, why he essentially disappeared again in 2004. It wasn't so much the heart attack he suffered that year, because he had long been aware of his mortality. "So many people I've known are dead now," Bowie said with a sigh during our 1993 chat, when he was 46. "Every day starts to become more and more precious. It really is a gift, life. It's a foolish man who laughs at it."

No, it was Bowie family values. As Bowie's carrot-topped alien character sagely declared three decades earlier in *The Man Who Fell to Earth*, "A man should spend time with his family."

He also had a deeper understanding of his family's predisposition to mental illness. Three of his aunts were afflicted as well as his beloved elder half-brother. Terry Burns endured a lifetime battle with manic depression and schizophrenia, and ended it all in 1985 by lying in the path of an oncoming train.

"He was a very intelligent, intellectual man," Bowie recalled. "The two sides of his mind were so opposite to each other that it always disturbed me inasmuch as I recognized similar traits in myself. So there was an ambivalence between us. I always wanted to push him away from me, but at the same time I always acknowledged the strong empathy that I had with him and what he was going through. I guess I always looked at it that I was the lucky one because I had these artistic leanings and I could express those things and all that."

He got teary-eyed, and I felt terrible. I didn't mean to make him cry! I related the story over the years until a doubly terrible thought dawned on me: What if he was faking? He is an actor after all. (And now I feel triply terrible committing these doubts to paper.)

"I never got closer to him," Bowie continued, dabbing his eyes. "I distanced myself too much from him. But it happened. I can't feel guilty about it. It's just something that happened, it's what I did. So I just have to know that up front and, if anything, try and learn from that experience, which is all you can do with your past. You can't hide it away and lock it away and pretend it never happened. All you can do is examine it for what it was. And if it's possible to learn from it, then try and learn from it."

We were talking about Terry because he was the subject of "Jump They Say," the first single from *Black Tie White Noise*. An elderly aunt, who had been tracked down by an enterprising journalist, later accused Bowie of cashing in on Terry's death. You can't win.

My head exploded when Bowie's publicist called in February 1993 to ask if I wanted to interview Bowie for *Black Tie White Noise*. A royal audience with the Thin White Duke? Waves of ecstasy and panic washed over me and I got little sleep as our big date approached. Much secrecy surrounded the project—not that the masses were clamoring for intel. Advance cassettes were not mailed out. I had to go to the publicist's house for a single playback. A bare-bones press release omitted the title of a classic rock song Bowie was covering. He did not want someone else to steal his thunder by also doing Cream's "I Feel Free."

And soon enough Bowie and I were swapping jokes at the Peninsula Hotel in Beverly Hills, with his faithful adjutant Corinne "Coco" Schwab hovering in the background to ensure the room temperature was to his liking. He looked appropriately aristocratic in his natty dark-blue suit, effortlessly sophisticated yet completely relaxed. He smoked the whole time, almost making me want to take up the habit. I had been in America for just six months and here I was, conversing with the guy whose novelty tune "The Laughing Gnome" was one of my first musical memories.

Naturally we discussed the new album, but much of the conversation was about his career—specifically his recent output, including *Let's Dance*.

Beneath the MTV-friendly dance beats, *Let's Dance* was one of Bowie's bleaker albums. The video for the title track drew the world's attention to the plight of Australia's Aborigines. It depicted a young couple confronting the humiliating realities of big-city life in Sydney, a metaphor for anyone caught up in the urban grind. But they have the last laugh, abandoning their modern-day trappings, including her shiny red shoes, to return to their ancient traditions. (Most of the people in the video, by the way, are dead now, I learned in 2013 when I visited the outback pub where he bravely mimed his song for hostile, piss-taking cattle farmers.)

"The lyric of 'Let's Dance' is incredibly dark," Bowie told me. "It's probably one of the darkest dance songs that you've ever heard. It's written in the minor—there's not a major chord in it—which is also traditionally the key to writing when you're writing a darker piece."

"Let's Dance" topped the singles charts on both sides of the Atlantic and showcased a relatively unknown guitarist named Stevie Ray Vaughan. (Coincidentally another guest guitarist, Eddie Van Halen, played on Michael Jackson's "Beat It," the song that "Let's Dance" replaced at No. 1 in America.)

The second video, for the remake of Iggy Pop's "China Girl," was also shot in Australia with Bowie and an Asian model from my very own New Zealand cavorting nude on the beach. The third video was a live version of "Modern Love," the track that opens *Let's Dance* with a Motownish flourish. Between the multi-pronged media exposure and his *Serious Moonlight* world tour, Bowie was hard to avoid in 1983.

There are only eight songs on *Let's Dance*, of which just five were brand-new. Besides "China Girl," Bowie covered the obscure post-glam rock track "Criminal World" and recorded a new, improved version of "Cat People (Putting out the Fire)," the song he had released the prior year for the *Cat People* movie remake. Vaughan was all over that one, and my other favorite, "Ricochet," with its semi-jazz bass and fragmentation of lyrics.

Contemporary critics liked *Let's Dance*, and it was the biggest seller of Bowie's career. But over time it came to be lumped in with his other '80s albums, viewed as a relatively lightweight R&B confection.

"In its time *Let's Dance*, I thought, was absolutely a stupendous album," Bowie said. "It's just it was a very singular album," the sonic creation of his co-producer Nile Rodgers, the funky maestro from Chic. "I gave Nile pretty much his own head on it apart from suggesting things like using a heavyweight rock-blues guitarist—Stevie—against the R&B patterns that he was putting down, which was really quite an interesting idea at the time. But other than that it was pretty much Nile's arrangements on *Let's Dance*."

Bowie removed himself even further from the creative process with the two follow-ups, the covers-laden *Tonight* (1984) and the unanimously panned *Never Let Me Down* (1987), admitting, "I don't know what happened there!"

Carlos Alomar, Bowie's longtime rhythm guitarist, had a better idea. "*Tonight* wasn't given much thought," he told me. "We had so much other stuff to do and had to rush through the studio real fast. It was 'just another album.' David didn't have much time for it—he just came in with the demos, and that was done and we did it."

Alomar and Turkish-born multi-instrumentalist Erdal Kizilçay claimed responsibility for *Never Let Me Down*. Bowie provided an overall concept, his old school chum Peter Frampton overdubbed some lead guitar, and then Bowie took the tapes from Switzerland to America for background vocals, Alomar said.

Bowie said his one regret with those two albums was that he wasted some good compositions, like "Loving the Alien" and "Time Will Crawl." "I was getting so totally indifferent about things at that time. It wasn't a very pleasant period for me," he admitted. *Never Let Me D*own was his last Gold-certified studio album in the United States.

Bowie promoted *Never Let Me Down* with the *Glass Spider* world tour. By most accounts, the highly choreographed extravaganza was his creative nadir. "I thought it was a bit beneath you," Tin Machine drummer Hunt Sales told Bowie in the presence of a *Q* magazine reporter in 1989. "I watched it [on TV] thinking, 'This is the guy who did Spiders from Mars.'"

But I was only four when Bowie broke up with the Spiders from Mars, the journeymen musicians who backed him during the *Ziggy Stardust/Aladdin Sane* glam era in the early '70s. And when Bowie came to New Zealand on the *Serious Moonlight* tour, I couldn't sneak out of boarding school to see his show 125 miles away like one of my buddies did.

So *Glass Spider* was my awkward first time. What did I know? I had no yardstick, and at the time thought it was similarly stupendous. I remember a chap named Spazz Attack most of all, which is maybe a sad commentary. The spiky-haired artiste was one of six dancers on the stage, along with Bowie's considerably younger girlfriend at the time, Melissa Hurley, and Toni Basil, the singer famed for her big hit "Mickey." The more I write, the worse I make it sound.

Most importantly for me, the *Glass Spider* tour marked my debut as a professional journalist.

A 19-year-old college dropout working in a clerical job, I was among the 80 or so fans who greeted Bowie when he flew to Auckland in November for the final show of the eight-month tour. In the ensuing crush, Bowie was spirited through arrivals into a waiting limo. In his wake stood crying schoolgirls with spiky Ziggy hairdos. Almost unnoticed, wheeling their baggage trolleys, were Frampton and Alomar. They boarded a charter bus.

A day after the show, I needed another Bowie fix. I could hang out at the Regent Hotel in hopes of a sighting. Or, a better idea, I could call his room. After some thought, it seemed more practical to lower my sights and ask the hotel to connect me to Alomar, who came up with the idea for "Fame," and whom I remembered from the "Fashion" video. He picked up the phone, I nervously said I was a journalist seeking an interview, and he said he would give me a break and talk with me the next day.

But that was a Monday, and I had to plead with my boss to let me take some time off. I was soon knocking on Alomar's hotel door armed with a shoebox tape recorder. He was relaxed, relieved that the tour nightmare was over, and clearly nostalgic for the dancer-free *Serious Moonlight* trek where the only weirdness that went on was Bowie taking boxing lessons. I didn't know it at the time, but Bowie and his tourmates had ritually incinerated the *Glass Spider* staging after the Auckland show.

"We were more of a family last time," Alomar said. "This time, because of the dancers, there was an initial intimidation between the band and the dancers because they were always seeking the camera whereas we were more straight-ahead playing."

As for the grandiosity of the whole enterprise, Bowie thought he was doing fans a favor. "This tour took $1.4 million a week," Alomar said, "and when you have that much money it becomes a point of, 'Am I going to plow that money back in and bring something to rock 'n' roll? Or am I just going to take the kids' money and run?' No longer can you just go on stage in just jeans and T-shirt and expect the audience to swallow that."

After about an hour, I took my leave and walked slowly along the hotel corridor hoping in vain that Bowie would pop out of his room and demand equal time. Back at the office, I transcribed the tape on company time and pitched my exclusive to the *New Zealand Herald*, the country's biggest paper. It was published the following Friday under the clever headline *A Guitarist in Fashion*, pretty much as I wrote it. Alomar correctly predicted that the next Bowie record would be "straight-ahead rock 'n' roll." But he was not invited to the party. Alomar's next outing was with Debbie Gibson.

The gloriously cacophonous Tin Machine marked Bowie's return to the traditional band dynamic he had last enjoyed with the Spiders from Mars. Sporting designer stubble and a double-breasted suit, he was backed by the equally debonair avant-gardist Reeves Gabrels on guitar and brothers Hunt and Tony Sales, the rhythm section on the Bowie-produced Iggy Pop album *Lust for Life*.

Their self-titled debut was loud, aggressive, and, unfortunately, somewhat humorless. Bowie's lyrics were also ham-fisted ("right-wing dicks in their boiler suits"), evidently the result of a band creed not to spend any time polishing material. The menacing opening track, "Heaven's in Here," was a popular choice at awards show performances, often degenerating into a melee of improvised distortion as Bowie sat on the drum riser in cool detachment. The cover of John Lennon's "Working Class Hero" was killer.

I rushed to the record store on the first day of sale to buy the cassette because I was worried it would sell out amid all the hype about Bowie's latest makeover. That was not a problem. Sales started strongly, and then collapsed. Tin Machine unfairly became a byword for ill-fated artistic detours, just as *Heaven's Gate* and *Ishtar* are derided by people who never saw the movies. There seems to be some nostalgia for Tin Machine now. It separated the real fans from the arrivistes, and helped pave the way for grunge.

But Bowie didn't do himself any favors at the time. He had already exhausted much of his post *Let's Dance* goodwill with weak albums, goofy film roles in *Labyrinth* and *Absolute Beginners,* and his camp duet with Mick Jagger on "Dancing in the Street." He also sent a lot of mixed messages. First, he claimed to be just one of the guys in the band and vowed never again to play his hits. But then he ditched Tin Machine the following year so that he could play the hits on a massive world tour. As the band finally set out on its own world tour in October 1991, on the heels of a poorly received second album that I never got around to buying, a *Q* cover story asked, "Are Tin Machine crap? Discuss."

Bowie remained fiercely proud of Tin Machine, and was still buzzing in 1993 about rave reviews for the first album from both *The New York Times* and *Los Angeles Times*. "I think that is one of the best albums of the late '80s, without doubt, without reservation, and I suspect it will be looked back as such in 10 years probably like *Low* was," he told me, referring to his experimental synth-driven masterpiece from 1977. "Listening to it against some of the more contemporary so-called rock bands makes them sound pretty timid in their way."

And that brought us to *Black Tie White Noise*. As he told anyone who would listen, the new album's beginnings dated from his wedding.

He wanted to compose some music that wouldn't offend either Iman's Muslim family or what was left of his Protestant one, ergo the opening track "The Wedding." But that was just one jumping-off point, and the album hardly offers a rose-colored view of relationships.

He also viewed the recording process as an opportunity to tie up loose ends by reuniting with blasts from the past. Rodgers returned as producer, though Bowie took more of an interest in the recording process than he had with *Let's Dance*. He also brought in ailing Spiders from Mars guitarist Mick Ronson, who played on "I Feel Free" and succumbed to liver cancer a year later. Tin Machine alumnus Gabrels played on one track and remained in the fold until 1999.

From a long-term perspective, Bowie's reunion with Mike Garson, the jazz pianist all over *Aladdin Sane*, was the most momentous. After he was purged in late 1974 as part of a break with the onerous regime of Bowie's former manager, Garson remained active in the West Coast jazz scene. Bowie bought a few of his newer albums, was duly impressed, and decided to surprise him with a "Guess who?" phone call from out of the blue. Alas, Garson immediately replied, "David," killing Bowie's hopes of hearing shock, elation, and disbelief on the other end of the line. He went on to become Bowie's music director. Like Bowie, Garson had undergone a lot of life changes. "He's no longer a Scientologist, which is a big difference in his life. I feel that he probably went through a lot of pain going through what he had to go through to get away from all that. Which is not an easy thing to get away from, Scientology."

With Tin Machine's metallic grind out of the picture, Bowie returned to his early passion for wind instruments: That's him on saxophone. The horn lineup was a nod to his first idol, Little Richard. Indeed, *Black Tie White Noise* was Bowie's blackest album since *Young Americans* in 1974. "Jump They Say" was an obvious talking point. So was the funky title track, with its references to racial strife and the 1992 L.A. riots. He feared civil unrest on a nationwide scale. His apocalyptic vision of America was a curious mix of Boer ideology and Public Enemy poetry.

"Anybody who's foolish to believe that race relations is gonna change into this great genial coming together are fooling themselves. At this moment in time the blacks have no interest whatsoever if the whites have any interest in coming together. They don't care. They don't want necessarily to have any equality with whites. They want their own thing based on a black economy. Which frankly is the only way that they can make it work over here, 'cause there is nobody anywhere who's gonna do anything about making a real and absolute and pure integration into society.

"The obstacles in the inner cities are almost insurmountable. It's quite incredible how everything's been structured. You just don't find any areas in white America that have the same amount of liquor stores on every block, the same amount of gun shops on every block that you get in those areas. It's like, 'Come on, do yourselves in. We'll supply you with the ammunition. You do it for yourselves.' Everything's geared to keeping them absolutely and completely repressed."

From his perch in Switzerland, Bowie had visions of swastikas. He was troubled by the resurgence of National Front–style violence across Germany in the wake of the economic fallout following unification. England seemed fairly immune to such conflict, having gone through such struggles in the 1950s—as depicted in *Absolute Beginners*, a really bad British film in which Bowie was the only highlight. But England's most important rock soloist was increasingly disdainful of his native land and "the poor English." His rare visits to Blighty were on the down-low, weekend trips to stay with childhood buddies and their families.

For the most part, Bowie was all laughs. He managed to pull off four convincing accents—a gruff Garson, the blue-collar Hull lilt of Ronson, a slightly fey Morrissey, and funky New York. I zeroed in on Bowie's positive frame of mind and lazily noted that great art is born of adversity. I wished him happiness, but surely he didn't want to get too comfortable?

"Maybe before I wouldn't tolerate negative things that happened to me on a day-to-day basis—which, of course, is absolutely impossible to carry out one's life always having intolerance to the negative. Negative happens! Shit happens! But I think when you become a little more relaxed about that and say, 'OK, it happens. It's not the end of the world. It's just something to deal with.' I don't think it makes life more comfortable. It allows one to let go a bit more, rather than trying to have absolute control over one's life."

Segue to my one brilliant question: You've fallen back to Earth? (A nod to *The Man Who Fell to Earth*) "Yes! The cat that fell—," he said, laughing uproariously before reaching the punch line of his in-joke. "I had a drummer once, Dennis Davis, in the mid-'70s, and Dennis could never remember the name of the film. And he always said [in thick New York patois], 'That film you made, *The Cat That Fell Down.*' I've always called it *The Cat That Fell Down.*"

That reminded Bowie of his thwarted film ambitions. He and Mick Jagger were supposed to star in *Dirty Rotten Scoundrels,* which eventually became a hit for Michael Caine and Steve Martin. Undeterred by the refusal of George Orwell's widow to allow him to make a musical adaptation of *1984,* he and Oliver Stone had hoped to do an adaptation of Orwell's *Homage to Catalonia.* Another director secured the rights, though nothing seems to have come of it.

Coco the guard dog eventually signaled that our time was at an end. We exchanged cordial goodbyes, and I felt generally good about myself for the next few years. Meet David Bowie? Check. Bowie did not tour to promote *Black Tie,* wisely preferring to keep the home fires burning. Bands in flannel shirts were more fashionable anyway. *The New York Times,* neatly summing up the dilemma Bowie would face for the rest of his career, said the album "stumbles because it tried too hard to be current." It debuted at No. 39 on the U.S. chart and sank to No. 100 in its fourth week. In the U.K., *Black Tie* hit No. 1, and "Jump They Say" became his last top-10 single.

I bumped into Bowie at a Hollywood party in the fall of 1995, when he was on tour with Nine Inch Nails in a bid for acceptance by the hard rock/techno/alternative crowd. I got to the postgig bash at the same time as Kelsey Grammer and his business manager, and was able to get ushered into the VIP area upstairs by engaging them in conversation just long enough to be considered part of Kelsey's posse.

Once inside, I saw Bowie sitting on a couch and waited for the right moment to ask whether he thought he would make the cut for the next class of the Rock and Roll Hall of Fame. The announcement was due any day. I nervously sidled up to him, and he barely turned to look at me as he replied, "I think it's very nice. I don't give it much thought, actually."

Huh? I wasn't asking for reaction, I wanted to know how he rated his chances. I quickly scribbled the quote on a cocktail napkin, and resumed my conversation with the amiable Kelsey who kept calling me "Gunga Din." The next day, sure enough, the Hall of Fame lineup was announced and Bowie was included. I guess he knew in advance and was giving me a scoop, which I missed. Oh well, the quote was still exclusive and lent some authority to my story.

The day after that was Halloween, a great day to see a Bowie concert. He did a gig at the 4,000-capacity Palladium, where everyone wore festive garb. The only downer was the opening act, song after interminable song by Keanu Reeves' band Dogstar. By the time Bowie came on, I had inched my way through the crush to about the third row. I sacrificed sound for vision; his vocals were totally muffled. As with the L.A. Forum show I'd seen three nights before, there was no encore, despite the crowd's pleas. After the show, I waited for the bus in the cold rain and schlepped my way back to my Venice hovel.

My favorite show took place two years later when Bowie played the Vic Theatre in Chicago. It was one of those "Blind Date" gigs sponsored by a beer company where the audience wouldn't know who was performing until the curtain opened. I was in the know, but my three guests were not. We were in the mosh pit when Bowie came on to general astonishment and performed "The Jean Genie." He was in a chatty mood. "Welcome to our place. Got a few minutes? We've got some old songs and some young songs, some you'll like and some you won't." The set list was exhaustive, and my pals were thrilled. I snapped a bunch of photos, which was verboten. A security guard spied me and frog-marched me out during the last song. He opened my camera to confiscate the film, but I had managed to extract it and shove it down my pants.

When Bowie and I reconnected in 1999 he was promoting *Hours...*, an album about his domestic troubles. Or, rather, an album about his fantasies of domestic troubles, since the despondent lyrics had nothing to do with his happy family life. If Bowie was long removed from the cutting edge, he at least gave the impression that he was pulling the strings of the hipsters like Kurt Cobain, Nine Inch Nails frontman Trent Reznor, and the Smashing Pumpkins' Billy Corgan. He was comfortable with his lot. "I'm very happy with the '90s, I like the '90s a lot," he said. "From around '89 onwards, virtually everything I've recorded or written has been done at the best of my abilities at any given time. I can look back on it all and feel quite proud of it all, actually. They're all very good albums."

Hours... was preceded by *Outside* (1995) and *Earthling* (1997). Both were ambitious efforts where the ambience and texture of the music were as important as the lyric. *Outside* was a concept album with a cast of characters headed by Bowie as a cop. Or something like that. It was meant as the first of a series of character studies encapsulating what life in the last decade of the old millennium was like. But Bowie got bored and moved on. He later threatened to formulate a follow-up from the 25 hours of tapes that he and producer Brian Eno worked up in Switzerland. *Outside* has a couple of great tunes like "The Heart's Filthy Lesson" (used in the movie *Seven*), but it's not what you'd call one of his go-to albums. *Earthling* has more durability—from the cover depicting an obverse Bowie in a tattered Union Jack frock coat, to the pulsing, urgent songs within. It yielded a minor hit collaboration with Reznor, "I'm Afraid of Americans," but the so-called drum-n-bass project fell victim to Americans' antipathy toward dance music. *Outside* debuted at No. 21 and *Earthling* at No. 39 on the Billboard 200. Within a month, both were well on their way to the bottom half of the chart.

Hours..., the weakest of the bunch, had an unusual genesis just like *Black Tie White Noise*. At least seven of the songs were initially written for a video game called *Nomad Soul*. Eschewing the obvious tack of writing yet another industrial soundtrack, Bowie decided he wanted to give the two-dimensional characters a heart and a soul by writing emotive songs with an emphasis on lyric and melody. "I took the idea of a representational 50-year-old looking back on his life, and I just went from there. In a way, it's a bit like a novelist putting together some short stories, a little collection of small narratives. The last thing anybody wants really from an artist unless they live in a saccharine world, is a really, really, really happy album, and I've never been good at making really, really, really happy albums."

The album died, of course. It debuted at No. 47 and was at No. 113 in its third week. He went on to release a relatively strong, if similarly uncommercial, pair—*Heathen* (2001) and *Reality* (2003)—and then returned to Mars. Or rather a loft apartment in SoHo, where he resumed his stay-at-home dad guise. As Iman told *The Times*, "I am *not* married to David Bowie . . . I am married to David Jones. They are two totally different people."

Bowie did emerge in October 2003 for one last world tour that was cut short the following June after he suffered a heart attack while performing at a German festival. He thought he had pinched a nerve in his shoulder, but tests showed he had an acutely blocked artery. He underwent emergency surgery and was hospitalized for about a week. He said in a statement that he couldn't wait to get back to work again, wryly adding, "I tell you what, though, I won't be writing a song about this one."

I agreed with his assertion in the statement that the tour had been "fucking fantastic" up to that point, although the North American leg got off to a rocky start in December when the first five shows were canceled after he was stricken by the flu. I was on hand for the default opener in Montreal. His voice was fine, but he was likely loaded to the gills with medication. He knocked back a sports drink, swallowed some pills, and blew his nose. "I didn't know if I could do the show tonight; I felt really ill, to be honest with you," he said toward the end. The French-Canadians loved "I'm Afraid of

Americans," but Bowie balanced the sentiments with "Heroes," a triumphant nod to his fellow New Yorkers. The *Reality* stuff was enjoyable; it's a pity the album spent just four weeks in the Billboard 200. In subsequent weeks I saw him play theaters in Chicago, Denver, and Los Angeles. And that was it for David and me.

In later years he popped up at his son's movie premieres, did cameos on *SpongeBob SquarePants* and pal Ricky Gervais' *Extras*, championed Arcade Fire just like he had flown the flag for Iggy Pop and Lou Reed decades earlier, and performed live for the last time at a 2006 charity event with Alicia Keys. EMI's reissues of Bowie's back catalog proceeded apace, culminating in an over-the-top five-disc configuration for *Station to Station*.

In January 2010 I interviewed Bowie's bald bass player Gail Ann Dorsey, who had toured and recorded with him since 1995. Our conversation inspired me to start learning the bass, notwithstanding her repeated warnings that early Bowie tunes such as "Hang on to Yourself" and "Cracked Actor" were extremely complicated.

Touring with Bowie was an education, literally, she recalled. "We went to the Motown Museum together on one of our Detroit shows, a little band outing. He often would do that. He's a very smart chap. He's interested in a lot of things, and reads a lot. I've been to several bookstores with him and various things. When we're out on the road he's always out looking for things, learning things."

Her choice of the present tense was promising. But like everyone else, she could only speculate as to his current activities. Unlike most of us, she had Bowie's email address and had just written to wish him a happy 63rd birthday. "I hope that he will return. I really don't know," she said. "I never pry into an artist's life or process either. I don't write to him and go, 'What are you doing?' Or call and go, 'Why aren't you playing?' You let people be, and you see where it falls."

Indeed, three years later, Bowie marked his 66th birthday by revealing that he would release an album called *The Next Day* in March. In this day and age where nothing stays secret for long, it was remarkable that not a word had leaked. All the players, including

Dorsey, signed nondisclosure agreements, though one would like to think this precaution was unnecessary. Leading up to the album's release, critics fell over themselves to hail both Bowie and his latest reincarnation—a bit like they did with Tin Machine. The man of mystery shot some sad videos, but otherwise did nothing to promote the album. *The Next Day* went to No. 1 in Britain and No. 2 in the United States, his best performance in two decades, and quickly slid down the charts. The album was a thoroughly enjoyable collection of conventional rock songs, which is probably the worst insult you can throw at Bowie. But like "the cat" says in *The Man Who Fell to Earth*, "I've proved enough. I've proved everything I'm gonna prove. I've gone as far as I'm going."

STEVE CROPPER: SOUL SIDEMAN

Steve Cropper usually comes near the top of "greatest guitarist" lists compiled by music magazines and aficionados. Jimi Hendrix, of course, reigns supreme, while Cropper jockeys for position with maybe Eric Clapton or Jeff Beck. But it's rarefied air up there, and Cropper stands out from the pack as a low-key sideman who prefers subtle rhythm guitar licks over flashy solos.

Cropper was the primary guitarist and one of the chief producers at Stax Records, the Memphis-based soul label that begat Otis Redding, Carla Thomas, and Sam & Dave. Millions have heard his name called out in the middle of Sam & Dave's "Soul Man" when Sam Moore exclaims, "Play it, Steve!" It's one of the most important examples of Cropper's work and also one of the simplest. The easily identifiable intro is just a series of two-note harmonies played up and down the neck. Any guitar rookie will pick it up within minutes, though it could take a few more years to duplicate Cropper's mojo.

Cropper once likened his style to that of George Harrison. "He's not fancy," he told me. "He's not trying to impress his mom or his guitar teacher. He's just having fun playing and that's what I like doing."

In the summer of 1962—at the same time the Beatles first entered EMI's recording studio—Cropper found accidental fame in his own right. The core members of the Stax studio band started working up instrumental jams during snatches of spare time between recording sessions, and label executives decided the tunes were worthy of release. And that's how Booker T. and the MG's became the biggest instrumental band in the world with breezy hits such as "Green Onions," "Soul Limbo," and "Time Is Tight."

With two blacks and two whites, the group was also a civil rights standard bearer in the segregated south. Organist Booker T. Jones was the group's nominal leader, while drummer Al Jackson Jr. kept metronomic timing. Lewie Steinberg played bass for three years until he was replaced by Cropper's childhood buddy Donald "Duck" Dunn.

As Stax's studio chief, Cropper co-wrote hundreds of songs, including Redding's posthumous chart topper "(Sittin' on) The Dock of the Bay," which he completed in the studio with the heaviest of hearts after Redding and most of his touring band were killed in a plane crash in December 1967. Cropper also collaborated with Wilson Pickett on "In the Midnight Hour" and with Eddie Floyd on "Knock on Wood." The intros for these two songs are basically the reverse of each other, testimony to Cropper's philosophy of "following the dots" on the guitar neck.

He recalled that his intros often had little to do with the songs themselves. "It was all about getting attention. 'Hey guys! Wake up, listen to this!' And then the song would start. The other is—admitting this, I'll probably get in a lot of trouble—but we designed a lot of those intros just to keep the disc jockey from talking over the record! So we do these powerhouse intros like 'Midnight Hour' and 'Knock on Wood,' 'Soul Man,' so that they couldn't talk over it! They talked until the singer kicked in, never listened to the music, never cared about it, I guess."

Notwithstanding his dislike of the spotlight, Cropper recorded a solo project in 1969. *With a Little Help from My Friends* featured such pals as Buddy Miles and Leon Russell who, paradoxically, were not credited on the hastily released project. Cropper left Stax the following year amid mounting creative and business disagreements and joined a short-lived label in Memphis where he produced albums for the likes of Jeff Beck, Rod Stewart, and Poco. After moving to Los Angeles in 1974, he became an in-demand session player, reunited for one more album with Booker T. and the MG's, and toured with Levon Helm. He reached a mainstream audience once again in 1980 with *The Blues Brothers* movie, where he played a member of the band reunited by Dan Aykroyd's and John Belushi's characters.

It's been an action-packed existence. "Having the memories to talk about, I'm a very fortunate guy," he told me in 2011, four months shy of his 70th birthday. "I literally don't have to make anything up."

Cropper shared his memories with me on two occasions. I first met him in 1994 just before the release of *That's the Way It Should Be*, the first album from Booker T. & the MG's in 17 years, and the group's last to date. He was still living in L.A. then, up on Mulholland Drive, but was about to move to Nashville, where he lives today with his wife and two children. The beefy, bearded, and ponytailed guitarist was the stereotypical charming Southern gentleman, regaling me with stories from the Stax days. But he didn't pull his punches when I asked him about Pickett's claim (in Gerri Hirshey's *Nowhere to Run*) that he alone wrote "In the Midnight Hour." After the interview was over, Cropper told me he would "kick his ass" next time he saw Pickett. (I'm not sure if he got around to that before Pickett died in 2006.)

What do you think of the Southern rock revival, particularly with the Black Crowes covering Otis Redding?

I think it's great. I'm glad to see it coming back. Black Crowes is a new band. They still have their Southern roots. You can tell that they were brought up on certain aspects of R&B, with songs like [Redding's] "Hard to Handle" and all. It sorta keeps the music alive.

Were you on the original "Hard to Handle"?

No, but I had a hand in it. I didn't get credited as a writer, no. But I definitely had a hand in the production of it. I was right there when it was done.

I read once that Wilson Pickett said you shouldn't have been credited for "Midnight Hour"?

He's said that more than once. He's completely crazy. He would never tell me that to my face. He respects me and loves me dearly and I don't understand where that comes from. That was my idea. That was definitely not his idea. He came in with a song called "Don't Fight It" and I brought him "Midnight Hour" and then the two of us collaborated on "I'm Not Tired." We wrote three songs the same night. [Stax co-owner] Jim Stewart and [executive/producer] Jerry Wexler were around when all that went down. That's absolute bullshit that I shouldn't get credited for it. What can I say? He did not write that music. He had nothing to do with writing that music. That's absolute crap. I can't believe that he's telling people this, you know?

It's more your song than his, in some ways?

Certainly. But that's not the first time. [Atlantic Records engineer] Tommy Dowd called me one time and said, "Have you seen the last issue of *Playboy*?" Or one of those magazines. Somebody made a statement in there that I shouldn't have been on "(Sittin' on) The Dock of the Bay." And I'm going, "Where in the hell did this come from?" I wrote all the lyrics and the bridge and did all the arrangement. The only thing I didn't write was the intro and the first verse. It's pretty amazing: He writes over three-quarters of a song and somebody says his name shouldn't have been on there.

When we reconnected on the phone in 2011, Cropper explained the only known downside to composing a classic. Redding is treated with such love and affection by the musical community that few dare record their own versions of "Dock of the Bay," which Cropper estimated had been played about nine million times on the radio. The handful of key exceptions includes Glen Campbell, Sammy Hagar, and Tom Jones. By contrast, "Knock on Wood" was a massive disco hit for Amii Stewart in 1979. Cropper's lighthearted plea? "Please cover it!"

But Cropper wasn't sitting around at home waiting for the mailman to deliver royalty checks. "I like going out and working for a living. I enjoy the money that I make on the road. I kind of enjoy that more because the money that comes from royalties and all is almost already spoken for: What the government leaves you is already designated to pay bills and that sort of thing. So [with] the money that I can make on the road I can do things in the future, save up and buy something. I like working for a living."

He has lobbied legislators on behalf of fellow songwriters hit hard by Internet piracy. He bore the theft of his songs "by every college kid in the United States, and then some" with equanimity. "I'd rather have a fan that likes my music and plays it, than not have a fan because he won't buy the record because he's gotta pay for it," he said.

"But I have to champion the songwriters, especially in Nashville," he added. "This is the songwriter capital of the world and these guys are living on a shoestring anyway, and to see them being ripped off of the money that they deserve it's just not fair. And I told the [Tennessee state] legislature, 'This is real simple. . . . If you or your grandkids or anybody could reach down on your cursor and punch and get free gasoline or free Coca-Cola, you and I wouldn't be having this conversation.' It's true."

Cropper and I were speaking about his new solo album *Dedicated: A Salute to the "5" Royales*. The project aimed to turn fans on to Cropper's hero Lowman Pauling, the "5" Royales guitarist/songwriter who was both hugely influential and tragically obscure. His death almost three decades prior had not even made the news. Among the group's songs was "Dedicated to the One I Love," which I had unthinkingly assumed originated with the Mamas and the Papas. Not so. The "5" Royales recorded it first in 1957, and it was covered on *Dedicated* by Lucinda Williams and Dan Penn. Similarly, I knew James Brown had a hit with "Think" in 1960 and that Mick Jagger did a version 30 years later. I did not know that the "5" Royales took it to No. 9, also in 1957. On this new album, Cropper revived Pauling's tune as an instrumental.

Other *Dedicated* collaborators included Steve Winwood, Bettye LaVette, B. B. King, and—alas—the annoying faux-harmonica player John Popper. Thankfully Cropper cut Popper's "million-notes-a-second" harmonica outro to a tolerable length on "My Sugar Sugar." On the other hand, Winwood hasn't sounded as soulful in 40 years as he does on the album opener "Thirty Second Lover."

Cropper and fellow producer Jon Tiven managed to get King into the studio during a rare day off for the bluesman in his adopted hometown of Las Vegas. After recording his duet with Shemekia Copeland on "Baby Don't Do It," King invited the crew to his place for six hours of eating and storytelling. "That was one of the greatest days of our life," Cropper recalled. What's his place like? "It's full of awards. Awards and guitars and records! It's kinda hard to walk through, but it's interesting."

The "5" Royales originated in North Carolina during the 1940s as a gospel group, and then reinvented themselves as an R&B combo in 1952. Between early 1953 and early 1954, they recorded such hits as "Baby Don't Do It," "Help Me Somebody" (heard on *Dedicated* as another Cropper instrumental), and "I Do" (redone by Queen guitarist Brian May). Chart action slowed in the years before the Royales' demise in the early '60s, but their gritty, plaintive sound was evident on King Records labelmate James Brown's early recordings.

Pauling also emerged as something of a guitar hero, teasing sonic bursts from a Les Paul custom that often hung at knee level. Cropper, turned on to the "5" Royales as a schoolboy, saw the group perform in Memphis when he was about 18 or 19. The photo on the cover of *Dedicated* shows a startlingly gaunt and well-coiffed Cropper about a year later, similarly hunched over his guitar.

"Every rock 'n' roll kid grew up on Chuck Berry stuff and all that, but I always went back to Lowman," Cropper recalled. "When I would get asked the question, how did you come about developing this style in the recording studio? I always went back to Lowman

Pauling. He was a guy that played rhythm, and then he would play a fill with little catchy licks that were melodic. I just sort of patterned myself after that. A lot of guys were great players and all that, but I just never took the time to try to emulate loud playing, let's put it that way."

In my defense and that of others largely ignorant of Lowman Pauling and the "5" Royales, Cropper said he had no idea his hero was dead when he started checking on him a few years ago. Pauling died on Dec. 26, 1973, his wife's birthday. He was 47. He had been working as a janitor when he suffered a seizure. He does not have his own Wikipedia page. One of his brothers is perhaps better known. Clarence Paul, a one-time member of the "5" Royales, went on to become a Motown songwriter who helped young Stevie Wonder become a star.

Dedicated was part of Cropper's master plan, to increase awareness of classic soul among young folks. "I think we're starting to lose a lot of that. I find that when we're on the road with the Blues Brothers," Cropper said. "Eddie Floyd was the one who always put it, 'We're gonna educate the new generation.' Because you don't wanna forget songs like 'Midnight Hour' and 'Knock on Wood' and those kind of things. You gotta keep 'em coming back. I felt like we were doing that with "5" Royales' music."

Cropper found himself in a similar bind with his own legacy, noting that his stateside renown has always been eclipsed by the enthusiasm of foreign fans. "You have moments of success in America, you have a career everywhere else," he said. "The most thoroughly educated audience that I have performed for would be the people of Japan. They have always been able to get in there and find out who played on what, even with albums with no credits or anything. They just find out who did what. It's amazing."

It was in Japan that Dunn died in his sleep in May 2012, hours after playing a gig in Tokyo with Cropper. (Superstitious R&B bassists might want to give the country a wide berth. Chic's Bernard Edwards also died in his Tokyo hotel room, in 1996.)

The MG's lost Jackson in 1975, the victim of an unsolved murder. He was shot five times during what his wife claimed was a home-invasion robbery. Interestingly, the Jacksons were on the verge of divorcing, and she had shot him in the chest two months earlier. A judge ruled that shooting to be in self-defense.

Following her husband's death, it was reported locally that Barbara Jackson was about to be indicted along with three others. Among them was alleged triggerman Nate Johnson, a.k.a. Nathaniel Doyle Jr. But nothing happened, and Johnson/Doyle was killed in a shootout with a cop the following year. Rob Bowman, the author of the definitive 1997 Stax history *Soulsville USA*, was stonewalled by the Memphis police in his multiyear quest for more information. Barbara Jackson still lives at the house. I found her number on the Internet and called her to ask if there were any developments in the investigation as of 2012. Nothing, she impatiently said, but requested that I write that Cropper is "a very kind-hearted young man."

As Jones pursued various solo endeavors in recent years, including the Grammy-winning albums *Potato Hole* and *The Road From Memphis*, Cropper reconstituted the band simply as the MG's, a backing group for other singers. Cropper, Dunn, Stax veteran Lester Snell on keyboards, and drummer Steve Potts toured Australia in 2008 with local singer Guy Sebastian, and with Eddie Floyd during the summer of 2011.

With Booker T. and the MG's unlikely ever to record again, *That's the Way It Should Be* will serve as a solid swan song and a template for how all records should be made. Cropper told me during our 1994 encounter that they completed it in two weeks merely by turning on the tape recorder and jamming. "We're pretty much two verses, a solo, and a couple of verses and out kinda band, y'know?" he said. Grammy voters were impressed, awarding the group the first statuette of its career, for a cover of Smokey Robinson's "Cruisin.'"

The reactivated group had been on a roll since 1992 when it was inducted into the Rock and Roll Hall of Fame and employed as the house band at the Bob Dylan 30th anniversary tribute concert later that year. Neil Young, who also played at the Dylan event, hired Booker T. and the MG's as his backing band in 1993. The tour brought them into contact with Young's opening acts Pearl Jam and Soundgarden, and I saw their stop in Los Angeles. Young, marking his anointment as the "godfather of grunge," was destroying his guitar strings as quickly as they could be wound on.

I asked Cropper if the Stax veterans wondered what the hell they'd gotten themselves involved with. "Well, everybody's got their way. Yank! That's his thing. What is he called? The godfather of grunge! ... I think Neil Young had me out there because I'm a fairly decent rhythm guitar player. I don't think he wanted me out there to be competitive or any of that kind of stuff—even though we had a lot of fun and he gave me a lot of space."

Can any of you guys sing?
Booker's a pretty good singer.
So why doesn't he sing on the new record?
Why do we wanna do that? Let me toot my horn. We were the world's best instrumental group for nine years in the '60s. Why would we want to sing and change that? Isn't it a much bigger challenge to say, "Let's try to get instrumental music back on the radio again?" I think that's a much bigger challenge because there hasn't been a market for instrumental music since about 1970–71. Booker's made albums, go out there and buy 'em. He's got plenty of albums out there he's singing on. I've got three albums out there I'm singing on. But when it comes to Booker T. and the MG's, they're not a vocal band. They don't need to be. I think if it ever comes about and we want to venture a little bit, maybe we'll do some stuff where we sing more or something. But I think right now, we want to revive Booker T. and the MG's, the instrumental band that it is.
How has the relationship among you three guys evolved over the years? Is Booker the leader? Or is it a democracy?
Somebody has to answer to somebody. We're all individual and we get together and we do this project. We certainly don't make any decisions without Booker. If there's a problem, Booker might be the

final say-so. It might boil down to that. He is Booker T. Jones, but we're all equal. We've always done everything on an equal basis.

How would you describe the personalities of the other two guys?

The personalities. Nobody ever asked me that question before. We're all family, we're all brothers. I'm an only child. I never had any brothers, but if I had any it would definitely be Booker, Duck, and Al and of course we lost Al in '75. Nothing has ever got to us where we have yelling and screaming matches with each other and all that sort of stuff. We don't always agree on everything, but we're intelligent enough to sit down and talk about it and nobody ever gets upset and it's not the end of the world. It's hard to get three guys that think so much alike that one can almost speak for the other in most cases.

Is it fair to say that there's no modern-day equivalent of the Stax Records sound, gritty R&B music that appeals to both blacks and whites?

Pretty much the music of the '60s that we made at Stax is a dead art. There's no market for it whatsoever and it's sad that none of these artists that made all those great records have a record deal. They sing just as good as they used to, people like Carla Thomas and Eddie Floyd and all these great people. William Bell. It's sad that there's just no place for them to go. I think you're gonna definitely see R&B moving back towards sounds of the '60s. Even the country people are doing it. If you take the steel guitar and the fiddle and some of the twangy vocal off of the tracks in Nashville, you've got R&B of the '60s, same drum and bass patterns.

Why have these superstars from the '60s fallen on comparatively rough times?

I think you gotta credit it to radio: They quit playing it. Somehow when music went into this disco format [in the late '70s], out of that came a whole 'nother type of thing. It didn't live very long, but it certainly did its damage while it was out there. And it went another way. Nothing ever survived that. It's easy to see why disco died, because they tried to make every record sound the same, and you can't do that. The same beat, the same tempo. That gets old after a while. There's no variety in disco.

It must have been great to work at Stax, but were there times when it was like working in a factory with constant pressure to churn out new recordings?

It was very much like going to church, so there was no factory atmosphere whatsoever. But in terms of what we had to do and the size of the roster we had, when you had six main guys in there tryin' to churn out records for 17 artists, it became a lot of work. I don't think it ever really did fall into a pattern of work until '68 when we sold to one of the bigger conglomerates [Gulf + Western] who wanted to all of a sudden make us a giant album company. Albums have 10 sides [songs] or more, so instead of working on an A and a B side, or three sides to pick from, we were all of a sudden working on 10 sides. And that's when the workload really got too much for everybody, and we had to start farming out stuff. And that's when we lost communication and that's when there was a breakdown in the direction of the company and all that sort of stuff. It took a lot of regrouping to get that back together. It took a while. Finally things started happening again. The Staple Singers started having hits and so forth, so that was a lot of fun. That formula that we had that worked so well seemed to get lost when they started spreading us all out and we started working with different musicians. They started cutting [recording] down in Muscle Shoals [in Alabama].

How did that affect you?

It affected enough of me to leave the company. I started a label in Memphis, which had minor success, and we made some bad business decisions and so forth. Finally I got frustrated with the whole deal and I moved to California. I've lived here almost 15 years.

What bands these days have the spirit that you guys had?

It's kinda interesting. When I went down to sit in with Pearl Jam [at a Pearl Jam show in Nashville], Eddie [Vedder] made a little statement before he brought me out. He made a comment that "with all of our success, so quick, we looked at each other and thought this is it. If it hadn't been for Booker T. and the MG's, we'd either all be dead or we'd be split up by now." I didn't know we had that kind of influence on them. They went out on the road with us and saw here are these guys that are still together after 30-something years, are still out there working and having fun and all that. They had a little meeting and said, "Guys, we gotta regroup and get our shit together because that's where it's at, if you can stay together that long."

You seem like such a rock. Have you always been so normal? Do you ever get carried away by the usual rock 'n' roll excess?

Hope not! [laughs]. It's a love with me and it's a very precious spot to be in. What can I say? I'm very proud of the stuff we've done and I'm very proud of the stuff that I do and work with and I try to set certain standards for myself. I don't try to go overboard, try to maintain. I don't try to be something I'm not. I don't think I'm something that I'm not. I don't always believe my press and all that sorta stuff, just say what you want to say. I try to stick to the truth when I can. All that Stax stuff was a very important moment in all our lives and I'm fortunate that I'm still alive to sit here and talk to you about it. A lot of guys aren't, for different reasons. If we can keep working on that, that's great.

GARTH BROOKS, CHRIS GAINES, & THE AIRHEADED REPORTER

Remember Garth Brooks? He used to be a big country star. Remember Chris Gaines? Who could forget the alter ego adopted by Garth for his ill-fated foray into rock 'n' roll, all dolled up like the chubby love child of Dave Navarro and Trent Reznor? The Airheaded Reporter is me, and this chapter's title is the result of a testy backstage encounter among Garth, Chris, and me at the American Music Awards in early 2000.

After nearing the 100 million unit sales mark in the United States with his easy-listening country pop, Garth had a "king of the world" moment and decided he really wanted to be a rock star. But he couldn't do it under his own name. The fans wouldn't go for that. So he invented a whole new persona, an Australian pop-rocker called Chris Gaines, and recorded a bunch of tunes with Rolling Stones producer Don Was. The resulting album was called *Garth Brooks . . . In the Life of Chris Gaines* although the cover reads, *Chris Gaines . . . Greatest Hits*.

People were probably too distracted by the photo to notice the discrepancy. The balding Oklahoman had evidently rifled through his wife's makeup kit and borrowed a wig from Phil Spector. He appears on the cover with mascara, a hipster soul patch of hair under his lower lip, and a cute mop of jet-black hair across his forehead.

The album, whatever its name, was billed as the soundtrack to an upcoming movie called *The Lamb*, which would star Garth as Chris Gaines. An actual soundtrack album was also planned, and maybe even more Chris Gaines albums. Confused yet? There is no doubt about one thing. The whole project brought Garth's decadelong magical ride to a screeching halt.

Even the pliant folks at music-industry mouthpiece *Billboard* could not contain their mirth as they allowed Garth and Capitol Records executives to dig themselves a big hole by explaining the concept. The funniest bit was the label's suggestion that it would outsell Garth's previous record, *Sevens*, which had sold six million copies at the time. Capitol planned to ship four million copies of *Chris Gaines* to U.S. retailers. It sold about two million. "It's just possible the buying public finds Brooks' pop music less compelling than his country material," *Billboard* noted in October 1999 after the album debuted at a disappointing No. 2 with a fraction of Garth's usual first-week sales.

Anyway, fast-forward to January 2000, when Garth appeared at the American Music Awards, a comically melodramatic event where he once refused to accept the top prize because he claimed it should have gone to Hootie and the Blowfish instead. The *Chris Gaines* record is dead, but what about the movie, the one set up at Paramount Pictures with Kenneth "Babyface" Edmonds attached as a producer? Reports had said it was scheduled for release by December 2000. Was Garth really still serious about bringing his hipster alter ego to the big screen?

But first let's get one thing out of the way. I don't hate Garth Brooks. I don't know his songs, but he seems like a principled fellow who did his best to do the right thing at every turn. You can't argue with his success. He has now sold 128 million albums in the United States (a distant third behind the Beatles and Elvis).

I saw one of his arena shows in Anaheim and was blown away. I even got caught up in the moment and bought a souvenir T-shirt (which I wisely never wore and eventually threw out). Despite the professional dictates of my job, I went along with the accepted wisdom that Garth (who refers to himself as such, in the third person) could walk on water. Was there a flaw? Probably, but even the late Patsi Bale Cox's excellent biography *The Garth Factor* failed to uncover one, despite some persistent digging.

Alas, Patsi forgot to mention Garth's showdown with me at the American Music Awards where he nabbed three prizes (not for *Chris Gaines*, obviously). As usual, Garth came backstage to speak to the press. This was pretty cool in itself. Most stars bypass the press tent, which makes my job easier, as there are fewer quotes to squeeze in the story. But Garth was always press-friendly. After someone asked a goofy question about baseball (Garth had a lifelong dream to play with a professional team), I chimed in with what I thought was a fairly straightforward question:

Does this, er, sort of make up for the *Chris Gaines* fiasco, perhaps, in some ways?

No, sir. And a little offended at the "*Chris Gaines* fiasco" thing in the same breath. People that think that's a fiasco are short-minded [*sic*], unintelligent in music, and don't know anything about taking risks.

Emboldened by applause from some of my fellow "journalists," Garth continued.

"He's a character in a movie that's coming out, in a year. When the movie gets here, it'll make sense. And then, trust me, anybody who does a movie in the future that has a musical entertainer in it will do it this way. They'll introduce their artist a year before the movie."

Not only was Garth a musical genius, he was also a Hollywood groundbreaker. It was an outrageous and nonsensical claim, but this was not the right time or place to dig any deeper into his distorted sense of reality. I fired off a quick follow-up question.

But the commercial sales must be disappointing, though?

Garth did not reply. He did not need to. The esteemed press corps did Garth's job for him by applauding him and shouting, "Yeah!" A veteran reporter chimed in, "I love that album." And then someone else immediately threw him another baseball question.

Garth addressed me in a quick, robotic tone, managing to invent a neologism along the way. He'd been on the defensive for months, and was clearly feeling the strain. He was also grieving the loss of his mother in August, and had just announced plans to retire. His marriage was on the rocks.

But his megalomania was finally out there for all to see. His prediction that his movie would rewrite the Hollywood rule book was so absurd you just had to write it off as one of the markers that separates celebrities from mere mortals. And I don't even mind that. I respect people who take risks, as evidently did *Rolling Stone,* which could have ripped Brooks but gave *Chris Gaines* a modest 2½ star review (out of five) with the advice that we should "give this Fortune 500 cowboy credit for trying something different."

I wrote a story about the exchange, and was labeled a "jerk," a "nimrod," and a "self-centered moron" by the fans on the *Planet Garth* website, where this chapter title was the title of the thread. Maybe "fiasco" was a strong word. On the other hand, it was probably an understatement for the bean counters at Capitol trying to account for the millions of albums returned by retailers. And we're still waiting for that movie, by the way.

GUNS N' ROSES: IN BED WITH STEVEN ADLER

Guns N' Roses were my favorite hard-rock band, but I was never able to secure an interview with them. Their publicist was very protective of her rambunctious clients. They were on the road or in the studio, she would tell me. In other words, most of them were doing copious amounts of drugs and therefore not in a position to talk.

The guys got easier to track down after the combustible combo started disintegrating. Izzy Stradlin was a gracious host backstage at a solo show in Tijuana in 1993, a year after he quit. A decade later Slash, Duff McKagan, and Matt Sorum happily did promotional chores for their new band, Velvet Revolver, and for various extracurricular ventures. Axl Rose—who keeps the Guns N' Roses name alive with a rotating lineup of no-name musicians—actually reached out to me. Or rather, the elusive singer unleashed his attorneys after he took a dislike to a story I had written. I ignored their letter.

Steven Adler was the easiest to get hold of. I simply cold-called the ousted drummer and he picked up. I received a tip in August 1994 that Adler had overdosed and was recovering at Cedars-Sinai Medical Center near Beverly Hills. I called the hospital with the intention of getting confirmation from a spokeswoman. But while waiting for someone to pick up, I decided I might as well get confirmation from the man himself. The operator answered, I asked to speak to Adler, and she put me through to his room.

Adler, a childhood friend of Slash's, joined Guns N' Roses in 1985 shortly after the band had been formed in Hollywood by Indiana natives Axl and Izzy. They paid their dues on the club scene, scored a label deal, and released their first album to zero acclaim. *Appetite for Destruction* started taking off about a year later in 1988 when label boss David Geffen persuaded MTV to play the video for "Welcome to the Jungle" in the wee hours. MTV's phone lines exploded, and Guns were on their way to the big time.

More monster singles followed—"Paradise City" and "Sweet Child O' Mine"—and *Appetite* went on to become the biggest-selling debut album of all time. According to Slash's self-titled memoir, "the feel and energy of *Appetite* was largely due to [Adler]." By the close of the decade, Guns N' Roses were headlining stadiums and opening for the Stones. They were the most exciting band on the planet. Pandemonium reigned wherever they played. Drug dealers and lawyers got rich getting them into and out of various jams.

But Adler's heroin habit was excessive even by the lofty standards of his debauched bandmates. It was so bad that Sly Stone—the crack-smoking, gun-wielding poster child for the perils of drugs—was drafted to lecture him about his wayward behavior. To no avail. After using up all his chances, Adler was kicked out in 1990 as the band tried to record its follow-up album. He took his former bandmates to court and received a $2.5 million payout three years later, providing an economic stimulus to the drug-dealing industry.

Which is how we got to talking. Adler, 29 at the time, had been at Cedars-Sinai for almost a week. He readily gave me the grim details. He had not overdosed, as such. He just wanted to get rid of his heroin and coke habit. "I'm just thankful that I'm alive and that I was able to get in here, and have them help me. They've been wonderful to me here, very sweet, very helpful. It's great waking up in the morning and not being sick," he said.

We discussed his sickness, his legal victory, his professional plans, and his real estate empire, and he accused Slash of being "a major fuckin' hypocrite cocksucker." He was lucid but his voice was slurred.

But he was clearly deluded if he thought a few days' stay at Cedars-Sinai would cure him of his addictions and their underlying causes. Sure enough, he goaded the Grim Reaper for many more years, as detailed in his 2010 memoir *My Appetite for Destruction*, which claims he survived "28 overdoses, two heart attacks, a couple of jail stints, and a debilitating stroke." It's understandable, perhaps, that Adler's detox attempt at Cedars-Sinai did not merit inclusion. Or maybe he just forgot it ever happened.

These days, with reality-show stints on *Celebrity Rehab* under his belt, he plays with his own band, Adler's Appetite. He and Slash are buddies again. But he has continued to struggle with his addictions, announcing in May 2013 that he had entered rehab after hitting the bottle "a few times and that is a few times too many."

Are you going to rehab?
Yes, well right now . . . It takes, like, five, six, seven days for stuff to get of your system. So I'm still on medication right now. Maybe Sunday or Monday [we spoke on a Friday], I'll be able to get out, and I'm going on a cruise to, um, not Barcelona—I went there a couple of weeks ago, beautiful place. But I'm taking my little brother on a cruise to, uh, oh man, what's that one island? By Mexico, I think. Oh, man. It's supposed to be really great. Like they have those cruise trips, y'know? Not Barcelona. Not Barbados. I can't believe I can't think of what it is.

I hope you remember before you set out!
[laughs] It's a really great place, from what I hear.

Do you have to do a rehab program? You seem to have a few problems, I imagine.
Well no, the only problem I have is that I use drugs, and basically all I really need to do is get the drugs out of my system. I'm not even getting high anymore. I'm doing it just to keep

myself from being sick. I'm sick and tired of being sick and tired, so I called up the doctor over here, a friend of mine, Dr. [name unclear], and he said he'd love for me to come down, and I've just been here ever since.

After you get released from Cedars-Sinai, will you stop taking drugs?

I pray to God. Yeah, the whole idea of coming in here and detoxing is to stay off the drugs. I wanna start working again. I've been trying to get hold of [former Whitesnake guitarist] John Sykes and I wanna put something together with John Sykes to get a band together with him is what I'd like to do.

Have the guys from Guns been in touch with you?

No, no. Actually, to tell you the truth they're pricks to me.

I thought Slash was still your friend?

We've known each other since we were 12 years old, and he treats me like shit. He's got a drug and alcohol problem, but he keeps putting me down. I ran into him a couple of times and all he would say to me is, "You're fucked up, look at you," while he's drinking triple vodka and cranberry juices. He's just a major fuckin' hypocrite cocksucker.

So you still feel pretty bitter towards the guys?

Well, I don't. But they do it to me. They won't be nice to me, so what am I supposed to do? I'm not gonna say anything that's not true. I want them to know how I feel, how they're making me feel, and what they're doing to me because obviously they don't realize it. You don't know somebody more than half of your fucking life, and grow up and have your dreams come true, and then just desert me like I never existed.

Exactly, because you were there right at the beginning. And you're not getting all the spoils.

I did. A hundred and seventeen thousand people is the biggest show. Plus we got to play with the Rolling Stones at the Coliseum. That was great.

Are you still getting royalties?

Oh yes!

You're not doing too badly!
No, no. I just received two and a half million dollars.
Do you still have that?
Of course! Well, actually, I had to pay my lawyers a big chunk of it, but it still left me with over a million and a half.
So what musical career do you have in mind?
Like I said, I'm tryin' to get a hold of John Sykes and [guitarist] Jamie Scott, [singer] Davy Vain and [bassist] Ashley Mitchell, who I'd like to put a band together with. But there's no way I can put a band together doing what I was doing with the drugs. The drugs got to be more important than anything else because I didn't wanna get sick.
Why did you take drugs?
I took drugs because I like it. But when you don't do heroin . . . See, your body makes its own opiate, and so I'm giving myself the opiate so my body doesn't automatically think, Oh, I just made it for him. So it stops making it because I keep giving it to myself, and it keeps thinking it's making it, but it's not. It's such a terrible, terrible fuckin' sickness. Every morning if I didn't save myself a couple . . . I wasn't shooting, I was smoking it.
Smoking heroin?
Yeah. And if I didn't save some for the next morning, my eyes would water, my nose would run. I'd be throwing up dry heaves.
Have you basically been taking drugs nonstop since 1990?
Basically, yeah.
Are you surprised you're still alive?
Thank God I'm still alive. I believe very highly in this that God does have something in store for me because if he didn't he definitely would have taken me a long time ago.
Have you become religious?
No. I'm Jewish. I believe in myself and I believe that there's a higher power than myself, and I believe that I've been around many, many years in other bodies, that my soul has been around. I talked with this psychic lady who's fabulous. It's really cool 'cause she tells me things I never said to her. I would not say anything to her and

she would tell me stuff, about what happened with Slash. She was saying that I'm gonna run into him again and he's gonna apologize to me and give me some stupid excuse, and that I should just go along with the excuse. She said we will never be friends like we were.

That's a bit sad, isn't it?

It's terrible. I miss them all so much.

Do you have friends now who worry about you?

Ever since that stuff happened with the band, when I would go out to nightclubs, I'd walk right up to the front door, the bouncer would give me a hug, say, "Hey! Stevie, how are you? Come on in!" After this shit happened with the band, I walk up to the front door, the same bouncer would tell me to get to the back of the fuckin' line.

That's L.A. for you.

It's sickening!

But do you have friends who worry about you?

I have one friend, his name is Steve Sprite. And my brother Jamie and my mom and dad. They've been really wonderful and helpful.

I thought they might be able to help you with your addiction?

Nobody could help me. I have to help myself. There's nothing anybody could do or say. It's all up to me.

So you're pretty confident this will be your last bout with drugs?

I hope so because I really, really do wanna start working again. That's the one thing I do have going on for me, that will keep me off of this shit is that I start working again.

I hope it works out—

Thank you, man.

Is it possible to get in touch with you just to keep track?

You can call anytime you like. I'll give you my mom's number, 818-xxx-xxxx.

Do you live with your mother?

No, but I'm there a lot.

You live in Beverly Hills?

I got a condo in Century City and a house in Malibu Canyon and a house in Laurel Canyon.

Wow! Three houses!

I wanna get another house. Actually, the house in Laurel Canyon, Martha Quinn is renting it out from me right now. Remember her from MTV? She's renting it out, and she wants to buy it. So I want her to buy it, and I'm gonna buy another house up on Mulholland.

Next to Slash?

I hear Slash is living up in Bel Air now . . . Oh, Mom and Dad just walked in.

ICE-T FOUGHT THE LAW

"Cop Killer" controversy was the silly summer story of 1992, a classic battle pitting a provocative rapper against a vast array of pressure groups in a debate over free speech, moral decency, police brutality, racism, and any number of other issues you could toss on the heap. Americans love to get riled up over such things, and the fact that Los Angeles was still smoldering from the "Rodney King riots" that past April as a presidential election campaign was in full swing added a few layers of stupidity to the whole unseemly mess.

"Cop Killer," a song about a deranged man's quest for bloody vengeance, appeared on the self-titled debut album of Body Count, a hard-rock side project formed by Ice-T, a one-time army ranger and jewel thief who decided that rap was a more lucrative venture. One of the stanzas in "Cop Killer" went:

> *I got my 12-gauge sawed off*
> *I got my headlights turned off*
> *I'm 'bout to bust some shots off*
> *I'm 'bout to dust some cops off.*

The record came out in March 1992, almost a year after Body Count premiered the song to zero outrage during the inaugural Lollapalooza festival.

But by June, it became big news after an official with the Dallas Police Association complained about the song in a column for the union's newsletter. (The official, Glenn White, years later defended Texas policemen who wrote tickets to motorists for not speaking English.) Local police associations across America, long untroubled by "I Shot the Sheriff" and untold violent Hollywood movies, expressed their outrage. But not all did. In fact, the debate offered an insight into the racially charged law enforcement situation in Texas. The Dallas Police Association's membership was mostly white. The National Black Police Association, also based in Dallas, defended Ice-T's right to free speech and backed up his insights into police brutality.

Soon the imbroglio went all the way to the top. The first President Bush said the song was "sick," and 60-something cultural icons Charlton Heston and opera singer Beverly Sills emerged from their crypts to protest the song at the annual stockholders' meeting of Time Warner Inc., the parent company of Ice-T's Warner Bros. label.

The controversy even reached my native New Zealand. The country's police tried to sabotage an upcoming Ice-T concert by contacting Interpol to see if any members of his tour party had convictions that could prevent them from gaining work permits. "I have no desire to have people who preach the killing of police, or mothers, come to this country to perform and will do what I can to prevent this," said Police Commissioner John Jamieson. In the end, Ice-T did come to New Zealand (and Australia), but did not perform the song, because—as was made clear all along—he was touring in his capacity as a solo rapper, not as a member of Body Count.

Ice-T made the cover of *Rolling Stone* in August, dressed as a baton-wielding cop. But by the time the issue hit newsstands, he had decided to remove the song from the album, citing death threats against Warner Bros. staff. No one was very happy. His fans, fellow rappers, and free-speech advocates said he had sold out; the white

Texas cops said the death threat allegations were false. The reissued album featured a newly recorded version of his old rap song "Free Speech." Left intact were such tunes as "Smoked Pork," a spoken-word skit in which Ice-T and bandmate Mooseman mow down some doughnut-chomping cops, and "KKK Bitch," in which Ice-T's character ravages the horny daughter of a white supremacist. Ice-T parted ways with Warner Bros. the following year amid a dispute over the artwork for his new rap album *Home Invasion*, which he put out on an indie label. Body Count released its second album, *Born Dead*, through Virgin Records in the fall of 1994.

That's when I interviewed him, with lead guitarist and "Cop Killer" co-writer Ernie-C sitting in, at Virgin's old office in Beverly Hills. The critics were lukewarm on *Born Dead*. *Rolling Stone* said a handful of tunes "resound with fresh thunder," but the band sounded "monochromatic and tired" and certainly wouldn't be confused with a more innovative outfit such as Metallica. *Q* described it as mostly "gloriously dumb fun," which was in line with my thinking. I was sucked in as soon as I saw artwork depicting a fetus in a noose. This was some funny stuff, clearly not meant to be taken too seriously.

But whereas *Body Count* peaked at No. 26 on the U.S. pop chart thanks to the "Cop Killer" controversy, *Born Dead* stalled at No. 74, and it had fallen off the Billboard 200 by the time we spoke. Ice-T blamed MTV for not playing the album's videos. But it surely did not help that his promotion efforts had taken a backseat to his movie career. He'd spent the summer shooting *Tank Girl* in Arizona. Clearly doing it for the money, he was cast as a half-man, half-kangaroo creature in this box office bomb. The album did go top five in Germany, bolstered by a European tour, and Australia. On the evening of the interview, Body Count played a gig at a half-empty club in downtown Los Angeles.

Ice-T—born Tracy Lauren Marrow in New Jersey, but raised by his aunt in a middle-class black Los Angeles neighborhood—formed Body Count in 1989 with Ernie-C, an old Crenshaw High School buddy whose real name was Ernest Cunnigan. The pair must have been real outcasts at school, black kids listening to Led Zeppelin and

Black Sabbath. Before long, Ice-T was discovering hardcore rock bands like Autopsy, Carcass, Crowbar, and D.R.I. (short for Dirty Rotten Imbeciles) even as he was pioneering "gangsta" rap with a series of hit albums offering glimpses of gang life in Los Angeles. He also established a bunch of solid acting credits, including 1991's *New Jack City*, in which he played a cop.

In 1993 he published a memoir, *The Ice Opinion*, co-written with Los Angeles journalist Heidi Siegmund. In that book, he said rap was basically like a telephone conversation between two buddies. Listeners are merely eavesdroppers and should be wary of taking any sentiments expressed too seriously. "I think sometimes people overintellectualize shit," he told me, essentially repudiating any role as a spokesman for his generation. The new album track "Last Breath," in which Ice-T raps about decapitating sleeping kids, was merely "a horror movie on wax," he said. "It means nothing . . . absolutely nothing. Some of this shit is just done out of fun. It's just some ill saying."

In 20 or 30 years' time, how do you think the whole "Cop Killer" thing will be perceived?

I think it is rock 'n' roll history. I mean, just simply because under the illusion of free speech we could be took through the wringer to the point where the president yells. Something happened. I don't know what happened. The people at Warner Bros. said we struck a nerve: You can't fuck with the queen's guards. You hit this threshold of free speech where they go, "Ah! Ah! Ah! It's free speech, but just watch what you say." I think people will look back and laugh about it. "Wow! That shit happened over that?" I remember when I first started making rap records and I used to talk what I thought was nasty. You take a record like "Let's Get Butt Naked and Fuck" (a.k.a. "Girls L.G.B.N.A.F." from his second album, 1988's *Power*) and compare it to the way people sing on R&B records now, it's nothing. So I think people will look back and say, "Wow! They got mad at Little Richard over that? Now they got mad at Ice-T over that?" It'll seem stupid . . . In Chicago there were people walking around with signs, "Ice-T was right" after a cop had killed some kids out there. I think it vindicates us from us just being some crazy motherfuckers yelling, "Kill the cops!" As soon as America is ready to kill the cops we will be an anthem. It's like a revolutionary battle cry!

The more the cops are violent, the more it makes you seem prescient.

But I'm not that greedy that I would want them to be violent to make me seem right. They're violent enough. I wish they would start treating people like human beings. That song was a wake-up call. It preceded the riots. It was like, "Listen up! People are complaining that they're ready to go after you. You don't hear me?" This is one guy, the Cop Killer. I'm talking about a neighborhood that is at this point. Nobody listened up. April 29 [the day the L.A. riots started]: It went down. What I said was real at that point. Whether people understand it or not. My neighborhood understood it at that point!

Since then we've had a change in presidents. Does the more liberal climate make things easier for you?

It's a weird climate. It can seem like it's cool, and then all of a sudden you can be picked out and hung in the town square. I believe when they moved on us, it was definitely a political move. It was like a Willie Horton–type thing. "We have an election. This record was made a year ago, let's pull it out. Warner Bros. has it, let's attack them, let's act like we are outraged. The cops are under siege. Let's act like the people . . ." It had nothing to do with the record.

Most of us live our lives and don't make a difference. In your case, while the whirlwind of attention might have been difficult for you on some levels, at least you made a difference.

Or go through the whirlwind and be killed. That would be a grand way to die, right? When you go that route you always have that little possibility. When I speak, I wanna shock people. I wanna bring people's attention to issues. But it's not a total blatant attempt to be in the news and all that kinda shit. That's way over what I'm tryin' to do. Some cheesy artists might have to do that. Like, this album [*Born Dead*] came out without looking for it [i.e., cheap publicity]. Now if they pick one of my songs out and make something out of it, then certain people think Ice wants that. That ain't what I want. I wanna make a record. I want it to touch you, feel it and move on, and maybe act on it. But I don't want to be on the fuckin' television and all that old bullshit. If I want to do that, I'll do a blatant publicity stunt. That's not a problem.

How would you compare and contrast both Body Count records?

To me, I'm happy with both records because what I equate success with is much different than what a lot of other people equate success. The groups we admired when we put out the Body Count album were groups like D.R.I. and Cannibal Corpse and Slayer, the real hard stuff, Autopsy and Crowbar. That genre may sell maybe 50 or 80,000 records and they blew up, like indie groups. When we came out with the first Body Count record, it sold half a million records; we were like, "What in the fuck? Anthrax didn't sell half a million records for five years." We were aware there was a lot of curiosity. We had sold a half a million before the "Cop Killer" incident and that just took us to another level.

How much did you sell after the "Cop Killer" incident?

About another 450,000. Almost the same amount. We almost sold a total of a million records.

Almost platinum, wow!

No, it's not platinum, because they're two different records. So you gotta go gold twice. Believe it or not, that first year was incredible—from playing in Raji's [a dingy Hollywood club] to [opening for] Guns N' Roses. Fuck, it was like a whirlwind. I can't imagine being on nothing like that, and doing the form of rock we were doing—cursing on every record, being aggressive. This new album, I mean we didn't get the commercial success in the States but in Europe we blew up. We were, like, No. 2 and 3. In Germany, we were top five. We've got two albums in the top 10 over there. United States, to put it point blank, MTV fucked us. We turned in two videos. They wouldn't play neither of our videos. We turned in two decent videos and we got no play. When you make a hardcore record that has no real radio tracks on it and you have no video, it's hard for people to even know you're out there.

I don't know what people expected. I don't know if people expected me to do another "Cop Killer" record. My attitude is why redo that song? That song is done. I think that would have been cheesy if we'd tried to do it. I don't know. But I'm happy. We've been doing our shows and it's kinda cool because the audience that's showing up to our shows now are like the audience I expected to get from the first place. They're very sincere fans that know what we're doing, that can quote words from the second record. "Fuck all those looky-loos, man. This is Body Count. We down with you. Fuck the bullshit." So, in a way it's kinda like we went into this pop audience first and now we're kinda back to this solid core audience.

What is your core audience? Typically white?

Of course it's white. But this year we've been getting more black fans showing up at the shows. White suburban kids usually probably ride skateboards, and then older metal people who have seen a lot of their groups kinda commercialize and are reaching back for what they feel is real. We've got real fans. They're not into the glamour of it. They're not into the bullshit. To me, I wouldn't trade a core fan for anything in the world, man. They're just down with the fuckin' mood. They know what time it is. They don't believe the hype, they're just with it.

As your career progresses, do you want to add to that core audience?

Not really. It'd be nice. Me personally, I've always said if I could move 200,000 records, 300,000 records, I'd be happy. That's a lot of records as far as underground goes. There's groups that are indie that sell 10,000 records, that's cool.

You've got a higher overhead, though, a posse to support?

Not really. You just teach the posse to live less expensive. Without going for this pop thing, I just found a way to work harder. I know how to make a pop record, I know how to make a fuckin' hit record. I know how to do that. All you gotta do is say something everybody fuckin' wants to hear. But I'm not gonna do that, so I stick with our shit. We're gonna curse on every record. We're gonna tell motherfuckers, "Fuck you!" We're gonna curse America out. But since I know I'm not gonna get rich like that, I'll do a book [*The Ice Opinion*] and then I'll do a movie and then I'll do this. Similar to what Henry Rollins is doing. Henry Rollins has never compromised, but he just works his fuckin' ass off. That's what I do.

That was a pretty good book, how did it sell?

To me, it was a success. If you say it was good it was a success. I was happy with it. I read it about six times before it actually came out. It's me, it's me. It didn't sell like Howard Stern's book [*Private Parts*], but who the fuck wants to be Howard Stern?

As you get older—how old are you now?

Oh man, ask me again and I'm gonna hit you with my cane! [He was 36.]

Oh. As you get older do you find yourself getting more mellow, maybe even a little conservative?

I find myself becoming more radical. Radical for two reasons. One is as I achieve goals and I'm starting to be able to make a better lifestyle for my family I can feel the contrast between living good and not having anything. I really feel a lot of pain for people who are still stuck. I'm not the kind of person who'll get a nice car and say, "Hey! That's me now and fuck all you." I'm like, "It's fucked up people don't have this." If people treat me nice it's fucked up that I have to be Ice-T to get treated like this. I'm still black but now I'm being treated another way. Bullshit! So I get more and more angry. And plus, due to the fact I am getting older, I realize I've got less time to talk. It's kinda like I'm sinking in this pond called life and at the last minute I'm yelling out my last "Muthafucka!" Fade out.

Is there something about Ice-T that would surprise us?

I think what would surprise people is that pretty much I'm a very peaceful person.

Why don't you drink?

I don't like how it tastes. I don't smoke. I don't yell. I don't do drugs . . . not even inhaled it, like Clinton. I don't argue. I don't raise my voice. I'm very, like, calm about everything. Not mellow, but it's kinda like I've learned how not to get mad at everything—just get really mad at certain shit. I've learned how to focus anger into a laser beam of rage. I've always been like that. That's why I took my name Ice. Some people would say, "Hey. He's so cool." Girls used to say if a bullet came to a party it wouldn't do nothing but part my hair. I've never got mad. But by me being so calm, I've always had the ability, if I did get mad, I'd night-blight a lot of people. I play videogames, I sit around. I love my kids. Come to my house, I've got flowers.

Do you have any excesses?

I like cars. When I was in high school I spent time working with auto bodies. I bought a lot of cars when I first started making money. I sold them now. My girl has a Range Rover, I've got a sports car, a luxury car. An Acura, turbo. It's more sporty. And I have a lowrider—a play car. And then I used to rob jewelry stores, so I like jewelry, y'know? But I splurge and then I stop. I've gone through that. Now all the money I have I spend on my three-bedroom house up in the hills. I spend my money fixin' it and trying to make it livable. And the rest of the *money, I loan* out—I give away.

Do you save or invest?

I have a little money in investments. My child has an investment thing. I've got life insurance. But I really don't have enough money to make extreme amounts of investments at this point—contrary to popular belief. I still own my publishing. I've been making some pretty good movies. I started my own record label. To be honest, this year I told my girl, "This year I'm finally at a point where I feel I'll be able to start really saving some money and making some investments." I came from zero. I was homeless, and then I was coming up through single apartments through this, that, and the other. I finally did something that some of these groups see in one year, and then people turn around and say, "Ice-T's not like us no more." I say, "Bullshit. You know what? I busted my ass." Everything I fuckin' ever did, they tried to stop me.

In your book, you say [censorship advocate] Tipper Gore is the only person you've ever called a bitch. Are there any other people who have entered your bad books since then?

Beverly Sills. She's the lady that got up at the fuckin' Warner Bros. stockholders meeting and said she hated us. How the fuck did she ever hear our record? Obviously a hired gun. But no, not really. "Bitch," man, the word means so little to black people. It's another word to us. White people don't use the word, so it like sends shockwaves through their bodies. But brothers call their wives bitches. . . . I've just been saying it since my father called everything a bitch: "Bitch this . . . My bitch . . . Damn, bitch."

And then we got into a lengthy conversation about the power (or lack thereof) of words. Ice-T agreed it was very difficult for fans to know when to take him seriously. "A rapper in one sentence will go from fact to fiction to reality to fact, in one fuckin' sentence," he said. "But the thing is, from an artist's point of view, I just have to write the stuff the way I talk. With all the criticism about the music, it's all an artist can do to still maintain himself. If you listen to the criticism they will remold you . . . And you'll become pop, they'll turn you into this little creature called pop and you'll be everybody's friend. My role model for writing lyrics is Prince. I'll never forget, I read an article where they asked him, 'Why do you write such nasty shit?' He said, 'That's how I think.'"

We reconnected a little over two years later in March 1997 when Body Count released its third album *Violent Demise: The Last Days*. I drove up a tortuous road in the Hollywood Hills to get to the tricked-out aerie that Ice-T shared with girlfriend Darlene Ortiz and their son. Like all good hosts should, he showed me some hardcore porn on his big-screen TV. It was the music video for the new single "Strippers." The new album was lighter in tone, he said, because "You can't expect a kid out here that's in [the upscale L.A. suburb of] Brentwood riding around in his father's BMW to feel born dead."

Some fans wanted him to write more "Cop Killer"-type songs, but Ice-T thought that would be "cheesy." Anyway, he never actually hated cops. "I just don't trust 'em," he said with a laugh. "You need 'em, but a crooked cop is the worst shit in the world. I don't have a problem with the police at all. 'Cop Killer' was a record about brutal cops. It was a record about a guy who lost it because the brutal police was fucking with him. I didn't know this cat I invented would become a hero."

Violent Demise failed to chart in the United States, but Ice-T's attention was elsewhere. Now in his 40th year, he was focusing on his acting career. He had paid his dues doing B-movies, netting perhaps just $30,000 per job after taxes and commissions. "Hopefully one day I'll get a chance to be in a movie with De Niro or somebody, I'll get a chance to flex," he said. He likened himself to multi-hyphenate filmmaker Orson Welles in his ability to segue from rap to rock to movies.

In the fall of 1997, Ice-T starred as an ex-con working for the FBI in *Players*, a short-lived NBC drama. The following year he had a small role as an ill-fated pimp in *Exiled*, a *Law & Order* spinoff TV movie. That gig led to a full-time role on another spinoff, *Law & Order: Special Victims Unit*, now running on fumes in its 15th season. He plays a thuggish cop who used to work undercover in narcotics and now gets to beat up perverts on a weekly basis.

In real life, the concupiscent Ice-T ended his 17-year relationship with the long-suffering Ortiz, moved back to the East Coast, and eventually married Coco Austin, an actress-model who was 13 when "Cop Killer" came out. Pictures of the blonde bombshell and her 39-DD implants are valuable currency in prisons.

Always on the hustle, Ice-T recorded another Body Count album in 2006—although he and Ernie-C were the only surviving original members. Two had succumbed to cancer and one to a drive-by shooting. He wrote a second memoir and starred with Coco in a reality show on the cable network that gave us the Kardashians. His acting in *Ice Loves Coco* is rough-hewn, but he somehow keeps a straight face while warning his wife that "Shakespeare isn't easy." Their love, though, is undeniable. Watch as they introduce their cute bulldog Spartacus (who has more Twitter followers than I'll get in several lifetimes) to a female suitor! Or as an emotional Ice admits that he cannot stand to be parted from Coco! Or as he fights a wave of jealousy after learning that she has a kissing scene in an episode of his show! But then watch him smile after he learns that the scene will be with another woman!

How do I know this? Because breathless recaps were published on the website of London's *Daily Mail,* reportedly the most popular online source of news in the world. It's true. Ice-T has turned mainstream pop culture into his bitch.

PHIL COLLINS: NO MORE MR. NICE GUY

Both times I interviewed Phil Collins he was married, albeit to a different woman on each occasion. If I were to talk to him again, I would say (with apologies to *Seinfeld*), "Phil, you're an Adonis! You should be swinging." And I'd offer to stage an intervention should he ever announce plans to abandon singledom and walk down the aisle for a fourth time.

Marital woes aside, clinical studies have concluded that Phil Collins is the most normal rock star on the planet, and he's happy to oblige in interviews. "If anybody in this business was to be closest to reality, if there was a box with all these rock stars in this box and the bottom fell out, I'd be the first out—purely because I've got my feet on the ground as much as I can possibly get them," he told me in 1993, during our first encounter.

Five years later Collins was mortified to be introduced to the world as the latest addition to a widely mocked subspecies, the rock star who paints. I attended a soiree thrown in his honor backstage at the Greek Theatre in Los Angeles. A simple watercolor depicting an abandoned rowboat on a sun-soaked desert island was unveiled by his corporate sponsor. It was an uncomfortable "Emperor's New Clothes" moment that he quickly defused by shaking his head and burying it in his hands as the guests surveyed his modest accomplishment. He joked that he was going to call the artwork "All washed-up and nowhere to go" before settling on "But I thought you packed the oars!"

If there's a reporter's microphone within 50 yards, a cheery Collins will speak into it, full of self-deprecating humor. *Q* magazine, which he read devotedly, once called him a "professional good bloke." When your hair falls out at an early age, you really have no choice but to drop the Eddie Vedder seriousness. Collins is one of those lucky guys who looks more handsome as he gets older. Free of the remnants of a short-lived civilization, he looks rather cutting edge. Oddly enough, his former Genesis bandmate Peter Gabriel went in the other direction: adorable back in the day, now a singing garden gnome.

It was with high hopes of mutual backslapping bonhomie that I showed up to interview Collins in November 1993 for his first album in four years, a collection called *Both Sides*. His music isn't my cup of tea, though I guiltily enjoyed his 1985 hit single "Sussudio." (Anything with horns in it is fine by me.) The new album was a chore to listen to, and I never played it again after the interview. Maybe I wasn't old enough to appreciate it.

"It's just songs about actually hitting 41, 42, looking back at the first half. Time out, intermission. Have your orange and a cup of tea," he said, awkwardly employing a string of sporting metaphors. "Now look back at the first half of your life, the goals you missed, the chances you didn't take. Will you get a chance to see through, or will you be sent off?"

Since I'm 42 as I write this remembrance, I gave *Both Sides* a spin to see if I could better relate to it. Nope, still got nothing. Every song sounds like a variant of "In the Air Tonight" but without the climax. Maybe it's my limited attention span. The 11 songs average six minutes each. This is the problem when you not only write all the songs and produce the album but also play all the instruments. Working alone in his home studio, Collins didn't have anyone to rein in his meandering impulses.

I didn't raise my concerns to him at the time. That would have been impolite. I took another tack that immediately backfired and turned the interview into a disaster. I emerged 30 minutes later feeling shell-shocked, knowing full well that Mr. Nice Guy was telling his handlers that I was a really awful person.

Of course it wasn't my fault, as I'd later tell people. When he announced his plans to divorce eight months later, I attributed his foul mood during our interview to tension with his second wife, Jill, even though he told me at the time, "I've got a great marriage. Jill's very understanding letting me write this stuff." However, after playing the interview tape in 2011, listening to it for the first time in almost 18 years, I can safely say that I lit Phil's fuse. From my first question—which was more of a statement rubbishing the syrupy sentiment of "Another Day in Paradise," his big 1990 ballad about the plight of the homeless—he was on the defensive. That turned into hostility, and I kept making it worse as I argued with him about some of his new songs.

There's nothing wrong with asking tough questions, but I failed to soften him up first, wrongly assuming that he would be goodhearted enough to roll with the punches. By the time I tried to mollify him, it was too late. A stock question halfway through the interview gave him the platform to vent. "What annoys you?" I innocently asked. He took a deep breath, walked over to a deli tray for some nibbles, and sat down again.

"I don't know you very well, I don't know you at all," he said. "It's this coming into battle. I feel like our swords are drawn and they got drawn quite quickly."

I gamely interjected that mine was a plastic sword, but he was in no mood for sweet talk. "Whatever," he tersely replied. And out came a lengthy screed about his frustration with the press.

"If you went out of here and I said to someone, 'What an arsehole, what a fuckin' cunt that guy was,' you—if you knew that—you would actually be upset, wouldn't you?"

I thought it best to go along with him and say yes, though I rather fancied the possibility.

"When someone writes something like that in print, that hundreds of thousands of people are gonna read depending on the circulation, why is that meant to not bother me?" he asked.

"I just feel that when there's that kind of criticism which is of a personal nature, I just find that it's extraordinary that the people that write that kind of stuff assume that you're not gonna read it and why do you take it all too seriously? And until right now I haven't been taking it seriously at all."

Right now? Did he mean right at this minute, and I'd picked at the scab? Or right now in a more general sense? I'll never know. Collins was unstoppable. Yes, beware when rock stars get on their high horse and spout idealistic slogans, but Collins was not like them.

"We should be skeptical of what we hear because there are a lot of rich arseholes that tend to write this kind of stuff and then say, 'Hey, but that's OK because I'm in my limo.' But actually, as it happens, I'm not one of them people, within the parameters that I'm allowed to work in.

"I go push the cart around the supermarket as a normal person, but when it comes to paying the money it doesn't really matter how much it costs. That's when I stop being normal, but at least I go out there and I push the cart around the supermarket. So I try my best, y'know what I mean?"

The cause of our discontent was the album's first single and opening track, "Both Sides of the Story." Collins had seen the 1991 movie *Grand Canyon* in which Kevin Kline's character gets hassled by thugs after his car breaks down at night in the crime-ridden Los Angeles suburb of Inglewood.

In Collins' song, "white man turns the corner, finds himself in a different world." An armed "ghetto kid" accosts him and asks, "Would you respect me if I didn't have this gun?" That's why he carries a gun because he wouldn't get respect otherwise. The song concludes, "We always need to hear both sides of the story." It's just one verse in one song, but it dominated most of our conversation.

"The guy that is getting mugged, in fact in my view . . . didn't even know this area existed," Collins explained. "This is like a glimpse into another world that he chose to ignore, chose not to believe existed. And he's subject to this assault.

"Now I believe there's a lot of those people around, and I believe that it is easy to say it's this kid's fault for doing that. I'm saying it's our fault for creating the environment that has caused him to be in that situation."

I was having none of this liberal claptrap, especially amid simmering tensions arising from the Los Angeles riots 18 months earlier. Well, hey, Mr. Rock Star, what do you know? When was the last time you ventured to south-central Los Angeles?

"What difference does that make whether I actually go there or not, if I know it's there? You're assuming, because I have money, that I actually cannot say this? You are saying that my feelings about the subject are off-balance mainly because what would I know?

"It really makes me mad this thought that I live in a fucking ivory tower. It really does make me mad. Everyone assumes that when you have money and you have success and you start cosseting yourself and buffeting yourself from real life . . .

"In England I drive myself to the supermarket. I do all that stuff. I live as normal a life as I possibly can and to me it is a normal life. People knock on my front door and I answer it. People are surprised. I live here, this is my house. I answer the fucking door!"

Collins, bless his heart, simply wanted to be taken seriously for a change. As a family man—not to mention a big taxpayer—he had legitimate concerns about society. The fraying of family bonds worried him. He blamed parents for their children's misdeeds, and he had firsthand experience of the evils that youngsters do. His first wife and three children lived in Vancouver, a historically tranquil city facing a street gang problem. One of his son's friends was blinded during a mugging. Along with everyone else in England, Collins was rattled by the horrific murder earlier that year of 2-year-old James Bulger by a pair of 10-year-old boys.

"I believe that implicitly, that we are to blame for a lot of the problems that we have; we are to blame as parents for not guiding our children and giving advice to our children as much now as we used to.

"At what point do you sort of say, 'C'mon guys, we all have to put our own house in order. When is the last time you sat down and had dinner with your kids? What was the last time that you actually sat down and saw the friends that your kids are hanging around with?' I've become more aware."

He touched on the generational divide in the album track "Sons of Our Fathers," in which he preemptively admitted that he sounded just like his dad, yearning for the old days. "I would love to go back, because I think the world was a nicer place to be," he explained.

He was also aware that even well-intentioned rock stars really have no vote. "I appreciate the fact that we're all tarred with the same brush. I don't want to be on a soapbox talking about this. What I'm doing [is] I'm saying, 'Excuse me. This bothers me. Does it bother anybody else? If it bothers anybody else let's all put our hands up and let's put our own houses in order. If I'm the only one, then you carry on.'"

But Collins' problem, as he admitted, was that no one took him seriously. If Neil Young had written "Another Day in Paradise"—which won the Grammy for record of the year—the song would be viewed much more positively, he said.

"It bothers me that people misunderstand and don't give me at least some credit for having some kind of intelligence," he said. "I don't think anything can arrest that perception. I think it's just too late; I've been around too long. In the same way that I have about the Grateful Dead, people have made up their minds about me. There's nothing I can do about it."

His credibility problem was so bad that people didn't believe him when he claimed he had a dark side. "I've been telling people I'm not so nice," he said. "For years now. They don't believe me."

How did one of the biggest-selling artists of all time end up in this sad situation? Collins' only crime was to write inoffensive, middle-of-the-road radio hits, make self-deprecating jokes, and smile a lot. And when was the last time Neil Young cracked a smile? Yet everyone worships the grumpy rocker.

Basically, people got fed up with Phil. He was unavoidable in the mid-1980s. While we were still recovering from his chart-topping ballad "Against All Odds," Collins unleashed hit duets with Philip Bailey ("Easy Lover") and Marilyn Martin ("Separate Lives"); the Grammy-winning album *No Jacket Required* with more big singles; and the massive Genesis album *Invisible Touch* with accompanying world tour. Ever charitable, he sang and played on Band Aid's "Do They Know It's Christmas?" and got more face time at Live Aid than the starving Ethiopians: He performed solo stands on either side of the Atlantic on the same day, and accompanied Sting, Clapton, and Led Zeppelin. The former child actor also found time to play a con man named Phil in an episode of *Miami Vice* where he uttered the immortal line, "You must take me for a right wanker, son!"

"I was everywhere," Collins said. "When radio stations started to advertise a guaranteed free Phil Collins weekend [sic], that's when I thought, 'Allo! 'Allo! How can I miss you if you won't go away?"

But Collins didn't go away. His fans did. *Both Sides* marked the beginning of his downturn. It went to No. 1 in Britain but did not crack the top 10 in the United States. In 1996 he quit Genesis and released *Dance into the Light*, which stalled at No. 21 in the United States. He remained a popular concert draw, and toured with a jazz-oriented big band in 1998. Disney came to the rescue in 1999 when it recruited him to work on the soundtrack to its *Tarzan* cartoon. He won an Oscar for his efforts. But in 2002 he released his first album in six years, *Testify*, and it bombed.

By then he was married to a Swiss woman named Orianne Cevey and they were living in Lake Geneva. He had divorced his previous wife by fax, or so the tabloids claimed. He vehemently denied the reports. "Of course I get crucified a little bit more than everybody else, than Rod Stewart would or Mick Jagger would, who kinda womanize their way around the world," he said, still playing the victim card when we reconnected for that *Testify* record.

Our second interview was a more pleasant affair. I was on my best behavior, and he was in a good mood. If he remembered our previous encounter, he was too polite to say anything. *Testify* was a reflection of his happy domestic life, filled with songs about love and Orianne's first pregnancy (the couple had two sons). But he was reluctant to describe it as "Phil's happy album." He noted that the track "Don't Get Me Started" took a shotgun stance against corrupt politicians, the gutter press, and religious zealots. (Sample couplet: "It's one man's god against another while the river of tears roll [*sic*] by.")

"Call me old-fashioned, but I still think that we are so sophisticated, aren't we, with our Internet, man on the moon, and space stations. And yet we're barbaric enough to still kill each other because of religious beliefs," he explained. "I just think that nothing's changed since the Middle Ages, in that case."

Returning to my unanswered question from 1993, I asked what else annoyed him. Collins admitted he had a short fuse, and was easily riled by displays of hypocrisy and racism. "The usual things that piss most people off, they piss me off," he said. "I expect to be treated fairly, the same as I treat people fairly. People are innocent till proved guilty rather than the other way around. I don't pretend to be nicer, better, more holier-than-thou than anybody else. I'm just slap-bang in the middle, I suppose. Normal."

He was fully aware that rock stars go through ups and downs, and that he had peaked in the '80s. He remained intensely proud of *Both Sides,* if bewildered by its poor reception. "It's at that point you realize, All these people, they like me for different reasons. They don't like me for the reasons that I hoped that they were liking me for, i.e., what I wanted them to like me for! Which is, as a writer of songs. They didn't see the beauty in that record that I did." He recalled that *Q* published a career-spanning discography years later and decreed that *Both Sides* would go down in history as one of his best yet. "And I thought, Thank you, someone's got it." (I wasn't able to verify this.)

He noted that no one seemed to be as judgmental about actors, the esteemed denizens of an honorable profession that he had tried with mixed success to crack throughout the years. "I remember reading a Jack Lemmon biography and discovering all these films of his I didn't know, or weren't successful, and yet he still was considered one of our great film actors. And yet his career was never, ever in danger of being anything other than Jack Lemmon, famous actor. In music you don't get that opportunity. You're either selling more, more, and more, or you're finished.

"I'm not in that marketplace anymore, and I'm quite pleased not to be, to be quite honest. I'm 51. I'm not gonna do the things that are required of me to be on MTV, if they were even thinking about having me on it, because I'm too old. As I come down after the top of the rollercoaster, there are all these other little things I can do. These things are not so high profile, they're not kinda things that put you on the cover of magazines, but it's writing a score for a film, writing songs for this, perhaps taking my big band out and doing this. I'm doing things for me, for my particular drive at this particular moment in time."

Alas, Phil and Orianne were over by 2006. He reunited with Genesis for a tour in 2007, and released a record of Motown covers in 2010. Maybe he should have done a Stax Records tribute instead, with a self-referential version of Otis Redding's "Mr. Pitiful." That was the tune he was singing by 2011. He was half-deaf, and unable to play drums as a result of a neck injury that restricted the use of his hands. In a *Rolling Stone* feature, he talked about contemplating suicide. A photo showed him glumly clutching a rifle, possibly re-creating Kurt Cobain's last minutes. But he was merely showing off his beloved Civil War memorabilia. He really needs to get out of his basement and start swinging, musically or otherwise.

QUEEN: THE SHOW MUST GO ON

When I spoke with Roger Taylor in 1993, the Queen drummer was 43 years old and out of a job. Two decades later, at the same age, I was in a similar jam.

Taylor entered middle age as a multimillionaire rock star, the jet-setting member of one of the biggest, most hedonistic bands of all time, and the writer of hits like "Radio Ga Ga" and "A Kind of Magic." As for my accomplishments, uh, never mind.

What we did have in common at 43 was an uncertain professional future. I had been fired after 23 years at Reuters, and Queen had lost singer Freddie Mercury to AIDS in November 1991.

Taylor and his surviving bandmates, Brian May and John Deacon, paid tribute to their flamboyant frontman by organizing a charity concert at Wembley Stadium five months later. They backed an all-star lineup that included Metallica, Guns N' Roses, David Bowie, Elton John, and Robert Plant. The performances with vocalists George Michael and Lisa Stansfield came out on a five-track album called *Five Live* in April 1993. That was Taylor's reason for calling me that month from England.

We spoke as the jury in the retrial of the four Los Angeles cops involved in the Rodney King beating continued its lengthy deliberations. Taylor was worried about the verdict because he had to be in L.A. the following week and did not want his visit marred by a sequel to the previous year's riots. The interview was a relaxed affair, a relief since Queen never went out of their way to butter up the press. When Mercury finally confirmed that he had AIDS, the day before he died, his statement noted that he was "famous for my lack of interviews."

We touched on sensitive topics such as Mercury's death and Queen's embargo-busting Sun City concerts in apartheid-era South Africa. And Taylor made my day by calling Pink Floyd's Roger Waters a "terminal arsehole." But the focus, naturally, was on the future of Queen. Everything was up in the air, but Taylor—unlike me at 43—wasn't lying around at home feeling sorry for himself.

His trip to L.A. was to collaborate with Japanese heavy-metal veteran Yoshiki on a single that came out the following year. He was also working on his third solo album (*Happiness?*) and a posthumous Queen album (*Made in Heaven*). He and May went on to perform together throughout the decade (John Deacon, particularly hard hit by Mercury's death, retired in 1997 and cut off contact with his bandmates). In 2004 Taylor and May teamed with Bad Company singer Paul Rodgers for a five-year run of touring and recording. More recently, the duo jumped on the talent show juggernaut on both sides of the Atlantic, with performances on *American Idol* and Britain's *X-Factor*. Taylor launched his own competition in 2011, seeking young performers for a "Queen Extravaganza" tribute tour. Which brings me back almost full circle to our 1993 interview.

Given that some of Queen's biggest moments have been in these sorts of extravaganzas, like Live Aid—
Rising to the occasion, it's called!
Is that perhaps a fitting finale for the band?
Well maybe. I don't know. People keep asking me, they say, "What are you going to do? Is that it? Are you going to stay

together?" We're all still friends. We're obviously in business together. We still sell records. We've got to finish one album yet with Freddie's voice on it. Together we're great friends. But at the same time Brian is pursuing a solo career at the moment, Brian May. And in fact I've been writing for the last year—well, since Freddie died really. I've built a studio at home here and I'm actually recording a solo album here, over quite a long time. So I'm looking forward to actually completing that, although it's quite a long way off at the moment. Whether we'll actually play together again I'm not sure, apart from in the studio. I really couldn't say.

Did Freddie complete the vocals for all the songs?

The three of us did all the harmonies—Freddie, myself, and Brian. But he's just so incredibly irreplaceable in a way. He was so big, bigger than life. He was a remarkably—he was a great person and we all miss him so much. We don't feel really that we could replace him. Having said that, it's great for the three of us to be playing with George Michael singing because, I tell you, he sang so wonderfully.

It can't be too much fun making that record without Freddie.

We haven't actually got ourselves into the studio yet to tackle it, because it's all stuff that was recorded before Freddie died. I know it's there, it's waiting to be finished, and in a way it'll be nice to get it finished, and it will also be really a matter of pride to make a really good job of it, a really decent job of it.

Does that fulfill your U.S. obligations with Hollywood Records?

It's not really a matter of fulfilling obligations, because if there is no more there's no more. That's it. That's your obligation. But that's definitely the last they're gonna get with Freddie Mercury singing. But who knows? Queen, whether it will continue in some other form, I really can't answer. But nobody's had any bright ideas yet.

I guess it's similar to the issues faced by the Doors after Jim Morrison died.

I suppose so. But I'd like to think we were—oh, I don't wanna knock the Doors—a more democratic organization maybe, than the Doors. I don't know. Maybe they were a democratic organization. But it is true that the three of us instrumentally play wonderfully together; it's like an old shoe. It just slots in and there it is. It sounds enormous, sounds like 10 people, and no one knows what the other is going to play next. There's no doubt about it. Like on the tribute thing, it was quite interesting, y'know?

Do you have any gems in the vaults that you may release in a boxed set?

God knows. I mean, I'm sure they'll drag out something. But usually if we rejected something, it was because it wasn't much good. No, I wouldn't want to bring out anything substandard, I don't think.

Just going back to that concert, how would you describe the emotions of you and your bandmates beforehand and on the day?

I can't speak for the others, but for me it was a helluva lot of work. It was such intensive work for about three to four months, but it didn't quite sink in that it was suddenly all over. I just went on holiday for about two months. It went too quickly to be emotional, almost. I was concentrating so much on making sure the thing went OK and then all of a sudden it was over.

Q **magazine ran a series of photos from the concert a few months ago, and you were in virtually every shot, looking very busy—**

—and extremely tired! I've never given more telephone interviews than I gave over those three months, with people ringing me at four and five in the morning from all over the world, saying, "Well, what if I do this?" Well, you do that. Let me get some sleep.

I understand Madonna was supposed to appear [according to *Q*]?

No. No. No. I'm afraid there's no truth in that. I can't really see what Madonna would relate to, at all. I know we don't relate to her! I don't know which song she would've done, but I'd like to hear it! We thought it apt that nobody should play "Another One Bites the Dust," because that was rather unfortunate phrasing there.

Do you have any poignant memories from the show?

I've got many poignant memories. It brought back old times, like playing with David Bowie out the front again. I think really probably the standout moment for me was when Axl [Rose] came on to join

Elton in "Bohemian Rhapsody," which I thought spoke volumes in a way. I thought that was a great moment. It made me smile.

Do you think the concert had any effect on AIDS consciousness?

Who knows? I think people were conscious, but it was a great platform at the time that we really had to take advantage of, apart from celebrating Freddie and his life, et cetera. We almost had a duty—we had the global platform—to bring to young people, just to remind them—not in a boring way hopefully—of the dangers. And if it did that at the time that's as much as we could have done. We must remember that in Africa, because it was aired in Africa, they don't have the educational awareness that we have or the efficiency that we have in the Westernized countries. So I do hope it did some good. There's no way to tell. There's no such thing as an awareness meter.

So you're fairly philosophical about the whole thing?

That's the only way you can be. You do your best, and hope you did a bit of good. There's nothing else you can do, and by worrying about it, you're definitely wasting brain cells, I think.

It's refreshing that you have such a realistic attitude.

It's the only way. We miss Freddie very much because we really were the greatest of friends and he was a part of our lives and we miss him like hell every day. But life does go on, and let's face it, we've been very lucky. We had an incredible career. We've had an incredible career.

What do you think some of the legacies will be, both of Queen and of Freddie?

I'm continually amazed at the young age of a lot of people that like our music. It's just quite extraordinary. I see 9-year-olds playing the *Greatest Hits II* and that's quite a big album with 9-year-olds, which I find staggering, which is absolutely terrific. I think at the end of the day, if your music's touched a lot of people and brought some kind of entertainment or enjoyment—whatever—affected them in some way positively, I think you're doing a good job as a musician. In 50 years from now, who cares really? It's interesting. At least we managed to bring quite a lot to a lot of people, which is good. Hopefully it's accessible.

You never lectured us with the music, which was nice.

I think there were a few messages in there, but hopefully they weren't sort of preachy. I can't stand being preached at especially by some piddly pop star, y'know? And I'm sure most people are the same! We took ourselves seriously in a way that we were proud of our music, but hopefully we weren't ever pretentious about it. We did have a sense of humor about it, there's a lot of tongue in cheek there.

I was reading some of the press accounts, and I know you guys don't get on too well with us.

To be honest, the last 10 years we could've given a shit, y'know? In fact it seems to be a rather better relationship than it was then. It doesn't really matter, no.

I guess press attention is good at the outset, but once you've got your franchise and your fans, it doesn't matter.

That's right. Really we found that there were two things. There was basically people and radio that were absolutely vitally important, and really nothing else mattered in terms of popularity.

But without the Queen name, Brian May is essentially starting out from scratch, isn't he?

In some ways he is, yeah. It's tough, isn't it, because the power of the brand name is extraordinary. Look at Roger Waters or even Mick Jagger, who finds it very hard to have a hit. I don't mean that in any derogatory sense, but [it's] the incredible power of the brand name to get across to the great mass.

They're two interesting examples because they've done lots of press. Roger Waters is still reliving his Pink Floyd days.

Yes, I don't think he should do press, actually! I'm surprised they let him out! I think he suffers from being a terminal arsehole.

What's in your future?

I'm doing this solo album, which I'm really sorta throwing myself into, and I'm doing this thing with the Japanese guy, with a few sorta film offers in the offing, which is all very interesting. I'm enjoying life. Life's actually pretty good, I must say.

How does the death of a close one affect you?

It affects you, but I find I'm at a stage in my life when I've lost quite a few friends now around me, not all from AIDS but some, some from just dropping dead and stuff like that. And it seems to be a period you reach in life when that happens. I'm just really trying to make some good music. I enjoy boats and I enjoy skiing and I enjoy my kids, and that's a pretty good life as far as I'm concerned. I don't have to go out and build walls or anything!

Rock 'n' roll is such a seemingly debauched industry—

You've gotta be tough to come through it!

And it's really had so few casualties, relatively speaking.

Well, I don't know. There's a lot of casualties really, I think. I always feel for the people that have really done too much of everything and never made it as well. That's like adding insult to injury. What do they end up doing, I often wonder?

What are your first memories of Freddie? You had a clothes store with him in Kensington?

Oh yeah, we ran a clothes stall in Kensington Market together, yeah. My first memories are of this very eccentric art student, incredibly theatrical.

What age were you?

I was 18. Long black dark hair, bright brown eyes, and tremendous belief in himself and a very sort of gymnastic person. He was very fit and alive and vibrant and a person who invented himself. He had absolutely invented himself. He was just terrific in every way. I can't think of a bad word to say about him, to be honest. He had a very strong character which got even stronger as he matured.

I imagine the band pressure must have got to you, though?

I never fell out with him really, because there was never a dull moment. He'd always laugh about something. I sold his jacket once when we had the stall together and he got pissed off about that.

Didn't you all have a problem over the royalties?

Never. We never ever had an argument over money. In fact, what we did was, we decided at some point—because we all wrote songs, especially in the last 15 years—whoever had written a song, every song we just called it "Written by Queen" and we split the money. There was never any argument over money. [In reality, the success of the Mercury-written "Bohemian Rhapsody" generated tension since the royalties were split equally with B-side writer Taylor.]

Was that the system from day one, though?

No, no. We just got together, and said, "Look, this is stupid." Somebody writes the A-side, somebody writes the B-side, somebody writes this, and then people are getting worried about what gets on the album because they wrote it. But if you can get rid of that at source—because we all contributed fairly equally, especially in the last half of our career, y'know?

Do you think it would have been harder for Queen to make it as big without Freddie?

Oh my God, yeah. I don't think we would have made it without Brian or myself either, frankly. What we had was a great mixture, it worked very well. And John. It just worked. There was a quiet one, there was a studious one, but we could all play well. And we understood music and it was a magical mixture. We were all completely different. I think Freddie, if he were here now, he'd say that. He was very much into the democracy of it. What makes a band? That's what makes a band, really.

Brian May said you lived the most extreme and extravagant and rock 'n' roll lifestyle. What do you think he meant?

Oh, I think that just means he's tight! No, I don't know. I live well, and I wouldn't put it any stronger than that.

Where do you live in England?

I live in the country most of the time.

In the stockbroker belt?

No, I'm just outside it, actually. I live in London a little bit. I used to live in London all the time, and now I live mainly in the country. I move around quite a lot, y'know?

You guys were all extremely private. Why was that?

We never tried to get publicity by any other means than our music. We weren't interested in parading our girlfriends or boyfriends or whatever in public. It just didn't interest us. We had quite enough attention when we were touring and we really weren't interested in publicity stunts or stuff like that. We'd just get on with life, we'd go out for meals, or we'd go out to clubs or whatever. But we weren't really a publicity-seeking band at all.

You had some bad publicity from playing Sun City.

Oh God. We really got a lot of stick for that, yeah.

Do you think in hindsight that was a bad move?

Interesting question. I'm in two minds. My logic tells me it wasn't a bad move. I think people don't understand. I think people who don't go to South Africa don't understand the country at all. I didn't. I know that. Until I went there, I didn't understand it at all. They see the whole thing in very simplistic terms. I think any sane person would agree Apartheid is wrong. Certainly we would. But in fact we had an awful lot of black fans in South Africa. And it's a long story and I don't really want to go back over it.

I went to Sun City two years ago and thought it was disgraceful as a tourist site.

I wouldn't go there. If I went on holiday, I wouldn't go there. The thing is, why the fuss about Sun City? It's really got very little to do with South Africa, for a start. It's a playground and it's a playground for black and white, which most people in the West don't really realize, I think. It's a rather tacky, Vegas-y place. We didn't make any money out of it anyway.

Have you been to South Africa since?

No.

It's a great place.

I hear Cape Town's one of the most beautiful cities in the world. I was expecting a lot of poverty, which I didn't see. There are parts of Soweto which are like Hollywood.

Not to glamorize it, but I wonder if you can tell me how it was with you guys when Freddie told you he was HIV-positive.

Well, I don't really want to go into that much detail actually. But obviously we'd been supporting him. We knew he was terribly ill. It was really only a confirmation of what we'd guessed. But actually hearing it is an appalling thing really.

When did you first realize he was ill?
I can't remember. A few years ago, and a few years before he died. But for quite a long time we tried to tell ourselves it was other things.

Did you think in the early days: Freddie, he's doing such crazy things, something is going to happen to him sometime, somehow?
No, we were all pretty crazy. We all lived very hard and very fast and we thought we were indestructible. I think probably we've all slowed down a bit now!

How old are you now?
I'm 43.

Well, that's not too bad.
Not bad.

You've still got a few years left.
We'll see, we'll see. I must tell you, I've got a recording session. I'm gonna have to run.

That's great. Thanks very much for talking to me. I hope it wasn't too painful for you.
Oh, no, no, no. You're Australian, right?

No, I'm from New Zealand.
New Zealand, I'm sorry. Kiwi. God. We only went there once [April 13, 1985]. I remember Freddie was pissed! He was drunk as a skunk. It was terrible. It was not one of our finest hours!

GENE SIMMONS: KISS MY ASS

I must have interviewed the members of Kiss about a hundred times. I visited Paul Stanley at his house, and I own Gene Simmons' pink bathrobe. But I've seen Kiss live just once, I don't own any of their classic albums, and I could probably hum about three of their songs, including the pop hit "I Was Made for Lovin' You," which Simmons despises. I have no excuse for my apathy. Dudes in makeup was never my thing. If you're not a fan by 17, you never will be.

I do respect the ability of co-founders Simmons and Stanley to keep the band together through multiple personnel lineups, and I appreciate their coming-of-age appeal to multiple generations of fans. They were always accessible to the media, despite lingering ill will over the critical opprobrium directed at them for much of their career. Simmons' hard-headed business acumen is an inspiration to us all, although a sweetheart lurks underneath his gruff, "sabra" exterior.

In 2000, I covered a two-day sale of Kiss memorabilia in Hollywood. Simmons and Stanley were cleaning out a warehouse's worth of costumes, instruments and other junk. I didn't mean to, but got sucked into the excitement and successfully bid $550 for a pink terry-cloth bathrobe that was given to Simmons by then-girlfriend Cher. Embroidered on the back was *Knights in Satan's Service*, for which Kiss was a rumored acronym. When I took it to be dry-cleaned, the little old Asian lady behind the counter doubled over in hysterics. I also paid $400 for a Kiss-emblazoned roadie case with two working keyboards and an old bra inside. Gene, if you want them back, they're yours for $10,000.

Simmons is the band's extrovert, a needy only child. Both he and Stanley are sons of Holocaust refugees. Simmons, 2½ years Stanley's senior, was born in Israel to Hungarian parents who split up when he was about 5. He and his mother emigrated to New York when he was 8½ and he changed his name from Chaim Weitz to Gene Klein. He once told a friend of mine that he and his mother were so poor that they slept in the same bed. This might have been a pickup line designed (unsuccessfully in this case) to evoke sympathy. "It sounds good," Stanley told me years later when I ran it past him. "When I met him he certainly wasn't sharing his bed with his mother. He was living in a nicer place than I did. Was it George Orwell who said 'the autobiography is the most outrageous form of fiction'?"

My first Kiss encounter was in 1993, a decade after the band had ditched its traditional face paint (the makeup would return for a reunion of the original lineup in 1996). Kiss had just released yet another live album, *Alive III*, which was ostensibly why Simmons and I were hanging out in a Sunset Strip conference room for an hour. More interestingly, Simmons revealed, the band was also overseeing a tribute record to be called *Kiss My Ass*, which featured contributions by the likes of Garth Brooks, Lenny Kravitz, and Anthrax. A hefty coffee-table book was also in the works. Simmons joked to me that the book would need legs. (The following year in a *Seinfeld* episode, Kramer unveiled a coffee-table book with legs on an ersatz *Live with Regis and Kathie Lee* appearance.)

At that stage, Kiss' lineup was rounded out by drummer Eric Singer and lead guitarist Bruce Kulick. They were subbing, respectively, for original members Peter Criss and Ace Frehley, who were in and out of the band multiple times through 2004. As of 2013 Singer was still in the band, while Tommy Thayer has been lead guitarist since 2003.

It's been almost 25 years since your friendship began with Paul Stanley, which makes it one of rock's more enduring partnerships. How would you trace the evolution of that friendship over the years?

It started off very much as a very one-sided relationship [in 1970]. I was looking for a lead guitar player for a band that I wrote material for and sang lead for, a band called Bullfrog Beer—this was when I was still in college—and Paul happened to be in the room. And when I was introduced to him, we didn't really get on very well. I don't think there was anything wrong with him. He thought I was full of myself, and of course he's right. We didn't really connect that first time. But later on we realized that each had something else to offer. Whatever piece was missing, then the other made up for. Whenever I see any of the other celebrated teams in rock 'n' roll whether it's [Steven] Tyler and [Joe] Perry, or [Mick] Jagger and [Keith] Richards, members seem to fight with each other. Then people have to go off and do solo records, and then maybe they get back together again, and they slag each other off in the press. I never understood that. Unless it was good business. Maybe that's what it's all about.

Maybe it's the creative energy that you get from that sparring?

No. Maybe it's just too much drugs that numbs your mind, and then makes you think that your friends are your enemies, and vice versa: that your enemies are your friends. But we never had that, fortunately.

Do you put the Simmons-Stanley duo up in the rock pantheon with those other duos?

Oh, hell no. I'm just glad not to be working nine-to-five. I never fool myself into thinking that this is anything more than just ear candy. If it means something today and means absolutely nothing tomorrow, that's OK with me. I don't think, ultimately really, rock 'n' roll means a hell of a lot except maybe it becomes a part of your life.

You remember back. It's almost like sign posts, street signs. When you're 20 or when you're 15 or when you're 30, whatever it is, a certain song can click off a memory. But more than that, I don't think it means anything. And with all the war chants and the peace anthems and all that stuff, ultimately I think a song's just a song. It can move people but then I don't think that if people aren't really interested in being moved, I don't care what the song is it's not going to happen.

Is it like the great rock 'n' roll swindle that you're perpetrating on us?

I don't think it's a swindle in any way, shape, or form. I think it is what it is. When you walk into a candy store and it says—clearly marked—candy, it's not a swindle, because you know what it is. A swindle is a wolf in sheep's clothing, or a sheep in wolf's clothing. A swindle is when you're buying something and think you're getting something else. I don't think we've ever deluded ourselves or our fans or enemies into believing or in any way even thinking that this stuff means anything. Ultimately I think Kiss music is no more relevant to the 20th century than football cheers. Kiss concerts are very much that way. People have often referred to Kiss concerts as almost like the bread and circuses that the Romans used to indulge in with excess and all that, leading to the point where you puke and all that. The one thing we've always had is a sense of not fooling ourselves or our fans. It's always been with camp.

When you go to a football game, whether it's European football or American football, there's a sense of nationhood, a sense of belonging. You root for your team, one team kicks the butt of the other team, and then you walk away. And then some philosopher someplace sits up and says, "But wait, what does it all mean?" At that point, you just have to beat the crap out of this guy because he misses the point of life. Life just is, and . . . doesn't actually have to mean something. If we just get by through another day without beating each other to a pulp them that's as valid as anything. You're eating a good sandwich or some dessert, and somebody says "It tastes good, but what does it really mean?" What are you talking about? I'm hungry, I'm eating something enjoyable. Basically I'm a strict believer in Epicurean hedonism—I had to do that so you have something to write about! You might have to go look it up! A life of pleasure. The pursuit of happiness and pleasure and so on.

So do you have orgies and things like that?

Everybody's done that in one form or another. Yeah, sure.

I saw a quote in *Q* magazine where you said you've had every experience up to but excluding farm animals.

Well, I have to add an additional. Nobody has ever been up my Hershey Highway, and that's off limits. My butthole is only for God. If somebody wants to take that only God can. Unless I find myself in jail, heaven forbid. But basically everybody's done everything. I'm a heterosexual. But other than that. And certainly there have been bowls of fruit here and there.

How about a mud shark, like Led Zeppelin [allegedly used on a groupie]?

That's so overblown and so silly. We actually stayed in that hotel [the Edgewater Inn in Seattle] a couple of times. This poor shark, what's sexual about this? This poor shark is dying, thrashing in its last death throes, and it's in a bathtub. Yeah, so what?

For better or worse I'd put you in the same category as bands like Van Halen—

A band I discovered. I produced their first demo, flew them to New York, recorded their demo at the 24-track Electric Lady Studios, and I couldn't interest anybody in the band. I was gonna really go through the record company route and shop them, but we had to go out on tour. We were touring, I think, *Love Gun* [1977] or *Rock and Roll Over* [1976], one of those records. I told 'em to hold on, I'll come back off tour and we'll try again. Or, take the tapes and get yourself a deal. I won't stand in the way. Within a month they were on Warner Bros.

—Like Van Halen, AC/DC, Kiss is meat-and-vegetables rock 'n' roll, no pretensions.

Yeah, I don't think the band has ever gone out of its way to try to do anything—quote—meaningful. I think it's a lot of crap. I'm really not interested in hearing a sociological point of view from a musician who, first, never learned to play an instrument properly which is what gives it the magic of rock 'n' roll in the first place. So where do you all of a sudden get this world knowledge? Everybody basically believes in the same thing—peace, not hurting anybody. Yes, the forests should not be burned down, because we'll all die. Nobody wants nuclear war. Yeah? What else is there? Be kind to each other. Everybody agrees with that, yeah. So I need some knucklehead guy, who's in a rock 'n' roll band because he doesn't want to work nine-to-five, standing up on stage saying: "Let me tell you what it's all about." There are enough pontiffs in the world as far as I'm concerned.

I've heard the story before: from Pearl Jam and Metallica and Mötley [Crüe], and you name it, Nirvana. They see the band [Kiss] at a certain point and they say, "That's what I want to do." It's all very heady stuff. I try not to take it too seriously, because you start having delusions of grandeur and start thinking you're the Beatles or something. But in fact I was watching *The Ed Sullivan Show* [in 1963]—most people don't even know what that show is—and I remember watching the Beatles on there, and being fascinated—not just the music, but the vibe, the look, the sense of unity that they had. They were an entity all to themselves. Their identity didn't depend on anybody else's. They looked differently but they were comfortable with who they were and I loved that strength, that sense of self. I can verbalize it now, but as a kid I just was drawn to it. I've heard the same things used when people first saw us.

I know this is gonna sound awful in print, so I just wanna say it: We're not the Beatles. I couldn't kiss their toes. But the language sounds the same. I understand the appeal. This ain't a popularity contest and that's one of the things I think that the band has always strived to uphold. Punk? We decided to completely ignore it, and it was an important piece of music that went by. But we decided not to play the game and stick razor blades in our eyeballs, or whatever. When green hair was the thing, we decided not to. . . . In essence you've got to basically be who you are, whether it's disco or punk or new wave or new romance or whatever. I think the bands that have lasted the longest have always by and large maintained their soul, their sense of who they are. You can change and evolve, but revolution for the sake of revolution is really bullshit. It's aimless. That rebel without a cause nonsense is a one-trick pony.

Are you on social terms with Peter Criss and Ace Frehley?

Every once in a while we see each other, but it's as often as you might see an old girlfriend that you broke up with many years ago. You grow apart and your lives change and you move on. Both Ace and Peter were good guys and never did anything wrong except to themselves. If you wanna say they both left, that's fine. If you wanna say they were both fired, fine. Or any variations thereof. The main point is I didn't want to play with them in the same band. If you're on a football team or a commando team, everybody's gotta give their heart, mind, and body. You can't have somebody straggling behind and say, "I'll catch up with you later." Doesn't work, because you may pass them the ball.

They must do OK from their share of the back catalog?

Ummm. I haven't heard good things. Everybody went through very high living standards for many years. A lot of the people you would think are really rolling in it are not.

That's sad.

No. Sad is when you get hit by a car. That's sad, because you have no choice in the matter. It's the whims of nature, the hand of fate, or whatever. When you do something to yourself, it's not sad. It's a choice. If you decide you wanna start drinking until you pass out. . . . Are they kicking themselves in the butt? Probably. I think everybody at one point or another goes through the process of thinking that everything revolves around them. I'm no different than anybody else. The problem is when you actually cross the line and think that nobody can exist without you, and then you see that things do exist very well without you, it really drives home the point in black and white that everybody's expendable. Everybody is. And you can always find somebody who believes in the same vibe, the same belief. Again, I'll go back to football. Your star player gets injured, you get somebody else who believes in it. And as long as they do it, the team will win. And I believe in teams.

Above tradition? It's always nice to have the original starting lineup, isn't it?

It's all semantics. It's the original lineup depending on when you hop on board the train. That train is constantly moving. You talk about the Beatles again: Who's the original lineup? Ringo? No, it's not. It's Pete Best. It depends when you hop on that train. Some bands have only had one or two changes, other bands have had more.

So Kiss is a partnership that you and Paul share control of?

Well, the more you've been in it, the bigger your stake. But everybody has a stake. This is not slave labor. Everybody's in it because everybody's very happy. I wouldn't want to get paid for something I didn't do, and it applies to everybody else. You talk to anybody who's around us; they all get paid very well. It's a very happy relationship and that's why there's no room for anybody who decides that their individual agenda is more important or above everybody else. And that means: "I want to go off to Bali on a holiday." No, you check with everybody to see whether or not the band's doing something. This is more of a marriage than any relationship you'll ever have with a girl.

Eric and Bruce have to buy into your ethos?

Bruce has been with us eight years [leaving in 1996]. Some bands don't last four years. Our last drummer, Eric Carr, was with us 11 years, and he passed away from cancer [in 1991]. And Eric Singer, our new drummer, has been with us a year and a half. It's all relative, if a fan buys *Alive III* and that's the first record he's bought by Kiss, this is the original lineup, for him. There isn't a band out there I can think of that didn't go through that process, whether it's the Stones or the Who or anybody. Sooner or later you go through the process because when the gun goes off when a race starts not everybody goes across the finish line. Not everybody has the same motivations. It's not even about stamina. It's about relentless, dog-headed, stubborn determination to cross that finish line. Not everybody has the same things inside of them when they start. In the beginning you think it's about money and then you get as much of it as you can stomach. Then you think it's about flesh—female—and whatever else you may want. And you can have as much of that anytime you want. Then you think it's about fame, and past a certain point you get your picture in a magazine or you get a good seat in a restaurant. That's really all there is.

What's in it for you now?
I realized secretly that it's always been about some other thing. Again, I don't want to make too much of the music, because I think a good song's just a good song and that's it, and shut up about it. It really does, sooner or later, come back to the songs, because if you take away the makeup and take away the bombs and the high heels and the costumes and the tongue or the drooling blood, or all the girls we fucked, all the stories and all the other stuff, the sauce is just not gonna improve the meal. You better have some substance going in. Which is why Sigue Sigue Sputnik and lots of other bands may have been interesting to look at, but nobody wanted to go into a garage as a 15-year-old kid and do those songs. It does come back to the songs. When I was a kid and putting the band together, I thought, "We'll write really good songs *but* I'll get laid! Or *but* I'll get a lot of money! *And* I'll get fame. *And* I'll get this, *and* I'll get that." Yeah that's all nice, but without that good song it's an empty victory.

You've always been portrayed as the business mind in the band.
It's such an unfounded reputation. I'm as much of a complete moron as anybody else. I don't know a single thing more than anybody else except I'm one of those guys that just doesn't want to be run over by a car. So before I cross the street I look one way, then I look the other way—all the natural stuff. Most people don't want to deal with details and I do because I don't want to be fucked.

Is that your Jewish refugee heritage?
I think everything that you are or could be is partly due to who you are and where you come from, what you've heard growing up and watching, and all that. And that doesn't negate that you could turn out to be a complete moron even though you had a real substantial background. But chances are at least if you have the

tools growing up, I think culture and upbringing are very, very important as to what forms the basis of who you are. But me as this business guy, that's really unfounded. It's very appealing to my ego.

It's hardly an insult.

Well, actually, in rock 'n' roll terminology, it is. Then people on the street may think, Oh great we're being manipulated. It's almost like there's some kind of sales or marketing plan. You wanna know something? I couldn't think of a stupider idea in 1973 to sit down and say, "You know what? Glitter and glam is dead. I have a good idea, let's put on makeup and go out there and try to do something." We were the only band out there doing that. As an opening band we invested every cent we had in the biggest show anybody had seen at that time. And we were opening up for bands like Rory Gallagher, Manfred Mann, Savoy Brown. You would have to have been a complete moron to think that that would work. We didn't have a clue that would work. We just had this sort of blind vision of something. I don't know what it is.

Does it help that you were on [the cocaine-fueled disco label] Casablanca Records, which was hardly run as a proper label?

It was not a record company in the traditional sense. There was nothing that was ever done by the book. It was the place of ideas almost like what I've read about the early mogul days of movies. An idea would catch on and then no barriers were too strong and no walls were too high. You had to get to that idea. Nowadays, unfortunately, music, records, movies really are fueled by market research and very careful analysis, and so everything tends to be a little safer. I didn't like [labelmates] the Village People, but the idea—one guy's like a cowboy and the other's like an Indian and so on—that was out there. It's way out there. Taking risks makes things more exciting.

Did you ever worry that the music would be subordinated to all the Kiss merchandise?

That's exactly a good point. It's a question that answers itself, actually. At the same time that people started to be concerned that it was becoming more of a toy factory than a rock 'n' roll band we felt the same thing. From the time that we put on the brakes to the time that the toy-making machine actually stopped, it took a couple of years. You can tell somebody to stop and they say, "We still have 50,000 to 100,000 pieces out there. Let them sell off and then we'll stop." That's one of the reasons we stopped it. I couldn't say I'm sorry about a single thing about it, because we had to do it. We were either going to do it on our terms or the bootlegs would appear and it would be substandard anyway. And we protected our makeup and our name and our logo. To this day it's the thing we pride ourselves on. It's almost like your signature, your name. Nobody should have access to that. You find a check or piece of paper with your name on it, your signature, you should be able to sue this guy's pants off. We sue everybody all the time, and without mercy. We will sue you so hard it will hurt your ancestors.

Is that why you've managed to avoid becoming too much of a parody, that you've been able to change course when required?
I think every artist, if they stick around long enough, to somebody someplace is a parody of themselves. The only way you can't be a parody is if you're a brand-new band and it's all fresh. But the longer you're out there, the more of a moving target you are. As soon as somebody doesn't like what you're doing they say, "Oh they're a parody of themselves." So I don't know if we are or aren't. But I think the last studio record we brought out, *Revenge* [1992], is as good a record as we've ever done. And I'm clear in my own mind, in retrospect, that the records we made in the '80s were real substandard records—although at the time I liked them. But looking back on it now, I think a lot of the records in the '70s were good rock 'n' roll records, one or two in the '80s but by and large not. But I think we're starting off the '90s the right way.

I don't like the poppier side of Kiss. This is a multifaceted band even though it's a rock 'n' roll band. This ain't Iron Maiden or Judas Priest or that one thing, good or bad. We've done ballads, we've done concept records, we've done symphony orchestras. We've done lots of different stuff. Invariably it comes down to being a rock 'n' roll band. I never liked the poppier side of it. I didn't like "Beth." I didn't like "I Was Made for Lovin' You"—our biggest hits. I was the one, actually, that pushed that song forward ["Beth"]. It was originally called "Beck," or "Becky." And I said, "You've got to change the name of this to 'Beth,' because people will think you're gonna be in love with Jeff Beck."

I see Paul can't quite hit the high notes on "I Was Made for Lovin' You."

I don't think that's important. How well you sing really is a warped idea in rock 'n' roll, really, because some of my favorite artists including Bob Dylan and even Tom Waits I wouldn't consider singers. So what? The great singers of the world—I don't own a single Pavarotti record.

You collaborated with Bob Dylan, didn't you?

Yeah. We have this track that we did, 24-track, that still needs a lyric, that he and I wrote together. It's sitting around. I just don't have the time to sit down and do something with it. But it'll come out. ["Waiting for the Morning Light" from Simmons' 2004 solo album *Asshole*.]

Are there any major misconceptions or fallacies about the band?

There is no misconception about the band as being sexist. We are. I don't think being sexist makes me the enemy. I believe in a lot of the same principles and, in fact, demand equal work, equal pay. The important issues. But how I look at women, I'm sorry, it's sexual. I can't help it. If you have a problem with that, talk to Freud. When I see a woman, especially an attractive woman, immediately the first thing I think about is sex before she even says, "Hullo, how are you? Nice to see you." It helps if she wears tight dresses, wears bras to lift her breasts in my general direction, and puts on bright red lipstick. And this kewpie doll is looking at me in the face, what am I supposed to think? It would probably help the cause of me not being as much of a sexist if girls dressed like truck drivers, very loose fitting clothes, dirty hair, matted. Believe me, I don't wanna even look at you.

You must be presented with a lot of temptations on the road that you have to pass up now that you have someone back home? [Former Playboy Playmate Shannon Tweed, his girlfriend since 1983, the mother of his two children, and wife since 2011.]

All assumptions are off. Don't assume anything about anybody. One of the reasons why I couldn't see getting married is because I couldn't see standing up in front of a preacher and saying, "I'm never going to have another woman as long as I live." I don't think that that's a promise that you keep.

So your girlfriend doesn't mind if you stray?

I don't think there's a single woman in the world who doesn't wanna slit your throat even as soon as you look at another girl. But my life and your life and anybody's life can't ever really depend on anyone else—not your mother, not your father, not who you share your bed with. Sooner or later you have to decide for yourself what you wanna do. Right?

That's a very Zen answer!

It's a real answer. You love your parents, and even they can't hold up the idea, "Look, don't do this, because it's gonna hurt my feelings." Well, wait a minute. Hurting your feelings and wanting to do something because I wanna do it, that's a guilt thing. Believe me, that's part of my culture.

So you're basically answerable only to yourself?

And to whatever higher power there is, I would say. And the laws of society. If you kill someone you should be killed. Don't take an oath you can't keep.

Did you keep a diary, like [former Rolling Stone] Bill Wyman did with his conquests?

Polaroids, actually.

Oh that's right, the 10,000—

It wasn't 10,000. Guys that use numbers like that lie through their ass.

What's a more realistic number?

Three [thousand].

Do you have any photos with you now?

No, I don't carry these things around. They're in big art folios.

At the end of each encounter, you tell them to sit up and you take a Polaroid?

That's a reasonable description.

Do you still do that?
Sometimes.
Who sees them? What's the historical value?
None. No historical value, except why do you keep keepsakes?
Because you think they may be of interest to future generations?
Maybe so, but I think if something really holds a memory for you, you keep it for yourself. I've got a box of marbles that I have in an old cigar box that I won in my neighborhood. Somebody made fun of the way I spoke English because I wasn't born in America, and then I played marbles and won every single marble at that game, and walked away. "Yeah, I talk funny, pal. But I got your marbles." For me that means something. I've got lots of keepsakes that bring back memories about stuff, and those photos absolutely are very happy memories.
Do you still have strong family ties to Israel?
My dad's there, my mother's here [in New York]. They're both happy as far as I can see. I bought 'em both houses, long ago.
Do you go there [to Israel]?
Haven't been there since I was 8 or 9. I know where I'm from. I guess at some point I'll go back. [He returned in 2011 on the Israeli government's dime while filming his reality show *Gene Simmons Family Jewels*.] I was born in Israel but that's an accident. And I'm proud of where I'm from, and so on, but it's no great achievement. I like to think I'm an earthling, and I was born on the planet. The idea of borders, some imaginary line someplace, has always been a strange concept.
Do your parents call you Gene?
Uhh, they usually call me by my Hebrew name, and publicly just Gene.
Was your family middle class?
Lower-middle. Nobody was poor. I don't wanna play that game. Even if you're poor you're still white. You have an added advantage. If you're poor and black that's as bad as it can get.
Will you return to the days of makeup and fire-breathing?
I still breathe fire, but just getting up on stage and putting the makeup on for no reason would be a cheap shot. It's too easy. There are too many bankers with checks they hold in front of your face

saying, "Do a whole tour." Then there's no difference between us and a Las Vegas act that goes and just does it for the money. Here's an extreme comment. . . . When I was a baby I used to wear diapers. Ten years ago I used to wear makeup. That was who I was then and I'm proud of that, but this is who I am now and I'm certainly proud of this. Just to go backwards for no reason is not necessarily appealing. I don't wanna close the door unequivocally. If somebody could show me a great idea to put it back on, I'd put it on. For a reason. I can't find a reason.

You could do it for a charity show?

Kiss has never really done that kind of stuff, because we believe as private citizens doing all that. Unfortunately, a lot of bands do charity shows because it's good for their career.

Did you ever get an operation on your tongue? Or has it always been like that?

No, it's just a big tongue. It seems to be able to do things that other people can't, for some reason. I'll show you . . . just a little bit, because if the floor's dirty. . .

What music are you listening to?

There's some awfully exciting music going on, and a lot of it very hard. Every year I like different records. Last year I liked the Helmet record [*Meantime*]. Pantera, I think, is doing very interesting stuff. I like some of the Toad the Wet Sprocket records. Urge Overkill's a very good new band. The main thing now is music has finally come back to being controlled by the musicians and the artists instead of the corporate mentality that says, "I need a single. . ."—the music-by-numbers routine. That's dead. Even MTV's dead. Heavy metal really is dead. Popular music is trying to redefine itself now.

You like this alternative music genre?

There is no alternative. It's mainstream. Alternative today really has moved into the mainstream, not because a lot of people buy it but because the songs have gotten better. Dinosaur Jr. all of a sudden is playing stuff . . . If you go into my car I'm listening to Firehose and Tragically Hip, today. Tomorrow I'll be listening to Urge or Counting

Crows. The idea, I think, always is that the big bands really have made good records. The [self-titled] Metallica record is a fine, solid record as a whole. Some of the Gun N' Roses stuff, I think, is real good. And I even like some of the rap stuff, not the idea that just any criminal can start rapping and become famous—although that's also true—but finally visually bringing to light this dissatisfaction with the status quo, the black dissatisfaction with being considered second-class citizens. Video after video after video, every black kid is pointing his fingers at the camera like a gun, and I'm going, "What the hell is bothering you?" I'll tell you what's bothering him. He's black, and that's not a popular thing to be in America, and that's bothering him. That message is finally creeping to the white consciousness. So that's made a big, big impact, whether you like the music or not. If you continue, I'll keep talking your head off!

I'm pleased that you're so hip. Are the other guys in Kiss as well versed?

Everybody loves different things. When I get sick of new music I put on Emitt Rhodes. You should listen to that: the American McCartney who never was. He was great. Or an old Love record, *Greatest Hits*. Great. And it doesn't have to be obscure. Dave Clark Five [the *History of the Dave Clark Five* boxed set], that just came out—I'm first in line. Recently we did a swing across the country where we did 40 cities in 30 days. They were parties. We signed autographs, hung out, and every once in a while the record company would take us to the stores. I went and got boxed sets from everybody—Pink Floyd, Nat "King" Cole, Patsy Cline, Brenda Lee, all that cool stuff. Frank Sinatra, absolutely.

You paid for them or they were free?

I'm in a band. I'm in Kiss. Life is free.

STRANGE DAYS DOG THE DOORS

The anecdote about Oliver Stone's *Doors* film inspiring me to come to America opens the introduction to this book. One of the few people unimpressed by my frequent recitation of the story was former Doors keyboardist Ray Manzarek, who hated the 1991 movie and abruptly broke off our conversation when I breezily mentioned how it had changed my life.

Things had been going well up until then because Manzarek loves to talk. We were chatting in September 2000 during rehearsals for a VH1 *Storytellers* episode that reunited the band's three surviving members for their first public performance since their Rock and Roll Hall of Fame induction seven years earlier. Manzarek, guitarist Robby Krieger, and drummer John Densmore were joined by a selection of singers filling in for Jim Morrison. Among them were Scott Weiland of Stone Temple Pilots, Ian Astbury of the Cult, Scott Stapp of Creed, and Perry Farrell of Jane's Addiction.

The November airing coincided with the release of a Doors tribute album, *Stoned Immaculate: The Music of the Doors*, a rather innovative effort featuring the aforementioned artists as well as John Lee Hooker, Aerosmith, and two "new" Doors songs. Sadly, it stalled at No. 72 on the U.S. pop chart.

I showed up early at the *Storytellers* taping to watch some rehearsals. Weiland, who has done his damnedest to die a gloriously premature death, was doing "Five to One," reading the portentous lyrics from a teleprompter for what he said was the first time in his life. "I wanna have to go to the restroom because it's loosening my bowels," he said for no obvious reason. The performers also listened to an old live version of the song to see how it ended. During "Break on Through," Krieger instructed Weiland to improvise on the too-edgy-for-radio "she gets high" mantra, "like Jim used to." As the rehearsal wound down, Weiland said, "I feel like I have an 80 percent chance of not letting you down."

During the break I chatted with Manzarek, softening him up by asking him if his keyboards dated from the bad old days ("those are not mine. Mine are all dead . . . but that is the exact same stuff I used") and why he was burning incense ("incense is all about altering the vibrations of smell").

Are there some Doors songs that are harder to cover? Maybe it would be sacrilegious to do them with a different singer?

No, I don't think it's so much a sense of sacrilegious. I think some of the songs are harder to play. They require a studio setting. Like "Touch Me," for example, that's a hard song to play in person. We tried it a couple of times, and that one just never locked in to what it was supposed to be. Each song has its own locked-in place, its Zen place, that Zen moment in time, and "Touch Me" never really got that Zen moment in time.

Are there some songs that bring back bittersweet memories?

You always think about Morrison. I miss that guy, man. He's always around. He's floating in the room here. The energy of Jim Morrison is always with us and I think all the singers are doing a real homage to Jim Morrison. They all love Jim, they love his poetry, they love Doors music.

But do we really need a tribute album when we already have the originals? Is your legacy in that much danger that we need this record to turn the younger generations on to the Doors?

You know what I find? I find that it's interesting to hear other people's versions of Doors songs. I've always loved other people doing

Doors songs. There's nothing sacred about a Doors song. There's nothing sacred about any piece of music. It's sacred in the conception of the music, but then anybody can do an improvisation on it. Doors music is like jazz. Anybody should play it. It's like saying nobody should play *A Love Supreme* by John Coltrane. Coltrane would be the first one to say, "Go ahead and play it. Enjoy yourselves. Get off on it."

Are you playing better keyboards now than when you did with the Doors?

Oh sure, yeah. I play better today. Robby plays better today. John's on top of it. We've been playing off and on here and there with all kinds of different people. I've been working with Michael McClure, a beatnik poet. With Michael he reads his poetry and I play the piano. So I've been just playing all kinds of stuff. So I think I was a better piano player than I was back then. But there was a magic to that time that will never be recaptured. It was like Paris in the '20s, America and England in the '60s, an absolutely psychedelic, magical place.

I kinda feel I missed the bus on all that.

Well, you know, the 21st century is here. The way I look at it is that it's now time to reinvent the gods, all the myths of the ages, as Jim says, to reinvent the '60s, apply it into the 21st century and take that Dionysian, psychedelic madness and riotous good time that we had and get it into the 21st century.

It's a bit hard when you have fire marshals at concerts telling people not to smoke. It's symptomatic of the fascist age we live in.

It is rather fascistic, isn't it? But so what? You always have to go up against the authorities. The authorities always want to maintain a status quo. They never want to break on through to the other side. The other side means an abandonment of everything they stand for—although certainly I'm for electricity and automobiles. Let's just power the automobiles without oil. Let's use some other way of doing it. Let's make electricity without burning oil. It's all the intellectual stuff we've gotta do. We've gotta save the earth, we've gotta replant, reforest the world. We've gotta clean up the rivers and the lakes and the ocean. Lots of organic things should be going on. No artificial fertilizers, no pesticides. That's all the stuff the hippies were into. That's all the stuff the 21st century has gotta get into.

That's great, Ray. I saw the *Doors* movie four times. That was my inspiration—

All right! Cool, man. I'm on.

Manzarek hated the movie because he thought it presented the Doors in too serious a light. Yes, the film does get overwrought at times and its focus on Morrison's poor performance in bed is unsettling. But if we'd been treated to a more accurate depiction of the band sitting around smoking pot and telling jokes it might have looked like a Beavis and Butt-head homage. It's easy to forget that Val Kilmer (as Jim) and Meg Ryan (as his girlfriend Pamela Courson) used to be hot, while the music remains as vital as ever. Manzarek's character, played as a geek by Kyle MacLachlan, gets put in his place during the burned-turkey scene when a fictional character played by Billy Idol sneers at him, "Yeah, fuck off, Ray!"

The script was based on Densmore's memoir, *Riders on the Storm: My Life with Jim Morrison and the Doors*, and Stone drafted Densmore as a consultant and gave him a cameo role. The book's version of events was bitterly countered in 1998 when Manzarek published his own, unimaginatively titled memoir *Light My Fire: My Life with the Doors*. The discord was a sign of things to come.

I hung around for the taping, feeling privileged to watch the relaxed trio merrily swapping reminiscences about their big hits. Densmore seemed to have the best memory, reciting Morrison's lyrics as he related the origins of songs such as "Break on Through" and "The End," and introduced the various guest vocalists. The singers did their best Jim Morrison impressions, but were mostly glued to the teleprompter. The standout was Perry Farrell, whose version of "L.A. Woman" was more interpretative. His song did not make the final cut. "Either I was off—or they were," Farrell said on Twitter years later.

***

There were plans for the Doors to play a handful of live dates in 2001 in both Europe and the United States. Instead, fans had to wait until September 2002, when the Doors received $150,000 to headline a Harley-Davidson 100th anniversary concert at a speedway in Fontana, a dodgy municipality east of Los Angeles. Densmore, suffering from tinnitus, was replaced by former Police drummer Stewart Copeland (who was soon axed after he broke his arm, then sued the Doors and settled for undisclosed terms). Up front was Astbury. According to one fan's review, attendance was less than expected because of a lack of publicity. Three weeks later, the same lineup played another Harley-Davidson event, this time at a park about 60 miles north of Toronto. "The crowd was a blend of middle-aged Harley bikers, beer bellies and mullets, with their biker wives. Mixed in were Generation-Xers with Doors t-shirts," one fan wrote. Were these lowbrow corporate events an appropriate relaunching pad for one of the most iconic bands of the '60s?

Krieger and Manzarek planned to keep touring with the new lineup. Densmore gave them his blessing as long as they agreed to promote themselves as the New Doors, or words to that effect, and did not use the original Doors logo. He was ignored. Krieger and Manzarek played a Las Vegas casino billed as the Doors, played late-night TV shows billed as the Doors, and announced plans to play in their Los Angeles hometown as the Doors. Occasionally printed in small type under the name was "of the 21st Century" as if that was supposed to clear up any confusion. Densmore later said he repeatedly begged his old high school buddy Krieger to make good on his promise to differentiate clearly between the two bands.

The drummer had already made known his feelings about protecting the Doors legacy in a widely publicized 2002 essay published in *The Nation*. He condemned the use of rock music in commercials, and proudly noted that he had recently vetoed licensing requests worth a total of $19 million from Buick and Apple. Under a long-standing policy, band decisions required unanimous approval. Densmore claimed to be speaking for

Morrison. (The singer went apoplectic in 1969 after his three bandmates agreed to license their biggest hit "Light My Fire" for a Buick Opel commercial that never aired.) Densmore also argued that he and his former bandmates were already rich enough. He even tithes his income to charity and writes big checks to a long-gone ex-wife, but both he and Manzarek doubtless thanked their lucky stars over the years that the Doors agreed from the start to split everything equally even though Morrison and Krieger were the primary songwriters.

Frustrated by his former bandmates' sneaky misadventures, Densmore filed a breach of contract and trademark infringement suit against them on Feb. 4, 2003, three days before the Los Angeles concert. He told me at the time that they could call themselves "the Windows, the Hinges," but not "the Doors." He said Morrison's elderly parents were "livid" about the reunion, and they joined a subsequent suit filed by the parents of Pamela Courson, with whom the Morrisons evenly split their quarter share. Manzarek countered in a separate interview that Densmore's suit was "frivolous." He and Krieger then sued Densmore, accusing him of breaching his fiduciary duties to the Doors partnership by blocking lucrative business deals. And thus began a five-year legal battle that ruined their friendship, tarnished the band's good name, bitterly divided fans, and enriched a lot of lawyers.

The Los Angeles show didn't exactly light my fire. Astbury looked silly mimicking Jim down to the moves, the leather pants, and the dark glasses. A video screen attempted to re-create the '60s by showing hippie imagery. The few highlights included Krieger's tasty flamenco guitar work on "Spanish Caravan" and an invite to dozens of kids to get up on stage and dance during "Soul Kitchen." But how excited can one get about a tribute band in a sterile indoor amphitheater? The *Los Angeles Times* was also underwhelmed. "[G]enuine sparks were minimal, furthering the sense that the whole affair was a sad replay of something that was once great," it noted.

The trial began in June 2004. Among the witnesses was Jim's father, retired Admiral George S. Morrison, who had been estranged from his famous son. Jim's younger siblings also showed up, much to Densmore's delight. A final decision issued in July 2005 went Densmore's way. The court blocked Manzarek and Krieger from using the Doors name or any version thereof and any images of Morrison. After various accounting issues were resolved, Manzarek and Krieger were also ordered to pay Densmore a total of almost $900,000, and $400,000 each to the Morrisons and the Coursons. The defendants appealed in September 2005. A split appeals court affirmed the ruling three years later. Manzarek and Krieger also appealed a ruling that they pay their opponents' $2 million legal tab. That was settled out of court.

The lawyers' clocks were still ticking in 2006 when a coffee-table book and CD boxed set were released to mark the Doors' 40th anniversary. In separate interviews, Densmore and Manzarek said they were not communicating with each other. Indeed, the warring parties planned to promote the new releases with separate appearances on opposite sides of their old stomping grounds on the Sunset Strip. A Doors management operative sat in on my phone interview with Densmore, and sent panicked text messages to the band's publicist, who in turn freaked out that I was venturing into verboten territory by asking about the legal battle. A planned interview with Krieger was canceled. I called Manzarek first, though. He was living the life of a country gentleman in Napa Valley, near San Francisco, having relocated with his wife, Dorothy, from Los Angeles a few years earlier.

When was the last time you communed with Jim?

In a waking state or in a dream state? The last time I communicated with him was a couple of days before he left for Paris in 1971, and I said goodbye to my good friend thinking that he was going to Paris to write poetry and to rediscover himself, and get away from being a rock star and get away from his drinking buddies and groupies, getting back to Jim Morrison, the artist/poet that I knew, that I put the band together with. We were doing poetry and rock 'n' roll the same way the Beats were doing poetry and jazz. That's why Jim and I started the Doors in the first place.

Subsequent to that, have you had dreams or out-of-body experiences?

I have dreams in which Jim's back, and curiously so does Robby. We talked about it. It's like, "My God, we're having the same dream!" We're in rehearsal on Santa Monica Boulevard and La Cienega in Los Angeles, at the Doors workshop, and who comes walking in, about 10 minutes late, 10 minutes after two, but Jim Morrison? We both turn and look at him, and say, "Hey, Jim! You're back!" Jim says, "Yeah! Of course I'm back." The first time I got together with him, I said, "Well, do you have any songs?" He said, "Ray, you bet I do." And that's where I wake up.

Are you all naked at the same time?

Naked at the same time? In the room? No, it wasn't a homosexual dream. I'm totally hetero. There would be no need to be naked with other men. But if I was in a playground and I was 10 years old, there'd be chances that I was running around naked.

What's the extent of your communication with Densmore and Krieger?

Robby and I play together in Riders of the Storm [the new name of the Doors of the 21st Century]. . . . When we're off the road, a couple of phone calls. We see each other often enough, so that it's not like, "Hi! What are you doing?" We all have our lives to lead, and Robby and I see each other on the road and see plenty of each other. We're not in close communication, but we're certainly good friends.

How about the other guy?

The other guy, not in communication with. These things happen in a rock 'n' roll band. If you stay together long enough in a rock 'n' roll band, something will go wrong.

Yeah, the whole male-bonding experience should be over by the time you turn 25, anyway?

It should be. You should find your significant other and cling to that person. I'm with Dorothy Fujikawa. We've been together for, hell, next year, December; it'll be our 40th anniversary of marriage, for God's sake. I met her at UCLA. We've been together since before the Doors got started. So I met Jim at UCLA and I met Dorothy at UCLA. My wife and my late singer, what a grand time I had at UCLA. I've got my buddy, I've got my pal, I've got my art partner, and she's also my wife, and of the opposite sex, so it worked out very nicely.

You've had the greatest life, but do you feel trapped by your legacy—that the brief existence of the Doors has overshadowed everything else?

No, it's been a marvelous life. The Doors have allowed me to continue to be creative, to do all kinds of things, to write books. I've got a new book that just came out, called *Snake Moon*, a tale of the supernatural set in the Civil War. I've got a couple of new albums out there that I've done, one called *Atonal Head* that's totally electronic. So the Doors allow me to engage in all kinds of artistic activities. I made a small movie—my directorial debut—called *Love Her Madly*, available on DVD. One of those direct-to-DVD movies. A very entertaining little flick about murder and madness and obsession on a contemporary college campus. . . . There's so many things, being in the Doors allows me to do all of that. It's been great, absolutely great. Of course, the first thing people want to know is, "Tell me some stories about Jim Morrison. Are they true?!" And I invariably say, "Let me hear the stories you've heard and I'll tell you whether those are true." Usually it's, "No . . . No . . . No . . . Yes . . . No . . . No . . . No . . . No . . . Double no . . . Yes . . . And I didn't like the Oliver Stone movie, because it was Oliver Stone in leather pants [*sic*] and not the real Jim Morrison in leather pants."

I thought enough time would have passed since 1991 for you to be a little more forgiving towards that movie?

Oh, no, never! Just yesterday, I was performing up here in the Napa Valley, at the old Napa Valley Opera House—what a great place, a hundred-year-old theater—and I was doing a benefit playing the piano and telling Doors stories. And one of the questions from the audience was, "What do you think of the Oliver Stone movie? Is it true?" I get that all the time, and I say, "No, that's not true. That's not Jim Morrison. That's Oliver Stone." Jim Morrison was a poet, an artist, sensitive, funny. Nobody in the *Doors* movie ever laughs.... We laughed a great deal. You see none of that in the film. You don't even get to understand the '60s, which is the real tragedy, what the point of view of the '60s was. So I'll be talking about that movie, bashing it, for the rest of my life.

Does that remain a source of discontent between you and Densmore as well, since he was involved with the movie?

Well, I don't know. That's a good point. I've never really actually talked to him about, "Do you in fact like the Oliver Stone movie?"

Well, he was in it for a second.

Well, Oliver had a way of seducing a lot of people. He seduced a lot of people with a lot of false promises.

Are there any disputes over songwriting credits?

Credits are no problem. Everything gets divided four ways, song credits and financial.

So even though Krieger more or less wrote "Light My Fire," he splits it evenly with the others?

Exactly.

Who does that work out best for?

The drummer!

You don't mind that?

That's the way it is, man. In the court of law, that's the way it is.

Then I got on the phone with Densmore. Note to rock stars: If you want to build our egos, sprinkle our names a few times throughout the conversation.

I just spoke to Ray Manzarek, and I get the impression that there's still bad blood.

Well, not on my side. But yeah, on his, because they're appealing. They didn't accept the decision. But it's almost over.

Why don't you guys come to an out-of-court settlement?

Tell that to Ray, would you, Dean? I'm all ears.

I thought it was metaphorical that he and Krieger will be on one side of the street on Wednesday, and you'll be on the other? There's this divide in case you accidentally bump into each other.

Oh, I didn't think of that. Sunset Boulevard as a Berlin Wall? No! Let me put it this way. With the three of us and Jim, some kind of magic muse came into our garage, and it was bigger than all of us. And that's why I'm doing this. I honor that. . . . People love what we created. I'm very interested in the future. I actually have a new jazz CD that just came out called *Tribal Jazz*, and I'm very excited about that. An artist wants to look ahead and I'm very proud of the past, and I'm also improving as a drummer, playing with 29-year-olds.

So you have mixed emotions focusing on the past with this 40th anniversary thing?

No. I don't have mixed emotions. I'm very proud of the past. Like I said, it was a magical combination of four people.

I know you shared the songwriting four ways. Are there songs that are quite clearly Densmore songs?

I think all the sections where Morrison goes off on his poetry and I sorta accent and accompany him. A lot of people comment on "The End." Bruce Springsteen said to me, "Wow! The drumming, so weird." No, he didn't say "weird." I would play real loud in a quiet section. I don't know why I did it. It just was right. It heightened the tension, or something.

I guess on "Five to One" too, when Jim goes off on a tangent?

Yeah. "When the Music's Over," I kinda get to show off a little. I'm an ensemble guy, though, with my playing.

You don't like the spotlight?

Well, I'm starting to change a little bit. I like spurring on the soloist as a singer.

Do you think this project could spur a meeting of the minds with the other guys?

Time is an incredible healer. The stupid appeal should wind up in a year or so. But if they're running off playing as Riders on the

Storm... it's OK! Anyone can play Doors songs, and they're the best at it, without the other two. Fine. The name is straightened out. Me and the estate just wanted the name back.

Theoretically, if the appeal is lost, you'll get a big check from Krieger and Manzarek? Or will you forgive them?

In one of these interviews Ray did say, "Oh John just made an easy pile of money." Well, I'm still waiting. It's only been three years, or something. The attorneys' fees? C'mon, Dean. You know what those guys are like! I'm so in the hole, it's ludicrous. But I will be evened out, supposedly, but I'm not counting chickens.

When you say you're in the hole, does that mean in general?

Oh, no. This lawsuit, which we're not supposed to be talking about because it's still going and my attorneys don't want me having my foot in my mouth. But just concerning that, I'm way in the hole.

I'd hate to see you end up on the street!

Oh, no. You're here promoting the 40th anniversary, Dean. I'll be fine.

I showed up at the big promotional event, but it was an organizational nightmare and I couldn't get into either the tiny bookstore where Densmore did a poetry reading, or later into the Whisky where Manzarek and Krieger performed Doors tunes. There was some free street entertainment: I watched a fan, in the spirit of noted cop-antagonist Jim Morrison, climb on the unattended motorbike of a sheriff's deputy for the amusement of his buddies. He was promptly arrested when the cop returned.

In 2010 the feuding Doors were on the promotional trail for yet another project, an appalling documentary narrated in a monotone by noted rock groupie Johnny Depp. *When You're Strange* traced the band's rise and fall, but didn't include much that fans didn't already know, and there were no contemporary interviews or analysis. The film was strictly for the PBS pledge-drive crowd with a passing interest in one of America's biggest bands. The major critics were underwhelmed, several noting that the script seemed to have been copied from the band's Wikipedia page. The *Los Angeles Times* said the film was "distressingly short on creative spark or historical illumination." Densmore, dressed in white to mark Ravi Shankar's 90th birthday, did a Q&A at the Grammy Museum and claimed that all three members signed off on the film after viewing it multiple times and deluging director Tom DeCillo with copious production notes. They should have demanded that Val Kilmer play Jim.

AEROSMITH: WINGS CLIPPED

In the fall of 1993 Aerosmith was the biggest band in America. Not bad for five former drug addicts who'd rocked harder than anyone in the 1970s and then crashed by the early '80s.

Thanks to a carefully crafted Kumbaya comeback plan revolving around rehab, counseling, and band meetings, the so-called bad boys from Boston were now holding their own in an era dominated by upstart grunge acts like Nirvana, Stone Temple Pilots, and Pearl Jam. Aerosmith's No. 1 album *Get a Grip* was still in the top 10 after 20 weeks, two singles were burning up rock radio, and the group was in the early stages of a world tour that would keep it on the road until Christmas 1994. A *Saturday Night Live* appearance was under discussion, and a substantial cameo had been filmed for the upcoming *Wayne's World* sequel.

The man who rescued the group from obscurity was unable to savor the moment. Aerosmith manager Tim Collins was being driven around the bend by lead singer Steven Tyler, and had checked in to a health spa. Tyler, Collins complained, would call him at all hours of the night threatening to quit unless his bandmates were fired. Tyler claimed that he was running the show, that he was the creative force in Aerosmith and the power behind their successful music videos.

The rest of the band did not take these outbursts seriously. Tyler's kvetching was the price they had to pay for their good fortune. He was the group's most recognizable member and the frenetic center of attention on stage. It was also Tyler's name on such top-10 hits as "Dream On," "Walk This Way," "Angel," and "Love in an Elevator." He wrote most of the band's songs with guitarist Joe Perry, and they were dubbed the Toxic Twins on account of their rambunctious behavior. Like all duos, theirs had its conflicts. Tyler was more driven, but also hyperkinetic and more at risk of burning out. Perry, two years his junior, paced himself like a long-distance runner, his life more balanced. But Tyler had an incredibly clear vision for Aerosmith, and dictated a lot of what went on.

"He's an Italian street fighter," Collins told me at the time. "He grew up in the fuckin' Bronx. He loves to fight, he loves to have havoc." Collins, six years younger than Tyler, described him as being like "my wayward son . . . Other days, it's like being a coach of the greatest quarterbacks that ever lived."

Collins grew up in Boston where Aerosmith were gods. He'd always wanted to be a talent manager and worked in the minor leagues with a few acts that never amounted to much. By the time Perry left Aerosmith in 1979, after his then-wife tossed a glass of milk at bassist Tom Hamilton's wife, the band had become a joke. The albums sucked, concerts were canceled because the guys were too wasted to play, and someone decided it would be a good idea for them to make a *Sgt. Pepper's* movie with the Bee Gees and Peter Frampton.

Collins set his sights on Perry, and secured an introduction through a mutual friend. It couldn't have been much fun trying to salvage Perry's lackluster solo career. No one cared about his albums or his club shows. Perry was a penniless alcoholic, variously living in a $25-a-week boarding house or sleeping on Collins' couch. His former bandmates, having also lost their money and their dignity, continued feebly with new members. Collins pressured Perry to get in touch with Tyler, and they hashed out their differences over the phone in 1984. Perry rejoined the band (along with rhythm guitarist Brad

Whitford, another Aerosmith refugee), and Collins now managed his heroes. He got them a deal with Geffen Records, whose A&R guy, John Kalodner, had once lambasted Aerosmith as "the new masters of American 'schlock rock,'" during a previous incarnation as a rock critic at the *Philadelphia Inquirer*.

One of the greatest comebacks in rock 'n' roll history got off to a wobbly start since sobriety was still some way off. The first album, 1985's *Done with Mirrors*, was a half-baked affair, although fans now fondly look at it as the last blast of classic Aerosmith, the last Aerosmith album not to feature help from outside songwriters. Perhaps for that reason it failed to sell. And, after years of half-assed performances, the band struggled to repair its bad reputation among tour promoters. More useful for Aerosmith's commercial rehabilitation was rap trio Run-DMC's Tyler & Perry–assisted cover of "Walk This Way" the following year.

Everyone cleaned up in time to record 1987's *Permanent Vacation*, which marked the emergence of the Aerosmith we know today: a ballad factory powered by outside songwriters. It was hard to argue with the Kalodner-driven change in direction after the band hit No. 3 on the Billboard Hot 100 with "Angel," a ditty that Tyler wrote with Desmond Child, a musician who had co-written monster hits for Kiss ("I Was Made for Lovin' You") and Bon Jovi ("Livin' on a Prayer").

In 1989, while bands like Guns N' Roses, Mötley Crüe, and Metallica were claiming Aerosmith's hard-rock mantle, Aerosmith replied with *Pump*. The rocking collection spawned six hit singles including "Love in an Elevator," the last great Tyler-Perry composition, and a yearlong world tour. Aerosmith played Europe for the first time since a brief excursion a dozen years earlier, and ventured to Australia for the first time ever. Afterward, the energized elder statesmen went on a retreat for a month, working hard to replace co-dependency with co-creativity.

In its first heyday, Aerosmith was the sum of Tyler and Perry's creative vision plus the autocracy of original managers Steve Leber and David Krebs. The comeback was more democratic. Whitford named several albums, Hamilton co-wrote "Janie's Got a Gun," a brooding revenge fantasy that earned the band its first Grammy, and drummer Joey Kramer came up with the concepts for some of the videos. No longer driven simply by money—although there was plenty of that—they loved what they were doing and were at the top of their game.

Tyler's combative ways, however, now threatened the band at a critical juncture. *Get a Grip* was potentially Aerosmith's last studio album for Geffen Records, which had taken a big gamble on the band when no one else was interested. In 1991 Aerosmith signed a lucrative deal to return to its original Columbia Records home after Collins and David Geffen failed to agree on a renewal and the mogul suggested that Aerosmith look elsewhere.

After *Get a Grip*, Aerosmith owed Geffen Records a hits album and either a new studio or live album. It could be years before it released a new album on Columbia, and Collins wanted to capitalize on the thrill of the new. He asked David Geffen for an early release, but the talks went nowhere. It wasn't the end of the world. Collins worshiped Geffen, eagerly looking forward to their lunch dates several times a year. And Columbia remastered and reissued the band's back catalog.

Get a Grip was a creatively modest follow-up to *Pump*. Tyler had been bedeviled by mental blocks during the songwriting process. He would ask his cohorts for their opinions and give them the silent treatment for a week if he did not like what he heard. Longtime fans hated the generic ballads, and the sexy MTV videos with Alicia Silverstone and Tyler's daughter Liv hardly compensated.

As the *Get a Grip* world tour kicked off in the summer of 1993, Collins complained that he was too busy holding Tyler's hand to approach Pearl Jam's managers about a possible opening slot on the trek. The other guys in Aerosmith would have dearly loved to display their hipster credentials by aligning themselves with the hot Seattle prospects.

Collins was also too fried to give his immediate attention to an interesting investment proposal from Hard Rock Café co-founder

Isaac Tigrett, who was setting up a new chain called the House of Blues. It was easy money. (The band did eventually invest, and it performed a blues set at the opening of the Los Angeles location in 1994.) The guys were becoming frustrated.

"We're dealing with a fucking crazy person," one bandmate said of Tyler. Chimed in another, "We're gonna get to a point where—just like we did with drugs—we gotta say, 'What is this life all about? Is huge success in the rock 'n' roll business something that makes up for total misery in your day-to-day dealings with people?'"

The guys pleaded with Collins to confront Tyler during their therapy meetings with celebrity drug counselor Bob Timmons, promising they would back him up. But Collins never said anything. He was appeasing Tyler, and that policy did not work out well for the world in the 1930s, the rest of the band noted. The best course of action, they reasoned, was to stay tight with each other and with Collins, and present a united front to Tyler. If that meant freezing him out, so be it.

"He's gotta get isolated so he has to start to deal with his own shit," a bandmate said. "He's either gonna fester and explode and freak out, which he needs to do. Or else he's gotta take care of himself. One way or the other, he's gotta get it together."

Collins did not work alone. His management company, boasting an army of creative consultants, media coaches, and archivists, was tailored to Tyler's requirements. They worked intensively with Tyler, studying old videotapes of *Saturday Night Live* and MTV Video Music Awards performances to see where the singer could improve his mannerisms and interview skills.

Evidently no one in management got the bandmates' memo about Tyler's onstage performance. They were embarrassed that he had scrawled "Get a Grip" across his navel, with an arrow helpfully pointing to his groin. "That's so fuckin' juvenile and so not hip and so not aware," said one of them. "All that stuff is what's holding us back and not letting us get to the next level."

Added another bandmate, "The bottom line is that Steven doesn't go up into his practice room and play his piano. He's not even into music. He's scared of it. He's petrified of going up there and not blowing his own mind with what he comes up with. Everything stems from that. I just remember when Steven was really tight with his music. Sure, he did juvenile stuff, but imagewise it was clear that that's where he was centered. He's kinda centered on the clown part of it now . . . to the point where his singing takes a backseat to all this fuckin' running around and strutting and humping the audience, and stuff."

Tyler was isolated from his own muse, and his bandmates agreed that had to be driving him nuts. The venom he was directing at Collins was his way of dealing with his own insecurity. Without music, Tyler was nothing. He was the music fanatic in Aerosmith. When the band was speeding away in the van after a gig, Tyler would be the first one to reach for the radio dial when the others might just want to chill out in silence. Tyler was seeing a therapist, but his bandmates complained the shrink was an incompetent yes-man. They said Tyler's sessions should be a few times a week, not once every few weeks.

To the outside world, Aerosmith was living a charmed life. *Get a Grip*, extending Aerosmith's reach to a new generation, went on to sell 20 million copies worldwide, and picked up two Grammy awards. *Wayne's World 2* flopped, but the Aerosmith scenes were the best ones. The band eventually fulfilled its commitments to Geffen with a hits package and a live album.

Not one peep about the internal rift was ever made public. This book contains the first revelation. The Aerosmith organization had survived greater calamities and knew it had to present a united front to the world. It also wouldn't be good for Columbia to realize it had been sold a bill of goods. "This band will be a band even if we're all in different parts of the universe," said one bandmate.

The Five Musketeers philosophy served Aerosmith well in August 1996 when another crisis did become public. The band, united this time, fired Collins during sessions for its Columbia relaunch. The break was unusually messy. Artists split with managers all the time (rarely do managers pull the trigger), but these breakups hardly ever make the news.

Collins went on the offensive. A big fan of David Geffen's advocacy efforts in politics and entertainment, he had taken a high-profile stance against drug use in the music industry. He turned his clout against his own band. Claiming to be "deeply saddened," he told the *Boston Globe*, "There's a certain element in the group that hasn't totally chosen sobriety." That was a massive allegation. Aerosmith were the poster boys for drug-free America. Say it ain't so!

Aerosmith countered in a statement, "Any inference [*sic*] that members of the band have backslid into drug abuse is ludicrous." Years later, the autobiographies by Steven Tyler and Joey Kramer each painted Collins as a manipulator. Kramer, who wrote his book with a former Collins employee, concluded that Collins was the sickest of everyone.

After promoting its publicist to manager, Aerosmith finally released *Nine Lives* six months behind schedule in March 1997. Among the album's hit singles was the steamy live staple "Pink," which the band performed at the Kids' Choice Awards in Los Angeles. It was surreal watching the raunchy rockers play for an audience of 8,000 excitable youngsters and their parents (not to mention a record 5.3 million viewers at home), but maybe a few of those moppets are now hardcore 20-something fans.

I was oblivious to Aerosmith during my youth until the Run-DMC collaboration, the first major confluence of rock and rap. The band played Peru and Paraguay long before it ventured to New Zealand for the first time in 2013, when it played a half-empty stadium in a remote college town.

In America, I caught about a half-dozen concerts: from big arena shows to club gigs at both the House of Blues in Los Angeles and the Hard Rock Hotel in Las Vegas. My abiding memory of the latter show was standing next to a woman who was bawling her eyes out as the band played "I Don't Want to Miss a Thing," the execrable chart-topping Diane Warren–written monster ballad that was memorable and forgettable at the same time. When I asked her why she was crying, she said it was the favorite song of a close friend who had died a few months earlier in the 9/11 attacks. A song or two later, she caught my eye again. This time she was gleefully flashing her tits at the band.

I liked Aerosmith largely because they had the field to themselves as colorful, dynamic, hard-rocking American road warriors. I would lazily write about them as America's answer to the Rolling Stones. But the band never sounds so lame as those times when a radio station thinks it's being synergistic by playing two Stones tunes and then two Aerosmith tunes. (In its defense, Aerosmith never encouraged the Stones comparison and the bands never shared a stage.)

"I think in a lot of ways, in certain subtle ways, we're still the band that no one wants to admit they like," Tom Hamilton said in the early '90s. "I just think that when we first came out, people thought of us as being cheap, and we're still fighting to prove ourselves in that way. A lot of people do have a lot of respect for us, but in other ways I think we're always gonna feel like kind of an outcast."

Part of the latter-day problem was that Tyler and Perry outsourced a lot of the songwriting. The duo alone wrote four of the 10 compositions on *Pump* and collaborated with Hamilton and Whitford on one song each. There was only one Tyler-Perry exclusive on *Get a Grip*, and none on either *Nine Lives* or 2001's *Just Push Play*. Their brand was being watered down.

In March 2002 I asked Tyler why Aerosmith needed to work with so-called "song doctors" like Child, Mark Hudson, and Marti Fredericksen. "I don't need them. It's fun," he said defensively. "Why use Viagra? Why do you go out with the girl with the big tits? I dunno. It's incentive! It kinda riles me up. I don't know what to tell you. Listen, it's always good to stir up the water a little. It was very frustrating for me to write with a band in the sense that everybody's too familiar and everybody's in a room. It gets to be a bit much. Everyone's playing all together. You wanna gravitate to people that also write lyrics that you can bounce your shit offa. It's just more fun.

"A year and a half ago we got in the studio with Mark and Marti and Joe . . . We fuckin' laughed. We laughed for 12 hours and then we left. We had a song. And all I remember doin' was laughing. Instead of it being work, it was more fun than it ever had been. I love that, man. I love it when whatever I'm doing just incites me to riot, when whatever I'm doing is incentive to come up with weird stuff."

Tyler was all over the place in the interview, which coincided with an upcoming VH1 tribute show. He wanted to get corporate backing and go into space. "Every bit of this fuckin' life is a dream. To make dreams come true is what I do. I'll be sitting in the basement goin' [sings] 'Dude Looks Like a Lady!' Who'd a thunk? It's just making it happen. We floated around the dark side of the moon for so long, I'd just as soon go back and it'd be a familiar place for me!"

He revealed that he was working on a solo album that could possibly come out in 2003, but he did not want to be tied to a deadline. "Sometimes you wanna just break away," he said. "I'm accessing areas of songwriting that . . . if I play something on a banjo in an open tuning, I don't wanna redo it on a Strat because that's what Brad plays." He was frustrated that the demos he worked up in his basement with his songwriting pals lost a little of their freshness when they were redone in a band environment, and he wistfully recalled that the demo for "Janie's Got a Gun" was "very interesting."

There was clearly a competitive tension in the band at that time. Tyler and I spoke barely an hour after I had interviewed Joe Perry. After Tyler learned about that interview, he demanded equal time.

In 2009, ahead of what should have been a joyous celebration of the band's 40th anniversary, Aerosmith was on the verge of another disintegration. The band had spent several frustrating years trying to record a follow-up to *Just Push Play* (a covers-heavy blues set *Honkin' on Bobo* was released in 2004). Along the way, most had been waylaid by health issues. In 2006, Tom Hamilton underwent a seven-week course of radiation treatment for throat cancer, and Tyler had throat surgery; in 2008, Tyler entered rehab; in early 2009, Perry endured emergency surgery after developing "unforeseen complications" with a replacement knee.

Things came to a head during the summer when Aerosmith embarked on a North American tour that was doomed before it started. Brad Whitford missed the first few shows because he hit his head while getting out of his Ferrari. Even before he returned to the fold, seven shows were scrapped when Tyler suffered an unspecified leg injury. Hamilton was also sidelined for a few shows after undergoing what was described as "noninvasive surgery." Then in South Dakota on Aug. 5, Tyler fell off the stage while singing "Love in an Elevator" and broke his shoulder. Most of his frustrated bandmates scattered to the wind, not even bothering to visit him in the hospital.

Tyler responded in kind. He hired his own managers—another thing he'd threatened to do during the 1993 rift—who informed the rest of the guys that their client wanted to take two years off. Tyler said he wanted to focus on "brand Tyler," which included writing his memoir and taking over as a judge on *American Idol*. Tyler's bandmates, not content to sit around for two years, threatened to oust him so that they could continue making music.

Perry hit the promo trail about the same time for his fifth solo album. He had recorded the songs quickly in Aerosmith's ample enforced downtime—some were initially targeted for the next Aerosmith record—with the help of an unknown German singer his wife had discovered on YouTube. Touring commitments would keep him on the road through March 2010. Everyone followed the same line of questioning: Is Aerosmith over? The prognosis was bleak. Perry said he had not written a song with Tyler in 10 years, and that it wasn't his fault.

"I'm down in my studio every day, writing, and for some reason he wants to write with people like Mark Hudson and whatever," he told me. "I haven't actually sat down with him. I finally got him to come down for one day, and we did it like the old way and it was encouraging because we came up with some good stuff. Basically we used to write songs—he would play the drums and put a microphone in front of him, and I would play guitar and record riffs. We'd come up with this stuff. And later he started playing keyboards because he could play drums on the keyboard and we would write songs like that. But for some reason, it just started 10 years ago, we never wrote again, no matter what kind of situation . . . I can't explain it. I don't see anything, at least from my end, that couldn't have been on an Aerosmith record. But without his input, it's just not that way anymore."

He did not think Tyler had heard his album. Communication between Tyler and the rest of the band was through emails sent by his manager.

A few days later, Perry's wife and I got into a public spat when I wrote a story based on some of her Twitter comments. Billie Perry decided it was a good time to tell the world that she did not particularly care for Aerosmith's recordings and had never listened to any of their albums in their entirety. "I am not a fan of Aerosmith's music without the live performance behind it," she wrote. "Honestly I have never listened to 1 CD all the way through. I listen in the studio when they record. I've never put an Aero CD on my player. I did order a few songs from iTunes, but have not listened." I facetiously noted that she was hardly being the "dutiful wife" and she ripped me on her Twitter page, but then deleted the post.

In November, Whitford and Kramer spoke to me on successive days in an anti-Tyler campaign orchestrated by a former publicist for the band. It was clear Aerosmith was going through a belated and public mid-life crisis not too different from the ugly one that tore the Rolling Stones asunder during the mid-'80s. I assumed Aerosmith would similarly get over it, and felt the bandmates were wrongly using the media to communicate with Tyler. Their threats to replace Tyler were ludicrous. Did they really think fans would pay good money to see, say, Sammy Hagar or Paul Rodgers sashay around the stage singing "Walk This Way"? Tyler's camp ignored numerous requests for comment, so the stories were inevitably one-sided. Still, it was good to speak for the first time with the low-profile Whitford and the newly minted author Kramer.

Whitford said he and Tyler had had a contentious relationship for many years, with neither of them anxious to talk to the other. "I just find him . . . very difficult to talk to. Most people say, 'How's it going? Nice day.' And [with Tyler] it won't be, 'Yeah, it is a nice day.' All of a sudden it's drama."

He feared Tyler might be back on drugs, though he had no evidence and it seemed an unfair allegation to make. "I suspect there's a lot more going on than we know about. He has a well-documented history of drug abuse, and I find myself very suspicious. I haven't seen him do this or . . . have any personal knowledge, but the isolation is very typical of addictive behavior, and his—what I call—irrational behavior."

"I get the sense that Steven has put us on his list of 'My Problems' and somehow we've created his problems, and that's the furthest thing from the truth," Whitford continued. "Time and time again we've supported him, and been backing him up for almost 40 years. I think there's times when we've been one of the things that he was always able to count on."

Kramer, who considered Tyler "my brother and my friend for 40 years," was reluctant to accuse him of getting back on drugs. "I think that Steven has just made some poor choices as of late, and he's got some bad influences around, and I think for the most part he's his own worst enemy . . . I just really hope that Steven puts the focus on Steven and gets healthy."

I asked Kramer if this was all one big scare tactic, a bid to shock Tyler back into the fold. "Not at all, not at all," he said, protesting too much. "Not by any means, not by any means."

Of course no one had made serious entreaties to prospective singers, underscoring the hollowness of their threats and the inherent media manipulation. As expected, Tyler did return to the fold, and the band launched a four-month tour of the Americas and Europe in the summer of 2010, ending just in time for him to begin his judging stint on *American Idol*. By all accounts, his new TV gig was well received, though I couldn't bring myself to tune in. His bandmates and fans had little choice but to indulge his self-branding efforts. He also released a solo single, which sank without a trace, and a memoir, which the *Boston Globe* described as a "barely literate hack job." The long-threatened solo album was put on the backburner.

History threatened to repeat itself in 2011 when Aerosmith returned to South America. Tyler slipped in the shower of his Asuncion hotel room and broke some teeth. But this time the concert was merely delayed by a day. His bandmates publicly marveled at his show-must-go-on ethos.

Indeed Perry, eager to enlist the media to promote his agenda when it suited him, now blamed the media for fomenting ill will with Tyler. "The media always wants to sling mud and lies at people's personal expense," he said on Twitter.

In March 2012, Aerosmith announced a 20-date summer tour to promote the excruciatingly conceived new album, which at that point was not finished or named. It wasn't even going to be on sale during the tour. Ignoring the sentiments of its 1985 hit single "Let the Music Do the Talking," the band did a lot of jawboning for the elusive recording.

Four of the guys (Whitford had another touring commitment, but no one noticed his absence) showed up at the Grove, a soulless Los Angeles shopping mecca, for a news conference attended by a few hundred onlookers confined to a pen by an army of anxious mall cops. The venue seemed better suited to a pop idol like Justin Bieber or Katy Perry. Or maybe it was an admission that Aerosmith was now more of a pop band. Someone forgot to turn off the lounge music blaring from the PA, and I couldn't hear anything uttered from a makeshift stage ringed by a Nordstrom, an Abercrombie & Fitch, and a Gap. But at least they all seemed friendly toward each other, and Tyler stayed upright.

Three weeks before the launch of the so-called Global Warming tour, Aerosmith performed on the season finale of *American Idol*. The kiddies were treated to the new single "Legendary Child" and a rushed, two-minute version of "Walk This Way." It was Tyler's last appearance on the fast-fading show. Fox failed to pick up his option for a third season, bringing to a merciful end a sad saga that almost killed off Aerosmith.

"Legendary Child," a leftover from the *Get a Grip* sessions, failed to stick at radio. It wasn't completely Aerosmith's fault. The song had won a high-profile slot in the summer movie *G.I. Joe: Retaliation*, but the big-bang sequel was suddenly and mysteriously pulled from the release schedule until 2013. So there was no chance of Aerosmith repeating the success it had enjoyed when "I Don't Want to Miss a Thing" was used in *Armageddon*.

Two weeks into the tour, Aerosmith bumped the album by two months until early November and told the world's biggest fib. The band cited a heavy slate of competing releases. Or, once again, maybe it really did consider feeble pop acts like Matchbox 20 and the Dave Matthews Band to be competitors.

When *Music from Another Dimension!*—terrible name, terrible cartoon artwork—finally came out after two follow-up singles also flopped, underwhelmed fans asked, "Is that it? It took you 11 years to come up with this drivel?!" And then the sad realization sank in. Aerosmith's 15th album would likely be its last given the members' average age of 62.

Tyler and his bandmates had long promised that the album's sound would be "vintage" and "lean" thanks in part to their reunion with Jack Douglas, the producer of early classics like *Toys in the Attic* and *Rocks*. Instead, *Music from Another Dimension!* featured a half-dozen ballads, including a Tyler duet with country-pop starlet Carrie Underwood. Maybe Aerosmith was taking its former manager's idea of democracy too far. The credits list 28 additional musicians and backing vocalists, including Johnny Depp.

For the first time since 1987, all five members of Aerosmith contributed to the songwriting. But so did six other writers, including the dreaded Diane Warren. None of them could surpass the efforts of the threesome who wrote "Shakey Ground" almost 40 years earlier. Aerosmith's cover of the old Temptations chart-topper was the only memorable tune. Unfortunately, it was available only to those who bought the Walmart version or the costly Japanese import.

Music from Another Dimension! received mixed reviews and was a commercial flop. It debuted at No. 5 with sales of just 63,000 copies. By contrast, *Just Push Play* started with 240,000 copies (No. 2), *Nine Lives* with 140,000 (No. 1), and *Get a Grip* with 171,000 (No. 1). In its second week, the turkey tumbled to No. 25 and Amazon.com marked it down to $5 for Thanksgiving shoppers. It quickly fell off the Billboard 200 after selling just 180,000 copies.

RAY CHARLES: BEST FUNERAL EVER

To date the only fresh corpse I've seen in real life, appropriately for my job as a showbiz reporter, belonged to a celebrity: Ray Charles.

I attended his colorful send-off in June 2004, and walked past his open casket on my way out as the sound system played his recent version of "Over the Rainbow." Sporting his trademark sunglasses and a dark suit, Ray looked better than he had six weeks earlier.

That was when the Los Angeles city fathers conferred historic building status on his recording studio and office complex in an inner-city neighborhood. Ray, battling liver cancer, showed up late to the ceremony in a motorized wheelchair. He had to be propped up at the podium by handlers as he mumbled a few remarks. "I'm a little weak now, but I'm gonna get stronger," he said. After posing briefly for photos with luminaries, including Clint Eastwood, he was whisked away.

Remarkably, his failing health never interfered with the work ethic that made him one of the most influential American musicians of the 20th century. Right up to the end he worked on *Genius Loves Company*, a duets album featuring Norah Jones, Natalie Cole, Bonnie Raitt, Diana Krall, and many others. I was scheduled to interview him at his studio in February after spending weeks with his publicist trying to nail down a slot. I showed up at the building wearing my best suit, and was walking up to the door when the publicist called to say Ray had been held up at the last minute and wouldn't be able to speak with me. I didn't mind too much since I assumed we would be able to reschedule.

A few days later, I received in the mail a typed note on classy Ray Charles Enterprises letterhead in which Ray said there had been an "unfortunate scheduling conflict" related to the recording sessions. "Please accept my apologies," he wrote. "I would like to make myself available to you to reschedule, if you are available. I know the life of a newspaperman is busy, just like the life of a musician in the studio. Regards, Mr. Ray Charles." Alas, it was not signed. Nor were we able to tee up a new time. When I saw him in the wheelchair at the ceremony, I realized we never would.

The ceremony came on the heels of a tabloid report in the *Globe* about Ray's terminal prognosis. It claimed funeral arrangements were being made. A longtime acquaintance of Ray's verified the information to me off the record. I had the difficult task of broaching the subject after the ceremony with Joe Adams, his business manager for 46 years. After beating around the bush with some soft questions—why isn't the historic-status plaque written in Braille?—I asked about the report. Joe calmly said the *Globe* seemed to know more about Ray's health than he did. But he admitted it was unlikely Ray would return to the road.

And then Ray slipped away on June 10, aged 73, in an unfortunate coincidence with the wildly over-the-top national mourning for Ronald Reagan, who beat him by five days. At least Ray's service was more fun than the multiple funerals accorded the former president. Ray's was an old-school gospel show with performances by B. B. King, Glen Campbell, Stevie Wonder, Willie Nelson, and jazzmen David "Fathead" Newman and Wynton Marsalis. Mourners at the First African Methodist Episcopal Church gathering included Eastwood, Johnny Mathis, Little Richard, Motown Records founder Berry Gordy, actor Steven Seagal—a late arrival in his trademark purple kung fu jacket—Jesse Jackson, ZZ Top guitarist Billy Gibbons, and actress Cicely Tyson.

Notice the absence of a key demographic? No young black stars came along to pay their respects. Where were Alicia Keys, Usher, Kanye West, Destiny's Child, John Legend, and so on? Maybe they were on tour or detained in the studio. But there should've been no excuses. None of those acts would have a career without the man who virtually invented soul music, conquered pop, jazz, and country, owned a business empire, and crushed racial boundaries. At least the rapper Ice Cube sent a wreath.

The no-shows missed a great musical and comedy gig. One of Ray's sons, the Rev. Robert Robinson, led the service, excitedly declaring at the outset, "We're here to celebrate today. So it's all right if you just clap your hands, stomp your feet, give God your glory. If you would do something for my family today, why don't you stand on your feet and give God your praise. We're here to celebrate God today!" And so we got up, clapped, cheered, and yelled back "Hallelujah!" to light piano accompaniment.

Robinson's frenzied recitation of Psalm 23, The Lord Is My Shepherd—". . . and I will dwell! I will dwell! I will dwell! In the humble Lord! Forever! Forever! And ever!"—garnered more cheering, and then the choir kicked in.

The marble-mouthed Jesse Jackson went on and on. "Now heaven has a maestro," he said. "Ray, when you first get there, before you meet Count [Basie], before you meet the Duke [Ellington], before you meet friends and loved ones, there's a man over there, across the river, who's giving sight to the blind." That got a lot of applause, although Ray did not feel unduly handicapped. He considered deafness to be a greater curse and generously gave to related charities.

Stevie Wonder, who considers his own blindness to be a blessing, recalled that as a boy he did not know Ray was blind. "As a matter of fact, when they [Motown executives] were saying, 'You should do this album about Ray Charles [1962's *Tribute to Uncle Ray*],' I said, Why? They said, 'Well, because he's blind.' Well, no, he's just great." Cue more applause, and Wonder's rendition of the gospel oldie "I Won't Complain."

Along with other speakers at the funeral, Eastwood zeroed in on the oft-noted "genius" of Ray Charles, a title bestowed on him by Frank Sinatra. "Certainly Ray was super-talented, but talent comes with a lot of work. I don't think I've met anyone who had a stronger work ethic than Ray Charles. He worked so hard to be a perfectionist, to entertain us all."

I had never seen Glen Campbell perform, so was thrilled when the guitar virtuoso got up to do "Where Could I Go But to the Lord," an old tune I knew from an Elvis Presley gospel record. Willie Nelson, one of Ray's chess adversaries, fought back tears as he sang "Georgia on My Mind." He joked that after his last chess defeat he asked Ray, "Next time we play, can we turn the lights on?"

Willie need not feel too bad about losing. In 2002 Ray battled former U.S. chess champion Larry Evans in two games that took almost eight hours, according to Valerie Ervin, the president of the Ray Charles Foundation. She told me Evans "was very nervous" that Ray was going to beat him. However, an analysis of one of the games indicated that while Ray was a very perceptive player, his adversary gave him a relatively easy ride. Ray owned several customized chessboards, one of which is at the Smithsonian and another on display at the new museum housed in his office complex. When I saw it, both white bishops occupied white squares, indicating something had gone terribly amiss during his last game. I later found out that it was a mistake at the curator's end. Ray always put his chessmen in special pouches at the end of each game.

I'm not sure if Ray ever played chess with B. B. King. But the bluesman had some funny anecdotes about other aspects of Ray's life. He once went to Ray's house. (Pause for effect.) "And he had the lights on." But overall, it was an emotional day for B. B. He was also overcome by tears, and someone yelled out, "Take your time, B. B." After the funeral, he was mobbed by autograph hounds outside the church. King spoke about Ray's devotion to his family, which was generous but untrue.

Ray, born Ray Charles Robinson, had 12 children from nine women during a period of almost 40 years (King has about 15 children). With his demanding work schedule and clear need for female companionship, Ray was not exactly father of the year and his far-flung offspring barely knew each other. A few years before he died, he gathered 10 of them in a room for the first time and told them he had set up a $500,000 trust fund for each child. That was to be the extent of their inheritance. Ray was paying forward the childhood self-sufficiency ingrained in him by his mother as his eyesight failed him. "He made it very, very clear to them that if you challenge my estate then my estate will go broke and you'll never see a dime," said Ervin, who scheduled and attended the gathering.

Ray's entire estate—including all his copyrights, master tapes, and rights to his likeness—went to a charitable foundation he had set up with a grant of about $50 million in 1986. Controlled by Joe Adams, who has since retired, it focused on needy and underprivileged children, especially those with hearing difficulties. In 2008, ignoring their father, Ray's children went to court seeking to win control of the marketing of his name and image, and a greater voice in foundation affairs. A year later, the foundation won a ruling affirming its rights and was also awarded compensatory damages and attorneys' fees.

Ervin told me the foundation did not pursue those damages and fees from Ray's children. "It's unfortunate that the children decided to challenge after what their father told them 2½ years prior to his death. . . . But I had to go by Mr. Charles' wishes that whatever it took, this is what it is and this is what it will be. And I followed his wishes and I filed the lawsuit to do what we had to do."

The duets album *Genius Loves Company*, by the way, was a smash. Released two months after Ray's death, it became his first chart-topper in more than 40 years. It was also the big winner at the Grammys in 2005, winning seven statuettes including album of the year. But while the foundation's vaults contain an astonishing array of unreleased material, it has stumbled with subsequent releases. A 2005 follow-up *Genius & Friends* featured freshly overdubbed vocals from the likes of Patti LaBelle, whose style was reportedly disliked by Charles, and *American Idol* winner Ruben Studdard. The deceptively titled *Ray Charles Sings, Basie Swings* (2006) had nothing to do with the latter legend, who died in 1984. The producers replaced the orchestral tracks from unreleased Charles masters with new arrangements by a big band that uses the Count Basie name. The 2010 release *Rare Genius*, released to mark Ray's 80th birthday, also boasted some contemporary overdubs as well as a previously unreleased duet with Johnny Cash. Unlike the previous two efforts, it failed to make the U.S. pop chart.

ISAAC HAYES: BALD AND BEAUTIFUL

Isaac Hayes gave me the courage to shave my head. Sitting on the patio at the House of Blues one afternoon, watching the sun's reflection on his wondrous dome, I realized that I could do worse than to adopt the look of the biggest soul singer of the '70s when it came time for me to face the music.

They talk about the importance of female role models, black role models, disabled role models. But the bald ones don't get the same glory. Hayes said he was the only bald, black entertainer back in the old days, and he made it safe for latter-day superstars like Michael Jordan to follow suit. "Let me tell you a secret," he said, grimly surveying my retreating troops, "Cut it all off. They never know when you go naturally, because it's gone anyway."

More importantly, I asked anxiously, do the ladies like the look? "Yeah, I think so. It's a phallic thing," he said with a rich, southern laugh.

"I could grow it back," he added, "but I don't like it. It's been way too long," and he wondered if people would recognize him if he was sporting, say, a 'fro. A furtive analysis indicated to me that he might be disappointed with the results if he stopped shaving, just like Elaine's swimmer boyfriend in *Seinfeld*. But I wasn't going to go down that route with my newly adopted guru.

Hayes laughed a lot during our encounter, not necessarily because I was amusing company, although that couldn't have hurt. He just seemed so relaxed, so engaged, so in love with life and with music. And when he wasn't laughing, he was melting my heart with that deep-fried Tennessee accent.

He was on hand for promotional events tied in with the opening of the House of Blues outpost in West Hollywood in April 1994. It may not look like it now, but the House of Blues was one happening spot for a good five years or so. The opening night alone saw Aerosmith perform a full-length blues set for the lucky 1,000 people inside. The day after our chat, it was Hayes' turn, and he waved at me from the stage at one point. A week later, James Brown and Bruce Springsteen were jamming onstage alongside Magic Johnson. It was almost like my second home during those early years, and I burned a lot of calories striding up the steep hill from the bus stop on Santa Monica Boulevard to the venue on Sunset. Hayes would have appreciated my exertions. He had been a self-described "health fanatic" for over 20 years.

"I work out, I pump iron. I eat right. I juice. I try not to eat salt and things like that and grease and cholesterol and fats and all that junk," he said. "It has helped me. Sometimes when you go to class reunions, it's embarrassing because you don't recognize somebody. And somebody else doesn't recognize me—not because of the bald head and beard—and they say, 'Man, you haven't aged at all!' There's a reason. Remember that rabbit food you used to tease me about eating? It pays off."

The day after our interview his grandmother turned 102 (and eventually made it to 105). He hoped her genes would rub off on to him. Sadly, they didn't. Hayes died of a stroke 14 years later while running on his treadmill at home in Memphis. He was 10 days short of his 66th birthday.

The obituaries followed a pattern, quickly covering his years as the world's preeminent soul singer before settling on his latter-day claim to fame as the voice of Chef, the randy fount of all knowledge on *South Park*. He quit that gig in 2006, reportedly claiming that series creators Trey Parker and Matt Stone disrespected Scientology, the religious movement he'd followed since about 1991.

Hayes took his superstition seriously. When we met again in 2005, to discuss a new hits album, he told me he was at the state of Clear level, which Scientology literature says involves "total erasure of the reactive mind." He was about to start working on his Operating Thetan levels ("a state of complete spiritual freedom," per the Scientologists)—"and that's a big deal for me.

"People don't know what Scientology is," he said. "When I got in Scientology, I didn't know either." He took a course about overcoming the ups and downs in life, and "it blew me away." But the Southern Baptist couldn't admit that to anyone. Pretending to be reluctant, he took another course, on personal values and integrity. He got defensive during the course, wondering who dared question his integrity?!? After that course, he decided to become a Scientologist.

"Scientology is an applied religious philosophy," he said. "Anybody can use it. You can be a Buddhist, you can be a Catholic, you can be a Muslim, doesn't matter. It will make you a better whatever you are. . . . It's a way of life. In fact, a Baptist minister got me into Scientology."

His Isaac Hayes Foundation brought Scientology-based study techniques to underperforming inner-city schools in America, in partnership with Lisa Marie Presley and with government funding, and he also built a school in Ghana, where he was made a member of a tribal royal family.

Scientology also helped him get over resentment stemming from his 1977 bankruptcy, collateral damage both from the demise of his label, the southern powerhouse Stax Records, and from his own financial mismanagement. He lost all the rights to his songs, never got another dime for either his own material, including "Theme from

Shaft," or the ones he worked on for others, such as those co-written for the '60s soul duo Sam & Dave ("Soul Man," "Hold On! I'm A Comin'").

"Excess was not the thing that contributed to all of that stuff. Bad management," he said. "When I say 'bad management' I assume responsibility for it even though I wasn't the culprit that executed it. I was wearing a lot of hats and I trusted the wrong people and that's what happens when those things happen, because creative people don't want to fool with business. But where the business is today you have to take a hand in it, otherwise things will get away from you. So that's in a nutshell what happened. But it wasn't the end. I never saw it as that, because my first love is musical anyway. If you're artistically successful and you get any kind of commercial success, the money will come."

He planned to reveal "the whole damn story" about his financial problems in a memoir. He was also planning to write a series of children's books called *The Adventures of Uncle Bubba*. In the meantime, his main form of income was touring and working as a radio DJ, but the work dried up after he suffered his first stroke in 2006.

Meeting Hayes—twice—was another one of those childhood experiences coming to weird fruition. I first became aware of him when I was about 5 or 6. He was one of the artists on a *Solid Gold* hits record that marked one of my parents' few music purchases. I played his contribution, "Theme from *Shaft*," over and over on a portable suitcase record player, and sang along as Hayes asked, "Who's the black private dick that's a sex machine to all the chicks?" But Hayes was huge long before the mid-'70s. He got his big break in the early 1960s when he joined Stax as a keyboardist at the label's Memphis studio. His first session was with Otis Redding. After patiently biding his time, he teamed with lyricist David Porter to compose some of the biggest hits for Sam & Dave. Hayes came up with the introductory horn line for "Hold On! I'm A Comin'" while Porter was in the bathroom. He yelled at his collaborator to hurry up, and Porter ran out with his pants around his ankles, yelling the words that would become the song's title.

But Hayes wanted to be a star in his own right and to incorporate strings and orchestras into his work, sounds seemingly at odds with Stax's bread-and-butter rawness. With his shaved head, dark shades, flamboyant clothing, and jewelry, Hayes certainly looked like a star, or at least a pimp. He released his debut album, *Presenting Isaac Hayes,* to little notice in 1968.

He broke through the following year with *Hot Buttered Soul,* whose four marathon tracks included a 19-minute version of the recent Glen Campbell hit "By the Time I Get to Phoenix." The album redefined soul music, even though three of the cuts were covers of pop songs. Extended monologues gave way to bluesy jams, raw soul, and soaring strings courtesy of the Memphis Symphony. *Hot Buttered Soul* sold more than a million copies, a staggering tally for a radio-unfriendly work targeted at the black audience. It made him one of the dominant black artists of the early '70s alongside Gaye, Stevie Wonder, James Brown, and Al Green.

The artwork, long an afterthought at both Stax and R&B rival Motown, was dynamic. The cover featured an aerial view of Hayes' head framed by his omnipresent sunglasses (a concession to his only flaw, his bug eyes). A thick gold chain necklace rested out of focus on his bare shoulders.

But Hayes also wanted to be an actor. He auditioned for the lead role of private eye John Shaft in director Gordon Parks' adaptation of Ernest Tidyman's urban crime novel *Shaft,* losing out to Richard Roundtree. The consolation prize was pretty good. He was recruited to compose the score, including the iconic theme song, an irresistibly urgent mix of wah-wah guitars and hi-hat cymbals spiced by the famous line,

They say this cat Shaft is a bad mother-/Shut your mouth!

The song and the album topped the U.S. charts in November 1971, four months after the movie premiered to gangbuster business.

The soundtrack vied for seven Grammys the following March, taking home three—including a pair for Hayes personally. He earned a one-minute standing ovation when he walked to the stage to collect one of his awards, a nod to his deserved superstardom after years of hard work in the trenches. But the industry's generosity extended only so far. He lost the key album and record of the year races to Carole King, who was riding high with *Tapestry*.

A month later, Hayes became the third black person to win an Oscar, after actors Hattie McDaniel and Sidney Poitier. But he had to overcome stiff resistance from the Academy's old guard to become eligible, since some claimed he did not really write "Theme from *Shaft*." "If I dictate to somebody what to write by playing on the piano or humming, I wrote it," said Hayes, who did not bother writing the arrangements on sheet music during the hasty recording sessions. "It took Quincy Jones, J. J. Johnson [the jazz trombonist who worked on the album], [fellow nominee] Henry Mancini to fight for me, as well as [screen composer] Dominic Frontiere."

His win ranks among the greatest triumphs for Black America. April 10, 1972: a date to remember. "Yeah! Yeah! I told you!" someone in the crowd shouted as Hayes jogged to the stage, dressed in blue tuxedo and tails complemented by an oversize fur bow tie. Hayes thanked his grandmother, his date for the evening, for keeping him on "the path of righteousness," and gave her his statuette as an early 80th birthday present. Rushia Wade and her husband were sharecroppers who'd raised Hayes and his sister in poverty-stricken rural Tennessee. Her trip to Hollywood must have been mind-blowing.

Hayes topped the American R&B charts later in 1972 with *Black Moses*, again in 1973 with *Live at the Sahara Tahoe,* and for the last time in 1975 with *Chocolate Chip*, his final gold-certified record. *Chocolate Chip* was his first (non-soundtrack) album under a contract extension that was so lucrative it aggravated Stax's perilous finances. At that time, Hayes was perhaps the biggest singer on the planet, depicted at the height of his powers—sporting traditional chainmail garb—in the film documenting the 1972 Wattstax festival at the

Memorial Coliseum in Los Angeles. For the most part he claimed not to be aware of his stardom.

"I was just so busy," he told me. "I was in the eye of the hurricane, so I wasn't aware of what was going on around me. I was writing, arranging, producing, performing. I wasn't aware of how popular I was until I stepped out of it and then began to walk the streets and see people rapt—'Wow!'

"It was quite amusing. 'Really? That's how you perceive me?' When you're on stage and you're performing that's almost what they expect. But when I find that my music had real meaning to people, that it had an effect on their lives, then I began to say, 'Well damn! That was some powerful shit.' One guy made a very interesting summation of that: 'You know why these people love you? Some artists are in the heads of people, in the minds. You're in the hearts of people, and that's what really counts. That's what longevity's about.' Interesting."

When I first interviewed Hayes in 1994, he had not released an album since 1988, nor enjoyed a hit single since 1973. Acting was his focus, and his recent credits at the time included a grab bag of modest performers such as the Keenen Ivory Wayans' satire *I'm Gonna Git You Sucka*, Mario van Peebles' black Western *Posse*, and Mel Brooks' *Men in Tights*. I preferred his earlier work, including his role as the title character in 1974's *Truck Turner*. He played a wisecracking skip tracer who deadpanned, "No, man. I'm a faggot," when a soldier asked if he had been in combat. Hayes was philosophical about the film-music imbalance. "But, you know, music is the original and, you know, you miss it. But I wasn't going to compromise myself until I found the right situation." Coincidentally, he had signed a deal with Virgin days before the interview, and released a pair of albums the following year, the vocal disc *Branded* and the all-instrumental *Raw and Refined*. The latter kicked off with an intriguing tune, "Birth of Shaft," a raw indication of how Hayes' trademark tune sounded in the early part of the jamming process. He was not happy with how the albums were handled, and he released no more new material.

* * *

South Park gave him a whole new audience, much to his amusement. "You work all your life struggling for artistic excellence, and some wacked-out late-night adult cartoon makes you hotter than you've ever been," he said backstage at the American Music Awards in 1999, just as Season 2 was wrapping up. The 2005 career-spanning compilation Can You Dig It?, the pretext for our second chat, included a DVD juxtaposing three Wattstax tracks with his character Chef's performance of "Chocolate Salty Balls." At that stage, Hayes was supportive of the archly satirical show. "You can't take it seriously," he said. "There's always a message behind South Park for the kids. . . . No one is immune from the wrath of Matt and Trey, but it's always so popular."

His tune changed after the airing later in 2005 of the infamous "Trapped in the Closet" episode, which mercilessly lampooned both Scientology and its No. 1 practitioner, Tom Cruise. Hayes left the show the following year, although there was some suspicion that his complaints about the show's alleged "intolerance" and "bigotry" were less his real opinions and more those of his Scientology minders.

His last years were, by all accounts, rather sad, as the stroke hampered his mobility and speech. Hayes died on Aug. 10, 2008, one day after irascible comedian Bernie Mac succumbed to pneumonia. I wrote both their obituaries. It was a tough weekend. Hayes, coincidentally, played himself in an episode of *The Bernie Mac Show*—I had become a fan of the late-night reruns—and they reunited posthumously on the big screen a few months later in the comedy feature *Soul Men*, about which the less said, the better.

Shortly before Hayes died, he wrote out the lyrics to the *Shaft* track "Soulsville," which I snapped up for a song at a charity auction. As for my hair, I finally applied the shears in 1998. The female reaction was not as advertised. I guess he omitted the bit about fame and fortune also helping seal the deal.

INXS: FLESH AND BLOOD

The phone rang late on a Friday night in November 1997 and a vaguely familiar voice delivered some startling news. "Michael Hutchence died," my sister said, calling from New Zealand. It couldn't have been a joke; she doesn't joke. She repeated the headline that scrolled across her television set. The INXS front man had apparently committed suicide in his Sydney hotel room. Stunned, I drove back to the office to help out my Australian counterparts with the breaking news. KROQ, a modern-rock station that had long ago abandoned INXS, cleared its schedule to play back-to-back hits. A rival rock scribe called in to offer some useless speculation.

I wrote a quick, 700-word profile that was filled with quotes from three interviews I had done with Hutchence, the most recent earlier in the year. It was decent wire copy under the circumstances: *INXS vocalist Michael Hutchence, found dead in a Sydney hotel room, lived a seemingly charmed existence as the handsome front man of Australia's most successful rock music export. From humble beginnings 20 years ago playing to unreceptive crowds in pubs throughout Australia, INXS went on to become an irresistible rock force and MTV favorite by the end of the 1980s.*

I skirted around the details of his death. Facts were hard to come by in those first few hours. Back home, I wrote another story, about rock 'n' roll suicides. It was 2 a.m. by the time I was done, exhausted. Michael Hutchence, dead at 37, naked and suffocated. Didn't see that one coming.

I congratulated myself on a canny move four months earlier: INXS had done a backstage meet-and-greet after a show at the Greek Theatre in Los Angeles, and I took time out from chatting up a pair of sisters to pose for a photo with Hutchence at the behest of a photographer hired by the label. Bassist Garry Beers then offered to pose for a shot with me. These photo ops are a music industry cliché that I try to avoid, but I'm glad I made this exception; otherwise I would have hanged myself too. A few years later, I went to great lengths to track down those color slides. And I continue to avoid goofy arm-around-shoulder shots with the excuse, "The last guy who posed with me killed himself a few months later."

I left out such first-person observations from my hasty profile. It also would have been nice to mention my INXS encounter a few months before that, as an unpaid extra on the video shoot for the single "Everything." Accompanied by a few hundred fans and professional extras who had wisely brought along food and reading material, I spent the better part of my Saturday doing an awful lot of waiting around. There was a line to get in the door and another one to sign a disclaimer. Then we sat for three hours while gofers occasionally came over to issue instructions and then disappear. Finally, we were herded to the set, a circular wooden grandstand looking down on a revolving octagonal platform. It was to be a simple performance video with the audience singing along while the band pretended to play along to a backing track, not exactly in the groundbreaking style of clips like "What You Need" and the MTV award-winning "Need You Tonight."

Take after take, we walked down from the top, sat down, sang, clapped, cheered, got up, and swayed. I rather enjoyed the audience participation bit; it was a step up from singing in the shower. The whole setup reminded me of the Rolling Stones' *Rock and Roll Circus,* where fans endured a multiday taping of a Stones-hosted all-star concert in 1968. During the frequent breaks, the INXS guys chatted with fans and signed autographs. Six hours later we were freed, tired but exhilarated. Sadly, I'm not visible in the clip, just one of the masses as the lens understandably zeroes in on the young hotties. Still, I consider it "my song."

"Everything" was the second single from *Elegantly Wasted,* the band's 10th album, and the video shoot followed the final stop of a two-week North American promotional tour. The record was unable to arrest INXS' descent from the spectacular, stadium-packing peak it reached during the late 1980s. With a possible assist from a performance on Rosie O'Donnell's talk show, *Elegantly Wasted* debuted at No. 41 on the U.S. pop chart—the same week that fellow modern-rock veterans Depeche Mode's *Ultra* came in at No. 5 with almost quadruple the sales. *Elegantly Wasted* fell out of the chart after just eight weeks.

INXS returned to North America in July, which is when I saw the Greek show. Hutchence's remaining days were dwindling, but he wasn't the only one in bad shape. Drummer Jon Farriss—the youngest of three brothers in the six-piece outfit—was going through a bitter divorce. Beers, in a rare moment of weakness, slept with a backup singer on the tour and was promptly divorced. Guitarist Tim Farriss, the eldest brother, was drinking heavily.

But the spotlight shone harshest on Hutchence, whose doomed romance with TV presenter Paula Yates had been tabloid fodder since the pair were snapped at an English hotel in March 1995. The photos of a rabid Hutchence beating and shrieking at paparazzi outside the hotel contrasted sharply with his image as one of the last rock gods standing. The melee resulted in an assault conviction and fines totaling 2,300 pounds (about $3,600 at the time). It also cost Hutchence his relationship with Danish model Helena Christensen, and Yates her 10-year marriage to "Saint" Bob Geldof. A week after she filed for divorce in December, Yates revealed that she and Hutchence were expecting a daughter. As part of the divorce settlement,

Hutchence and Geldof exchanged nearby homes, a downgrade for the latter.

In September 1996, two months after Heavenly Hiraani Tiger Lily Hutchence was born, a police raid netted an opium stash at the couple's house. They were arrested, but claimed the drugs were planted while they were out of the country.

The drugs case was still open in February 1997 when Hutchence and I discussed *Elegantly Wasted* on the phone, and it was closed without charges filed the following month. Hutchence admitted people in England probably regarded him as a bit of a cad. "Errol Flynn—me—all the best," he said with a laugh. "I could have done without some attention recently. But it's OK. You get through. If you know who you are, and who you're with, and what people really are, that's all that matters."

"Are you secure in your public persona?" I asked.

"It depends what country I'm standing in. In England there's no control at all, because you've got a bunch of oiks in pubs getting pissed and writing fiction about you. What can you do about that? It's not even suable. There's an absolute carte-blanche, inverted version of freedom of the press there. I was just in Hong Kong and talking to a woman there, Rosa, who's a political activist. She was horrified at the cynical exploitation that the words 'freedom of the press' mean, considering she'll probably do five years when the Chinese come in there [in December 1997]. It's sad, isn't it?"

Unbeknownst to me, Hutchence and his sloppy-drunk girlfriend were on heroin. Not surprisingly, he wasn't about to reveal that tidbit to me, and I didn't push him very hard anyway. I felt bad for my fellow Antipodean. In hindsight, some of his comments indicated he was in a bad place. But I didn't read too much into them at the time.

His lyrics on *Elegantly Wasted* were more introspective and narrative than usual, to the surprise of his bandmates. "He was never really like that before. He was always a lot more cryptic person," Jon Farriss recalled years later.

"I'm Just a Man" was among the album's more personal songs, a slow-burning cry for help. "It's a song about blood is thicker than water, that you can find a way through whatever happens, no matter what happens—and I have," Hutchence explained.

While he claimed to have a great relationship with his family, the singer was actually estranged from his mother and half-sister. The pair later unsuccessfully sought custody of his daughter and published a tell-all book. On the other hand, Hutchence had reconciled with his father, and dined with him and his second wife the night before he killed himself.

"Searching" was another personal song. "Sometimes you just get to a point where everything is so black and dark," he said, "you're just looking for . . . that thing that keeps you going, that keeps you believing."

He denied the record was bleak—and there were indeed some power-pop moments. "It's a bit like the blues," he explained. "These things can liberate you." I asked if anything gave him the blues. He claimed to be fairly happy overall. "The usual stuff," he said. "The world seems to be running faster than it can stand."

Paradoxically, the band's waning fortunes proved a welcome distraction from lines of inquiry into his domestic life. It's easier to explain commercial setbacks than personal ones. He optimistically mentioned INXS in the same breath as peers like U2, R.E.M., and Depeche Mode. But his band had fallen behind, unable to keep pace in the new generation of alternative rock. He attributed INXS' slippage to the laidback ethos of Australians.

"You go around, you go around, you go around, and before your brain turns to vegetable soup you just have to sometimes say, 'Look, what's more important? Selling another million records? Or being real about yourself? What do you want in life?' We're just the kind of people—I think it's the Australian in us—some things we just don't care about that much. And other things are more important to us. You pay a price for it, but as long as you accept that, that's OK. We're realistic about it, and now we feel very charged up. And we're gonna go out there and put a lot into it and see what happens. We're one of the hardest-working bands in showbiz, I can tell you that. That's fact. You just don't want to become *Spinal Tap* where you're sitting around in a room and it's just insane and you lose all context . . . That's just called blind greed, feeding something that shouldn't be fed."

He half-seriously said it was all part of a master plan to peak with *Kick*, the 1987 album that yielded four top-10 singles in the United States, including the No. 1 "Need You Tonight." (Atlantic Records in America hated that record when it was delivered, pleading with INXS manager Chris Murphy to get the band to start over. He ignored the executives and wisely did not apprise his charges of the label's distaste.)

"We wanted to make an accessible, big, fucking record and we did," Hutchence said of *Kick*. "Bigger than we even realized, though it was going to be [big], that's for sure. We usually know what's going to happen when we put it out. We don't have false hopes. We're pretty earthy because we know what a public is and that's where they are.

"Occasionally, though, you get surprised, and we might get surprised with this one [*Elegantly Wasted*]. I think this one is lining up OK . . . Hopefully the fans that we used to have will find out about it and get into it again, and hopefully we'll get some new ones. I don't expect it, but it would be good if we did."

It was hardly a ringing endorsement. But it was hard to fight the sales tallies. INXS made some questionable career moves in the wake of *Kick*. The 1990 follow-up, *X*, was basically a *Kick* knock-off, although the first single, "Suicide Blonde," topped a couple of charts. In 1992, INXS released *Welcome to Wherever You Are*, a tasty offering often considered the band's most interesting album, perhaps its version of U2's *Achtung Baby* from the previous year. While it flopped in the United States, *Welcome* did quite well in Europe, debuting at No. 1 in Britain. Hutchence considered it his favorite, alongside *Kick* and *Elegantly Wasted* (inevitably; an artist always says his new album is his best).

Instead of touring behind *Welcome*, INXS went straight back to the studio to record its least-loved album. *Full Moon, Dirty Hearts* was the band's answer to the grunge bands. Hutchence was enthralled by Nirvana and was convinced INXS had to follow its lead. His bandmates were less impressed by the Seattle sound. The album also featured duets with Chrissie Hynde and Ray Charles, and a rather desperate cover photo depicting the elegant rockers dressed down in plaid. It debuted in America at No. 53, the same week Pearl Jam's *Vs.* held down the top spot as Nirvana and Smashing Pumpkins rode high with new releases. It spent just five weeks in the Billboard 200. Hutchence said the record stores "virtually didn't even know it existed, let alone anybody else. It was completely buried, along with *Welcome*."

A selection of tracks from *Welcome* and *Full Moon* appear on *Live at Barker Hangar*, a digital download taken from the Los Angeles stop on a brief theater tour of North America in 1993. It marked my first INXS show because the band rarely ventured over to New Zealand. I got to the Santa Monica Airport venue in style, interviewing Hutchence in the back of a limo that drove us from the band's digs at the Four Seasons Hotel. The 20-minute encounter was videotaped for an electronic press kit that I was never able to track down. Many of the questions pertained to the songs that would appear on the as-yet untitled and unfinished *Full Moon*. So it was all theoretical, talking about songs I hadn't heard. He suggested we pick up where we left off on the way back after the show, but that was going to be difficult logistically.

The two-hour show was probably one of INXS' last great stands in America, before its groove rock was swamped by the grunge monster. The place was packed with 4,000 beautiful young people just looking for a good time. I was able to get to the front because a girl next to me fainted and I carried her to the security zone at the stage, where I stayed after my annual act of not-quite-selfless charity was completed. Almost half the songs were from *Full Moon* and *Welcome*. There was an after-party but I didn't stay for long, feeling insecure in a place filled with Perfect 10s.

The publicist told me the next day that Hutchence liked the interview, but she thought it was vital that we go deeper into the new tracks and the reasoning for their tour, which also took in similar venues in Australia and Europe. We accordingly reconnected five days later when I called him at his Chicago hotel. He was checked in as Mr. Shake.

He admitted to some unease with the band's recent promotional strategy. "It's kinda weird. We had an album out without touring; now we're touring without an album. I suppose it's a bit strange . . . It's not a profit-making experience, that's for sure," he said with a laugh. "We're basically running around the world pretty quickly and saying, 'Hi! Remember us?'"

Aware that it been neglectful of North America, the band did return for a monthlong trek later in 1993, though some of the dates were reportedly scrapped because of poor ticket sales and the illness of the Farrisses' mother.

We shared our surprise that the unfamiliar stuff from *Full Moon* seemed to go over well with the L.A. crowds. Among them was "Cut the Roses," a response to the resurgence of neo-Nazism across post-unification Europe. "It's prevalent," he said. "The graffiti tells you, to start with." Its lyrical content was a far cry from the band's recent big single "Heaven Sent," an ode to a sexy librarian.

I felt stupid asking him, but I needed a sound bite about his sex-symbol status. He claimed not to think about it, apologized for being boring, and said that if he did come across strutting and preening he was doing it tongue-in-cheek. Of course, the critics seemed to take him at (pretty) face value, which annoyed him.

"I wanna be respected for my talents. I just don't believe I get enough respect for my vocal abilities and songwriting abilities sometimes. So fuck 'em all! I just sometimes feel as though I don't really hang out with the right journos and go to dinner with them or kiss their ass or something.

"People discovered us. *Rolling Stone* didn't, *Spin* didn't. It wasn't till after we played with 10,000 people in front of us that everyone said, 'Oh, we'd better go down and review these boys.' And journalists hate that . . . It wasn't like we were a little band playing down in a local bar in New York and [noted critic David] Fricke came down from *Rolling Stone* and went, 'Hey! I love these guys, I'm gonna make 'em big.'"

* * *

Eight years later Hutchence was dead. INXS returned to Sydney in November 1997 to rehearse for a 20th anniversary tour designed to shore up faltering support among hometown fans: The band had not cracked the local year-end chart since 1991. On Nov. 22, the day before the tour was scheduled to begin, Hutchence hanged himself with a belt in his room at now-abandoned Ritz-Carlton. His death was ruled a suicide. Because he was naked and a book about autoeroticism was found in his room, there was some talk that he had died accidentally in the act, and Paula Yates promoted that angle. But Hutchence was clearly depressed, caught up in a custody dispute between Yates and Geldof, and facing Christmas kept apart from his daughter. The autopsy found traces of cocaine, alcohol, and the antidepressant Prozac in his blood. After an angry call to Geldof, Hutchence left a voicemail with his manager in New York saying, "I've fucking had enough."

Along with Yates, mourners at the nationally televised funeral in Sydney included ex-girlfriends Christensen and Kylie Minogue. Errol Flynn would have been impressed.

Yates died of an accidental heroin overdose in 2000, and Geldof ended up adopting Tiger Lily, whom he raised with her three older half-sisters. "Michael hated Bob in the end so much," Tim Farriss said in a 2014 Australian television interview. "To think that he would end up as the sole parent of Tiger Lily would have been the most horrific thing he could have imagined. But luckily for Tiger she had Bob in the end."

Geldof couldn't let Hutchence rest in peace. "Why put a noose around your neck?" he asked in the 2001 song "Inside Your Head," which rehashed the unusual house-swap settlement. Hutchence's old mates in U2 adopted a more subtle approach a year earlier with "Stuck in a Moment You Can't Get Out Of," which got a mixed review from Andrew Farriss, Hutchence's songwriting partner.

"I couldn't think of a better way for people to honor Michael's memory than to write songs about how they felt about the guy," Farriss told me in June 2001. But, "Michael's . . . an awesome singer and great songwriter and he deserves to be seen in that light, not as someone that necessarily got in a moment they couldn't get out of."

Farriss—the middle brother—and guitarist/saxophone player Kirk Pengilly were in Los Angeles to promote a two-disc anthology called *Shine Like It Does*. They even played a brief acoustic set for staffers at Rhino Records, with Pengilly on vocals for the title track, "Never Tear Us Apart" (which required two attempts) and "Mystify." I taped the performance on my cheap Sony tape recorder, which did a great job. The bespectacled Pengilly's a good-looking, cerebral fellow, but not a rock god like Hutchence. By that time, INXS had toured Australia and New Zealand with singer Jon Stevens, but they were reluctant to bring him into the fold full-time. The band also did gigs with Terence Trent D'Arby and local hero Jimmy Barnes.

Farriss and Pengilly—chatting with me in a Rhino conference room—were surprisingly dispassionate about Hutchence. "I don't really actually think of the death," Pengilly said. "We all went through, at different stages, all the emotions that you do go through after a death: anger to sadness to even joy. You go through them all. With everyone, it affects everyone differently. The period of time that it takes to get through that differs. I think most of us are pretty well out the other side too."

Certainly, Andrew Farriss was over it. "I've lost people in my life, and I'm sure as my life goes on—and I hope I live for a few more years—I'll lose more people around me too. The difference, I suppose in this particular situation, is that he was someone of public notoriety, and therefore the intensity of it all goes along with that . . . Life happens. We happen to be in it, all of us."

They were chomping at the bit to make music. That's what musicians do, and these guys were at the top of the game. They likely missed the touring income, especially the non-songwriters and those going through divorces. But they had no immediate prospects until reality TV called. *Rock Star: INXS*, which aired during the summer of 2005 with Dave Navarro as host, was an *American Idol*–inspired competition to find a new singer. I never tuned in, but not because I had a problem with it. Unlike some dismayed fans, I understood that this was a fun way for the guys to move on with their careers. I assumed they would choose wisely, and I didn't need to suffer through the fabricated dramas that are the hallmark of reality shows. The winner was a Canadian chap named J. D. Fortune, who'd apparently once been homeless. He sang on the band's fall 2005 album *Switch*, which shockingly debuted at a worthy No. 17 in the United States. The whole project—TV show, album, and world tour—kept the band busy for three years.

In 2009, Fortune told a TV gossip show that he had been fired from the band and abandoned at the airport in Hong Kong. He also admitted to doing cocaine while on tour. Over my objections, a woman at Reuters picked up the story without getting a solid response from INXS' people. It smelled fishy to me.

Indeed, as of early 2011, Fortune was still in INXS as its touring singer and was helping write its next album. His outburst evidently earned him a scolding from his patient bandmates. "He's obviously had to pay for it. He's buried his head in his hands," Jon Farriss told me in February of that year. Added Beers, "You have to hit a wall to change direction."

Farriss, Beers, and I were dining at The Palm restaurant in West Hollywood. Beers, who lives in Los Angeles with his Realtor girlfriend, and Farriss were promoting a new album, *Original Sin*, featuring guest vocalists doing heavily recast versions of old songs. Fortune was among the singers, along with a mixed bag including Rob Thomas of Matchbox 20, Ben Harper, Nikka Costa, and some exotic foreigners. The idea was "to remove the preciousness of the singer thing. Let's get as many singers as we can," said Farriss, who shepherded the project.

The first couple of listens were rather painful for me, deconstructed versions of "Mystify" and "Kick," among other tunes. I told the publicist it would be a waste of my time doing an interview and then writing it up. But I wanted to meet Beers since I was learning bass, and Farriss since he'd co-written the wonderful ballad

"Disappear." I also wanted to stick it to Reuters by eating grilled salmon on the company dime at a costly restaurant.

Beers, a fan of Motown bass player James-Jamerson and Led Zeppelin's John Paul Jones, offered to help me out with my bass. It was a generous offer I reflexively turned down because I figured my dismal playing was best kept a secret. He recommended I listen to his playing on "Bitter Tears," "The Loved One," and "Kick." For his part, he was learning lead guitar by watching YouTube clips.

I asked lots of deep questions as they dined on lobster bisque and crab cakes. Farriss complimented my dedication and complained about the state of sound bite–driven music journalism. "I love these sorts of conversations. Really there's not enough of it anymore, Dean. There's not. Twenty years ago, there'd be a lot more interviews that would be more like this where you sit down and have a good talk about something. It's not so formalized. You'll ask that, we say that, and all that sort of shit."

Wisely, they didn't expect the dance-heavy sound of *Original Sin* to be widely accepted in America. I could certainly see it catching fire among stoned ravers in Europe. The reviews were brutal, and I quoted some harsh ones from Australian newspapers to balance my story. It debuted at No. 49 in Australia, and did not chart in America.

Naturally, the subject of Hutchence came up. "The older you get, the more people that you know die around you that you love," Farriss said, echoing his brother Andrew's earlier comments to me. He revealed that after Hutchence's death, the rest of the band holed up in group sessions with psychologists who were "able to make everyone feel safe about sharing their fears and stuff about Michael," and then move forward. "What was born out of it was the TV show."

The band "never got derailed completely," added Beers. "But obviously it was a very painful period for us. We're a family and we lost a brother, in a very awkward way. It wasn't like you got to say goodbye, or you really understand why and how."

Perhaps, more importantly, added Beers, "We're enjoying each other's company again, really playing well. It's a pretty bright future right now for us, which is ironic that you can say that after all we've been through . . . We're kinda used to changing course and doing the hard work it takes to do what we need to be invigorated ourselves. We just hope that people enjoy coming along for the ride as we do it."

Alas, it seemed that Fortune's ride was over. Both he and I lost our jobs around the same time, in mid-2011. INXS teamed up with Ciaran Gribbin, a Northern Irish singer/songwriter who sounds like Bono. He relocated his young family to Australia so that he could write with Andrew Farriss. In January 2012, three days after Hutchence would have turned 52, the new-look INXS premiered a patriotic ditty called "We Are United" for a big Australia Day crowd in the federal capital of Canberra. Not even Hutchence could have made it sound sexy.

By November 2012 INXS bowed to the inevitable, announcing during a warm-up performance for Matchbox 20 in Perth that it was breaking up. This time would indeed be the last time. Maybe it was 15 years too late, but you can't blame 'em for trying.

BILLY IDOL, INTERNET ICON

P oor Billy Idol. The English punk rocker embraced the Internet long before most other musicians, but he was ridiculed for his efforts. Way back in 1993, when a cadre of tech-savvy folks grandly referred to the largely theoretical mass connection of computers as "the information superhighway," Idol released a concept album called *Cyberpunk*.

The title was a nod to the science-fiction genre popularized by the likes of William Gibson, who coined the term "cyberspace," as well as Rudy Rucker and Bruce Sterling. Idol, evidently nerdier than his trademark spiky hair, lascivious sneer, and death-defying substance abuse indicated, said he started reading their books in the early '80s. He devoured scientific journals and concluded that fiction was fast becoming fact. According to the quaint wording of the album's press kit, "Cyberpunks refuse to buy into the one-to-many form of communication. For $500, you can buy a computer and a modem and participate in many-to-many computer network communication, where there are no 'reporters' or 'readers,' only individuals sharing information instantaneously . . . Jack-in to the continuous global conversation in Cyberspace!"

Oblivious to all that mumbo-jumbo, I interviewed Idol—now sporting dreadlocks—in a North Hollywood rehearsal studio where he and his band were gearing up for a European tour supporting, ahem, Bon Jovi. ("It's the only tour that's selling in Europe apart from U2, so I think we lucked onto the right thing," he said.) The word "Internet" was not used during our hourlong chat. In my ignorance, I was more concerned that his new esoteric bent might mean fewer strippers in his music videos.

Although Idol recorded *Cyberpunk* on an Apple Macintosh in his Hollywood Hills home, he admitted that enthusiasm for computers outweighed his prowess. But he knew more than I did, and patiently explained how to use the Mac-compatible floppy disk that accompanied the CD. "Click, click, you're in! Instant jack-off time," he said, referring to the "nude fucking chicks" that would appear on the screensaver. (If a butterfly in a distant land had flapped its wings at a different angle, Billy might have made billions through Internet porn.)

Artists like Todd Rundgren and The Orb were also embracing interactive technology, but Idol complained that their visions were too complicated. "Our idea of doing it was to draw people into it rather like myself who aren't computer-friendly really, whose idea of computers is kinda backward, who think that they're kinda dangerous," said Idol, who generously included his (since-disabled) email address in the CD booklet, idol@well.sf.ca.us.

Cyberpunk, whose first single was a cover version of the Velvet Underground's "Heroin," had just debuted at a lowly No. 48 on the Billboard 200. It fell off the chart in seven weeks. Reflecting the critical consensus, *Q* magazine described it as "the comedy album of the year."

Idol was less concerned about the poor reception, and more excited about sharing his enthusiasm for "virtual reality" and conspiracy theories. He pointed to a television in the corner and said, "that box is no longer gonna just be sitting there as something you just watch. You're gonna start interacting with it, and that's gonna happen before the end of this decade. So I think we're very much in the beginning of a cyberpunk time. And I think, Yes! Fuck! It's nice to be the herald."

He segued excitedly into a discussion about SIMNET, which allowed the U.S. military to conduct war games through virtual reality. "It's gonna make them even more expert at war. It's gonna make them even more capable of destruction. If that's not gonna affect our lives, Jesus Christ, what is?" I felt like I was attending a Zig Ziglar motivational seminar. Idol was on a roll. "Doesn't that make you want to sing about it? It did me. I just went, 'Fucking hell! This is gonna get crazy!'" (Once again, maybe instead of singing about it, he could have made a few more billion developing drones for the U.S. military.)

He calmed down when I asked if he was a prophet or a pioneer. After some thought he replied in a serious tone, "I think I'm just enjoying myself, mate. I'm trying to take myself to a new level, and my music. . . . You've got to keep moving, you've got to keep doing things, you've got to keep yourself alive, first, before you can do anything for anybody else."

Idol recalled how he had come to America 12 years earlier to reinvent himself after his song "Dancing with Myself," which he recorded with his previous band Generation X, died "a horrible death" in England. He promised himself he'd stick it out for a year and braced for some hard times. But the tune became an unlikely club hit in America, so he knew he was on to something. "I was standing in Hurrah [a New York nightclub] at the bar and then 'Dancing with Myself' came on," he recalled. "I couldn't believe it. People rushed to get to the dance floor, chairs were pushed, tables went over. I was the only person left at the bar. It was like, 'That's why I'm here.'"

There wasn't too much science involved. Although he came of age during England's punk rock revolution in the late '70s, Idol considered himself a purveyor of rock 'n' roll dance music, following in the footsteps of Elvis Presley, Little Richard, and the early Beatles. "That's what I always thought rock 'n' roll was. It wasn't just listening to it. That was wrong. That's what I kind of hated about a lot of hippie stuff was that people sat down and watched it. It isn't just cerebral is it? People fuck to it. I thought that was the idea of music."

Solo stardom came quickly for Idol, abetted by his trusty guitarist Steve Stevens. His self-titled 1982 debut album included the hits "White Wedding" and "Hot in the City." The following year he did even better with *Rebel Yell*, its title track, and the moody ballad "Eyes Without a Face." MTV couldn't get enough of the bad-boy rocker and his cartoonish antics. *Whiplash Smile*, recorded in a haze of drugs and debauchery, followed in 1986, and the supposedly more-mature *Charmed Life* in 1990.

Just before the release of *Charmed Life*, while riding his Harley-Davidson, Idol ran a stop sign at the corner of Fountain and Gardner in Hollywood. He was hit by a car, almost lost his leg, and underwent at least five operations. A virtual cripple, he was filmed from the waist up for the music video that accompanied his song "The Cradle of Love," and took to the world's concert stages with a cane.

His modest film career took a hit, though. He was supposed to play Jim Morrison's best friend in Oliver Stone's movie *The Doors*, but the shooting schedule could not be adjusted and his role was downgraded. (Despite aspirations of big-screen stardom using his real name, William Broad, Idol's biggest role was as himself in Adam Sandler's *The Wedding Singer*.)

On the evening of April 29, 1992, when Los Angeles was going up in flames after four white policemen were found not guilty of beating black motorist Rodney King, Idol was at home doing his first recording session for what would be the *Cyberpunk* album. "From my house you could watch," he recalled. "It was like L.A. was replaying the Gulf War. It was weird, some weird karma. Rent-a-thug. The government, the enemy of the people, is attacked by the people it really fears, its own people. I was reading this book by Noam Chomsky. It's fucking great, it's called *What Uncle Sam Really Wants*, and that's what he says. He says that the American government is always protecting itself from its biggest enemy—the American people." He giggled as he flexed his impressive literary muscle for me.

The riots inspired him to write "Shock to the System." The song was initially going to be about Galileo, the shit-stirring astronomer largely ignored by rockers since Queen made him the star of "Bohemian Rhapsody."

"I had a whole other idea for a set of lyrics, which was about Galileo proving the fallibility of the Pope by discovering those planets, rather like [the sci-fi novels and film adaptations] *2001* and *2010* where God sends a sign," Idol said. (I've never read or seen *2001* or *2010*, so can't be sure what he's talking about; I'm pretty sure Galileo merely discovered a couple of satellites orbiting Jupiter.) "By Galileo seeing these two new planets," he continued, "when the Pope had said that there was only ever going to be five, it was almost like God proving the fallibility of the pope. So I was really into that idea—shock to the system."

Instead he chose to glorify the carnage with such lyrics as, "Hell of a night, L.A., it really was. Oh, what a riot. I said yeah, come on. It makes my life feel real." The song has an unmistakable sense of exhilaration, reflecting the temperament of its creator. He took some flak for expressing such fond memories, but he claimed merely to be an observer.

"I think I saw two things—horror and a sense of glee. It was weird," Idol said. "People were actually being heard, they seriously didn't think justice had been served so they did something about it. I thought it was kind of wild, whatever it was whether it was right or wrong, whether it was good or evil, ugly or beautiful, it was wild, weird. Weird.

"The other thing about the riot was it shook the whole world up," he added with mild hyperbole. "Once L.A. rioted, Atlanta went. They started rioting all over America. It really showed you that L.A. isn't just Tinseltown and Hollywood, and that's what the song's talking about as well. It's not just a few fucking actors and a few rich people in Beverly Hills. There's millions of other people here—a lot of them suffering. That's when the journalists had to take notice, didn't they? For once that there was a load of other people here."

Another song, "Tomorrow People," was aimed at the American government: "the world's rent-a-thug," he reiterated, and the creator of "global oppression."

"The first thing they did after the Soviet Union fell under was attack Noriega," he said of the Panamanian leader overthrown at the end of 1989. "If America itself wanted to solve things by negotiation that would take away from their power, so they have to win by fighting so that they can be bigger than their opponents . . . Continuing with that idea is a suicidal idea, it'll only end in some sort of karmic comeback. That's what I think."

That's all very well, but I was worried that Idol was going to end up like some hippie peacenik and disavow his life of sleaze. He quickly calmed my fears, noting that one of the videos for "Heroin"—apparently six videos were made—has "definitely got me with three chicks in a hot tub." It was confusing. Computers and sex. Whoever heard of such a thing?

I felt more comfortable asking him personal questions about his demons and so on. The heroin and the cocaine and the drinking almost killed him during his initial burst of stardom in New York. So he and his patient girlfriend Perri Lister decamped to Los Angeles in 1987, and he dialed down the hedonism when their son Willem was born the following year. But L.A. is not a safe haven for reformed party boys, and the bad habits returned. Perri eventually left him, unable to forgive his flagrant womanizing. For the sake of his son he was trying to keep it together. He recalled that Oliver Stone would urge him to stay excited about the world, otherwise he might just as well be dead inside. "That's partly what I'm tryin' to do. I'm keeping myself alive really."

He stopped doing heroin a few years earlier, but jokingly (I think) said, "I could always do it again, though. Got a line?!" Alcohol was his big vice. "I'm hoping that if it's true that there's better living through science and chemistry, someone will usher something in pretty soon . . . and I'll be able to go on boozing," he said.

The DIY ethos of the punk rock revolution had served Idol well. But, just short of his 38th birthday, he admitted to some artistic insecurities. "Even Bowie said he's always battling with his mediocrity. Christ, if he's battling with it, what do you think I'm doing?" It was a delicious line that the *Los Angeles Times* included in its year-end survey of memorable quotes.

As the interview wound down, we were both a little bored. This was back in the day when I used to prolong interviews for the sake of it, forgetting that it just meant more to transcribe later on. I watched Idol and his band rehearse and didn't feel good about the whole project. The following night, Idol played at Prince's now-shuttered Glam Slam club downtown. He came on after midnight, wearing a polyester space suit and dark shades. His hourlong set began with "Dancing with Myself" and mixed oldies like "Rebel Yell," "Mony Mony," and "White Wedding" with some unloved and quickly forgotten newbies. We partied like it was 1985.

I wrote about Idol exactly a year later when he overdosed on GHB outside a Sunset Strip nightclub and spent a few days in the hospital. His publicist told me he was "feeling a lot of remorse and shame about the whole thing." The next—and last—time I saw him was on Sept. 13, 2001, during an unfortunately timed nightclub residency at the Roxy Theatre. He wisely did not mention the terrorist attacks. Given his enthusiasm for conspiracy theories, that could have been awkward, albeit good copy. "Karmic comeback," anybody?

At 45, Idol was in great shape, though Stevens looked anachronistic with the makeup and the hairspray. At one point during the trip down memory lane, Idol stared at me as I was looking sullen (my default setting). He started laughing and then I did too. When the people are under attack, what else can you do?

PUTTING THE "SEX" IN SEX PISTOLS

Do you feel uncomfortable when two people start making out in front of you? What if it's two guys? What if it's two members of the Sex Pistols, the punk rock band that shook up the stale music scene in the mid-'70s?

Steve Jones and Glen Matlock got hot and heavy when I interviewed them backstage at a festival in 2002, groping each other and engaging in bawdy banter while I tried to ask deep questions. It was my own version of *The Bill Grundy Show*, when Jones called the band's drunken inquisitor a "dirty fucker" on live British television in 1976. I chalked up my experience to a pair of straight guys taking the piss. That's what middle-aged Englishmen do.

I'd been allotted a few minutes to talk with them during the one-off Inland Invasion punk rock festival at a 65,000-seat amphitheater in a remote desert hellhole 60 miles east of Los Angeles. The Sex Pistols, making their first U.S. performance since their 1996 reunion tour, headlined a bill that included Blink 182, the Offspring, Pennywise, Bad Religion, and veteran acts like the Damned and the Buzzcocks. Matlock and Jones were joined by drummer Paul Cook and irascible singer Johnny Rotten, who made sure to tell the crowd that "no fucking way" did the band have anything to do with the event's corporate sponsors.

I met Rotten, born John Lydon, once, and that was an accident. It was a summer evening in 1993. He was at the King's Head, a pub favored by homesick British expats in the coastal community of Santa Monica, when I walked in with a buddy. The place was packed apart from an empty table conveniently next to where Rotten was sitting with two pals. My buddy and I bought beers, headed over to the table, and chatted amongst ourselves. I soon caught Rotten's eye and we talked amiably about beer. He then introduced himself as "John," and one of his cronies, one of them being his brother "Martin Rotten." I pretended not to know who he was, and I think he enjoyed the anonymity of being another Englishman out for a pint.

But it was all too much for me. This was a guy I'd worshiped in high school during the early '80s, long after the Sex Pistols first broke up. So when I excitedly blew cover, the conversation took some weird turns. Rotten said he didn't like me (cool!) and that I was gay (not so cool). He launched into a diatribe about how he didn't want to be linked to any movement, including punk, and for some reason revealed that he had just got some free Nikes.

I would have followed up, but a big-breasted woman (his wife?) came over and they split. Martin tried to take his glass of beer out of the pub, but the bouncer hauled him back inside and the party hung around sheepishly at the door while he finished his drink. Rotten had wisely left his half-full Guinness at the table and I finished it off like I was drinking a magic potion. All I got was a bad cold a few days later. I did interview him on the phone a few times in later years, but there was no way I was going to bring up that story.

I also caught the Sex Pistols' 1996 reunion stop at the Hollywood Palladium, when they raced through most of their catalog in 55 minutes. It was a pleasant piece of classic rock nostalgia, not exactly a revolutionary punk moment. Rotten got pissed off with a "wanker" who was trying to get into the spirit of things by spitting at him. He told him to do it to the earnest guys in Pearl Jam instead. Which brings us up to 2002, and my near-threesome in the desert.

What does it take logistically to get the Sex Pistols together? I know you guys aren't close personal buddies.
GLEN: Sometimes we're into doing it and sometimes we ain't, y'know? I'd like to do it all the time, I would.

Is it like four guys getting into an old comfortable shoe?
GLEN: It's like an old comfortable shoe with a nail coming through. . . . There's a whole load of history and baggage that we share and nobody else in the whole wide world shares, so there must be some kind of empathy there.

How long would it take for you to make another album?
STEVE: A week. It's just finding the right week.

Is he grabbing your ass?
GLEN: He is!
STEVE: No, I'm not. That's me phone! Look! Just for the record . . .

Do you have anything on the horizon?
STEVE: No plans. People keep offering us stuff.

It would be good to have the money.
GLEN: Of course it would. We love money.
STEVE (to Glen): I wanna make love to you.
GLEN: Before the show.
STEVE: I don't want to wait until after the show either.

Have you seen each other naked?
GLEN/STEVE: Yeah.
STEVE: He has a lovely big cock.

How would you describe each band member's personality?
STEVE: Mmm, sexual [giggles].

Tell me about Paul.
GLEN: He ain't in this band. It's just me and Steve.

I left the lovebirds alone and retrieved Matlock's cigarette stub for my collection of really pointless rock 'n' roll memorabilia. It was still boiling hot by the time the Sex Pistols came on after sunset. Someone tossed a beer at Rotten, who responded: "There's some dopey arsehole there who's got more money than sense. If you're gonna buy beers, fuckin' drink 'em, ya wuss! Be a man. Hide in the crowd, you fucking turd."

I reviewed the show in an evenhanded report that began, "In true punk spirit, rowdy music fans pelted the Sex Pistols with beer on Saturday as the one-time scourge of the British establishment played its first U.S. concert in six years outside Los Angeles." I also included references to Rotten's other outbursts (against his drummer, President Bush, and a fan whose only sin was to have long hair: "You're in the wrong fucking building, Lemmy."). I later heard that Sex Pistols management was annoyed by my story and I was placed on the bad-boy list for a few years.

All was forgiven by 2007 when the band played a private show for 500 fans at the Roxy Theatre on the Sunset Strip. It was like déjà vu, sweaty as hell and full of acrid one-liners from Rotten, who guzzled red wine from a bottle and had trouble remembering the lyrics. When a young woman bounded onto the knee-high stage and hugged Jones in the middle of "Submission," Rotten quipped, "Steve Jones always gets the fat ones!" After another woman tried to get up, Rotten went on to plead, "Can the ugly birds stop getting up on stage? It's fucking embarrassing!" Toward the end, after complaining of stomach cramps, he took a lengthy bathroom break that he said left him "15 pounds lighter."

In the home stretch a dude next to me tossed his cocktail at Rotten, and it hit him square on the face. When the band returned for the encore ("Anarchy in the U.K."), Rotten angrily said he'd kill the "coward" if he did it again. I had a pleasant chat afterward with the culprit, who was thrilled to get the shout-out from his hero, and I gave him some brief worldwide infamy by quoting him in my story. His name is Manuel Vasquez, if you're reading this, Johnny!

JOHN CALE, DOUG YULE: VELVETS UNDERGROUND

The only time I spoke with Lou Reed I quickly regretted it. It was in 2003, after he had been inducted into the RockWalk, a process that involved pressing his hands into a framed section of wet cement for display on the footpath outside a guitar store in Hollywood.

Reed allotted a few minutes to the handful of reporters there. I had no pressing issues, so facetiously asked if he worried about the risk of confusion between his old band the Velvet Underground and Velvet Revolver, the new Guns N' Roses spinoff. He answered with a lengthy Black Angel's Death Stare that made me feel pretty insignificant for a few days.

But at least I didn't compound the indignity by asking him for his autograph afterward, as my starstruck colleagues did—and what a puny scribble it was. (Mind you, if I'd known he'd be dead a decade later. . .) That night he played a theater gig at the Wiltern, invited a tai chi master to prance around the stage, and ordered security guards to eject a chattering fan who had apparently annoyed the freaky backing singer Lou was toting around the world, an oddity named Antony.

Fortunately, two of Reed's former Velvet Underground colleagues were less curmudgeonly. John Cale, Reed's sometime nemesis, spoke with me in 1993 after the band's original lineup reunited for the first time in 25 years. In 1997, I called Cale's replacement, Doug Yule, to discuss a reissued album. To this day, the two VU alumni have never met.

Cale, a Welsh-born viola player, co-founded the Velvet Underground in 1965 with Reed. The lineup solidified around guitarist Sterling Morrison and drummer Maureen "Moe" Tucker. Taking their name from the title of a smutty book, the stern-faced, leather-clad foursome soon became the toast of the New York art scene, providing a grimly satisfying alternative to the flower-power anthems of the hippies and peaceniks. Their avant-garde improvisation, rooted in basic '50s rock, was a massive influence on David Bowie, punk rockers, and the so-called alternative bands of the '80s and '90s.

Their best-known album is the first one, 1967's *The Velvet Underground & Nico*, which was nominally produced by their patron Andy Warhol. Nico, the pop artist's throaty German protégée, added funereal warmth to such ditties as "All Tomorrow's Parties" and "I'll Be Your Mirror." Reed explored the hard-drug culture with "I'm Waiting for the Man" and "Heroin," a song he wrote in college. A reading of Leopold von Sacher-Masoch's fetishist novel of the same name inspired "Venus in Furs." The album has come to be known as "the banana album" on account of the peel-off banana sticker on the Warhol-designed cover. The banana became the center of a lawsuit in 2012 when Reed and Cale—the legal owners of the Velvet Underground entity—sued the Warhol estate for appropriating the design in tacky merchandise. (The parties reached a confidential settlement in 2013.)

It's sad to think that more people own VU banana T-shirts, refrigerator magnets, and iPad cases than the album itself, which peaked at No. 171 on the chart. The 1968 follow-up, *White Light/White Heat* (No. 199), marked Cale's swan song, but not after he got to narrate "The Gift," a comical ode to a hapless college kid whose brain is accidentally sliced open by an old flame.

Reed ousted Cale and replaced him with the less-confrontational Yule, who played bass and guitar. This lineup released two albums,

1969's *The Velvet Underground* (No. 197) and 1970's *Loaded*, which did not chart, and then Reed quit the group to become a mainstream rock star. Yule was left in charge of a revolving lineup of players until the flailing enterprise was put down in 1973.

Cale went on to release dozens of solo albums, produced recordings for others, including the Stooges, and briefly married fashion designer Betsey Johnson; Tucker raised a family and worked at a Walmart in Georgia; Morrison earned a doctorate in medieval studies and became a tugboat captain in Texas; Yule ended up in the Pacific Northwest making cabinets and drawing plans for store fixtures.

Reed and Cale papered over their differences to reunite the original Velvet Underground lineup in 1993. Their brief European tour included a few dates opening for U2. A live album, *MCMXCIII*, was released later that year. But by that stage the principals had fallen out again, killing any chances of additional touring or recording.

Yule, at that time living simply in the Seattle-area community of Bothell with his wife and young son, was not invited to participate, cementing his status as the group's forgotten member. "When the reunion came out and they were traveling, people would say, 'How come you're not with them?'" he told me. "And I had to resolve some of that, and I did deal with some of my old feelings. It did hurt me at the time, it's the 'be asked' kinda thing where you'd like to be asked even though you know you're gonna say no, because you can't afford to go for one reason or another. But you still would like to be asked."

Cale and I spoke just before the release of *MCMXCIII*, when additional touring seemed a possibility. He said the reunion had been "somewhat" unchallenging. Tensions with Reed were obvious. "Ideally, what we wanted to do was for the four of us to contribute and have something that was the product of the four of us, not be second-class citizens and be sidemen," he said.

Why did you reunite? It all seems to have happened quickly and begs the question why didn't you do it earlier?

I guess it's still a mystery. If you think of string quartets, whether the Juilliard String Quartet or the Guarneri String Quartet, these are people that are really intensely involved with each other all the time because rehearsal and practice is really essential. And here we are someone who can pick up our instruments after 28 years and still get it all together in a short period of time. That kind of makes it a natural phenomenon.

Which elements of the stage performance were similar, and which were different from the old days?

One thing I missed was Lou's dancing. Lou's the dancer. I kinda wished he'd done more of that. When you have limited objectives like we did, I think we did a lot of work in a very short period of time. We achieved what we set out to do which was very important. There's nothing that we did that we didn't want to achieve and we didn't set out to do something that we failed at. So from a nuts-and-bolts point of view, we did what we set out to do. So there are no complaints there.

Was it a bit weird doing stuff from the albums that you weren't on?

It wasn't so much that it was weird, but I kind of missed the collaboration. I'm a collaborator. There were two [new] songs: One was a funny song that was a throwaway ["What's Wrong With This Picture?"] and then there was "Coyote," which really didn't demonstrate what we were like as a band very much. We just made it sound competent. It didn't have the magic of "All Tomorrow's Parties" or "Venus in Furs" in it.

When were they written?

They were written in rehearsal, by the whole band.

Do you think there will be more collaborations along those lines?

Well, I certainly hope so. That's what we're about. Playing the catalog is fine; I mean we're very good at it. But what I think more of our mission is, is to provide stuff like "All Tomorrow's Parties" and "Sister Ray" and the more adventurous stuff.

Did you hang out together after the shows, or did you go your separate ways?

We had a lot of fun. Sometimes we'd hang out together, sometimes we wouldn't. Nothing pretty much gets in my hair when

I'm out there. Everybody seemed to have their families with them, so everybody was happy. When we got to open for U2, that was the least satisfying from a musical point of view for all of us. It was impressive to run into U2 and study their organization and their modus operandi and to see that this is a band that may have as many problems as the next band but you never know about it. Nobody finds out about it. They are so disciplined, and they have a great time. They enjoy themselves. Going swimming in Lake Geneva was very entertaining. It's a great way to do a heavy tour like that and have a good time. But in the last analysis, they're the least satisfying shows because you cut your set down to an hour, and those people are really not there for you. They may enjoy you and may revere you but they're really not there for you. And you don't know where things are from a technical point of view. You do not have the run of their equipment. It's a limited sort of satisfaction in a way.

How has the band's relationship with each other changed over time? Are things still the same as they were in 1965?

Very much so. You're just aware that nobody's changed, everybody has the same pattern. It's just now that you've got a certain amount of understanding of it and hopefully patience for it, so that you can get past the initial shock of realizing it.

Was it difficult for you and Lou to return to a band dynamic after successful solo outings?

I can imagine it was difficult for him. I sympathize with his position in that he was definitely the most famous of all of us, and having been in his band where he pretty much can dictate what happens. When it comes to Velvet Underground nobody can dictate what happens, because we're all such fiercely individual that it wouldn't work. And that's not the way to get the best out of us anyway, because we like puttering around and trying different things and so on. You can't get control over that. That's just the waiving of an imagination.

Can you describe the other guys in a nutshell?

Moe has a heart as big as all our doors. Moe is just unbelievable. She hit those drums, it was monstrous. There's nobody like her in the world. Sterling likes being thrown in the deep end. He likes being given problems, he likes solving problems. The more you throw at him the happier he is. Lou can never get his guitar loud enough. There was never a single note that came from his guitar that wasn't a beautiful sound. He finally got himself a setup where that amp will do anything he wants. It sounds gorgeous.

Would you work with them individually?

Yeah, it was so much fun working with them that I do want to do something with the two of them, Sterling and Moe. I think if I do a band album, I definitely want to do it with them.

But not with Lou?

Of course. If the Velvet Underground wants to pursue another project, that's fantastic. But I mean separately from that.

How did you and Lou either overcome or harness the creative differences you have with each other?

By respecting each other's space. There was too much work to be done. We wouldn't have been able to do it, if any of that was happening.

How would you describe those creative differences with Lou?

I don't think he really understands it, and this forces it into an even smaller window of magical opportunity, that if it doesn't happen within a really small window then it's not gonna happen. If you look at the stuff we did on the "banana album," that was the result of a year's work, of one day a week for a whole year of just playing this material over and changing the arrangements. That really took a lot of patience and doleful work of sitting around and trying this and trying that. When I look back, that's a lot of really constructive labor. We didn't have that time this time, we didn't have that luxury. All we had time to do was to get our technical aspects together and lock them in, and make sure that whatever happened we didn't sound like somebody who couldn't tune their instruments.

What do you mean about Lou not really understanding it?

I think there's a valor to mistakes, and that kind of muddling along—changing ideas and trying different things—is something that you've really got to do all the time rather than just when the Velvet Underground are together. What the Velvet Underground really was, was four individuals puttering around, trying to find something a little different, and trying this and trying that. When you have different instruments and stuff like that then you have a lot of ground to go over before you arrive at the finished product. I don't think the finished product for the Velvet Underground is just bass, guitar, drums. There are all sorts of different things that you can try, that we have tried. In the end, even if we had time that's not what we would have ideally wanted to do. Ideally what we wanted to do was for the four of us to contribute and have something that was the product of the four of us, not be second-class citizens and be sidemen. We know what that means. What we're really best at is coming up with original stuff. When we first played together it was improvisation, and that was much more interesting than knocking out well-honed rock 'n' roll songs.

So you were unchallenged in that regard?
Somewhat. Yes.

Now that the tour's done, what's your state of mind?
It's done. I'm happy that we found that we can do that. It's obvious what we haven't done, which is come up with new and original stuff that continues in the vein of all the stuff that's on the first two albums, and that's it. It's clear what wasn't done and needs to be covered.

Would you do it again?
Yeah, no problem.

Is there a U.S. tour on the cards?
Not at the moment. I think we're waiting to find out what the album does. I guess we're hoping that things go well enough that there'll be some interest. I know that there's interest in us doing it here. It's always been something that we've debated a lot about, and at the moment we're just not addressing it.

Does it frustrate you that you never got commercial recognition at the time?
No. Spilled milk. We were never very good at doing things for money anyway. I think we were doing things because we were excited about the ideas that were there. Because we didn't work on ideas this time, it leaves us still that hurdle to cross, because we're very good at that.

Is the back catalog selling well these days?
No. The sales are not anywhere near what you'd think they were.
Do you listen to the Velvet Underground records much?
No, not at all. I don't think I'll listen to this one very much either. It's kind of in your face most of the time. It's not something you put on and sort of relax to.
Is there much stuff in the vaults?
I don't know that there's that much. There's probably more in the bootleg department than there is in the vaults. I was just given bootlegs of the tour! We had a meeting about [reissues] but I don't remember very much, because there was so much bureaucracy. It was tiresome.
Did the reunion work out nicely, financially?
In many ways, in many ways. I'm glad that the record is there as a document. "Yeah! That's what we sounded like." It sounded pretty healthy to me.
The Velvet Underground is described as the most influential band of the last 20 years, do you agree with that?
I have no idea. I buy that [Brian Eno's oft-repeated observation that VU's few fans all went out and formed bands of their own], but it's very difficult for me to see where the influence is. I don't know any bands with violas in them, that many. And I don't see anybody that really has arrangements that are like any of ours. I don't think "Sister Ray" is ameliorated by many people. So it's really a little stretch to say that it's influential. Maybe universal acclaim is one thing, but not reflected in sales is a little category that the record companies would love to take advantage of. It's a palliative. As long as you keep talking there is no recession everybody believes it. It's the same kind of category that you talk about people that are influential when they're really just liked a lot. The one thing was that we never had a record that really reflected how we sounded. There was always something that was going on. We tried so hard to make it difficult for them to record us on *White Light, White Heat*. We were intolerable. That's one of the weird things about this recording that made me twitch every once in a while, I thought, Hey, we're making it really easy for them to record us. There's something unrevolutionary about it.

What bands today convey the Velvet Underground ethos?

I don't think there's anyone, really. I don't have that grating feeling from them [bands like Nirvana, Soundgarden]. Tom Waits sort of gets my goat a little. Tom Waits has a way of presenting material that's really interesting and aggressive—a little more aggressive, I feel, than Nirvana.

Do you think much about Andy Warhol?

I do, yeah, every once in a while. Positively, always positively. What a gentleman he was. All this new talk today about the data superhighway, all of Hollywood is so happy that this is happening, that television and telephones have united so that they can find more markets for their useless old programs that are lying in vaults, they don't know what to do with. Everybody's gonna be famous. They're going to have these couch potatoes with cameras on the TVs and they're going to be able to talk on the telephones visually with people. I like the superhighway, as a data retrieval system to get information. But the way democracies worked in general is to provide people with so many choices that there is no choice. That's a pretty cynical view, but that's the way the data highway is gonna be.

The live album, recorded mostly during the second of a three-night stand at the Olympia in Paris, peaked at No. 180 on the U.S. chart in December. The band never played together again. Sterling Morrison died of non-Hodgkin's lymphoma in 1995, two days after turning 53. A few days later, it was announced that the band would be inducted into the Rock and Roll Hall of Fame the following year. Yule, once again, was left off the list.

Yule and I spoke on his 50th birthday in February 1997. Coincidentally, he was given a violin that day and a career change was born. The self-confessed "late bloomer" went in to business making and repairing violins, violas, and cellos. His experience was documented in the 2009 short film *The Violinmaker*. He also performs with an old-time string band called RedDog.

Hailing from Long Island, New York, Yule was playing with local bands in Boston when he got the call to join the Velvet Underground.

He had seen the band once and was fairly impressed but in no way could be described as a fan. He was just happy to play in a band. "There's nothing I've ever experienced that's as satisfying as the community of a band that travels together and works together. It's a nice feeling to belong someplace and know where you belong," he said.

After the Velvet Underground broke up, Yule toured with Reed for a year, "and then we had a falling-out. He decided I was being disloyal by wanting to be in a band by myself. So he hasn't spoken to me since then, since '75. I talked to Maureen and Sterling a few times over the last 20 years. When Sterling was dying, I talked to Maureen on the phone a few times. It's been a peripheral kind of thing; they pretty much do what they do. Our main contact has been through the lawyer who handles all of the business and management or suits or whatever they do."

His last communication with Reed at the time of the interview had been in the mid-'80s, when Yule was working in a shop in Brooklyn. Reed was doing a book signing in lower Manhattan and Yule stopped by to say hello on his way to a nearby tai chi class. But the line was "humungous," so Yule stood at the window and looked in for a minute. Reed "kinda looked up and saw me and he kinda looked back down again and finished signing, and then he looked up again at me and gave this kinda half-nervous smile, and kinda waved and I waved, and that's the last communication we had."

(In 2009, Yule joined Reed and Tucker for a Q&A at the New York Public Library to promote a Velvet Underground coffee-table book to which they had contributed. A year or two beforehand, the trio had gathered for a memorabilia exhibit that later became part of the book. "Other than that we exchanged an email or two and that's the extent of our interactions," Yule wrote me in an email in 2011.)

Yule only learned that Morrison had been sick when, four or five weeks before he died, the band's lawyer called to say that Morrison was in remission. "And then a week after that, I got another call—I think it was from Maureen—that it had popped up again. They had thought it was gone, but it wasn't and he had weeks left. I called, but he was on morphine and really unable to talk. So I spoke to [Morrison's wife] Martha and I spoke to Maureen, but I never really got to close things with Sterling. Somewhere in my mind, I always believed we would get together again and play some music, but it was not to be." Yule did not attend Morrison's funeral. It cost too much money to fly to Poughkeepsie, New York.

Even though Yule played on more songs than Cale, distribution of performance royalties (as opposed to the songwriting royalties that went mostly to Reed) was weighted in favor of the original members. In a good year, Yule received $10,000. "That's a lot of money when you had nothing before," he said. "It's the difference between my wife having to work and not having to work. That's what's been the big payoff for me is that she's been able to stay home with the baby and she can go to school now. We're not rich, but we get by. We pay the bills, we live in a little house that's not ours but at least it's comfortable." (Yule had a four-year-old son at the time, and four grown children from his first marriage.)

Yule considered himself a musical facilitator for Reed, posing less of a threat to his musical dominance than Cale, "who was another big thinker—and I'm not a big thinker. I used to think I was, but I'm not." Both Reed and Yule were heavily influenced by pop music from the '50s, including doo-wop and basic four-chord rock 'n' roll. Additionally, Yule was heavily into folk and bluegrass in high school and then returned to rock 'n' roll when the Beatles came out. "I was always fairly mainstream. I have a very melodic sense as opposed to a dissonant sense. I'm less experimental and I'm more conventional in my musical tastes. I did have classical training in grade school and high school—but nothing really extreme—and church music, because my mother was in a choir and I sang with her."

Our conversation centered on *Loaded*, which was being reissued with an extra disc of outtakes. Yule was disappointed with *Loaded* at the time of its release, in part because Tucker was busy being pregnant and her role was filled by a handful of drummers, including Yule's brother Billy. The tracks also underwent much editing as various producers and engineers came and went. He much preferred the third album, which was a true collaboration among the four members at the same time. That album's relative mellowness, with melodic tunes such as "Candy Says" and "Pale Blue Eyes" and recorded in Los Angeles, accurately reflected the band's positive frame of mind. They stood in sharp contrast to the visceral cuts from the first album.

But by the time the band started recording *Loaded*, its debut for Atlantic Records after it had been dropped by MGM's Verve Records imprint, manager Steve Sesnick's divide-and-conquer mentality was weighing on everyone, Yule said. "Just the fact that he could say, 'We're gonna record an album without Maureen,' and we would do it indicates how much control he had over everybody, as opposed to what I would have preferred to see happen, which is, 'No, no. We can't do that, we'll wait till she's ready,' which we could have done."

To Yule's shock, Reed abruptly left as the album was being finished, allowing Sesnick to install Yule as the puppet leader. "I was like a Pavlov's dog in those days; sometimes it's still that today. He would say, 'Wanna be a star?' I'd just smile and say yes."

The plan was to make an album "loaded" with hits, and indeed "Sweet Jane" and "Rock & Roll" are the closest the band got to mainstream radio fare. Yule handled the vocals on the seductively warm opener "Who Loves the Sun" as well as "New Age" and "Ride into the Sun." The sessions also yielded the pop classic "Satellite of Love," which turned up on Reed's 1972 album *Transformer*. All the songs on *Loaded* were credited as group compositions when the album first came out, thanks to Sesnick. But Yule said Reed was the actual writer, fair and square.

"Lou wrote the songs and that's undeniable. He put the words down; he invented the melodies out of his mind. He would have a melody and he would not know how to chord it—and this didn't happen all the time, because most of the stuff was simple. But occasionally that would happen. I'd say, 'Sing a harmony for me' and I'd put chords to it. I helped him to get out what he was trying to do at the time. We all did it that way. We'd help arrange cooperatively as a group."

No, Yule did not have his own cool Velvet Underground memorabilia or boxes of old recordings gathering dust under the bed. He sold four acetate recordings to a collector in Japan and believed they ended up on some bootlegs. A daughter had a few posters. He said he was recognized by his name, usually in checkout lines, but never by what he looked like. He did put his Velvet Underground experiences on paper, but wasn't happy with the results.

The reunion and Rock and Roll Hall of Fame snubs, oddly enough, helped him move on. The Velvet Underground was a small part of his life, one of many defining points. Once he examined his unresolved feelings and said to himself, "It really does bother me not to be called and it really does bother me to be, sort of, the fifth Beatle," he felt better. "Once you let go of that and say that, a lot of that hurt has gone, and then you can get on with life."

DANCING WITH IGGY POP

In April 2007, Iggy Pop celebrated his 60th birthday by playing a show with his reunited rock band the Stooges in San Francisco. It was not only a milestone for the so-called "godfather of punk," but also a significant event for me.

I had seen him maybe a dozen times, but had never had the opportunity to join the traditional crowd-participation segment when fans get to dance on stage during a song. This time would be different, I vowed. I watched most of the show from a prime position on the floor of the stately Warfield, and slowly moved toward the front as the show progressed. The opening licks of "No Fun," a tune from the band's self-titled 1969 debut, were my signal, and Iggy invited fans to join him. The stage was hardly a Marines-style obstacle course, but I just couldn't get a footing and my quest looked pathetically doomed. Just then a fan above me held out a hand, and hoisted me up. The hand belonged to a girl.

About two dozen people were already on stage. I got my bearings, looked out into the audience, and basked in my sudden rock stardom. I sauntered over to guitarist Ron Asheton, who was doing his best to stay away from the masses, and watched Iggy contort himself. As usual, he was shirtless. W-shaped waves of veins rippled across his chiseled torso. His blue jeans seemed sprayed on and his long straight hair well shampooed. If this is what a lifetime of drugs and decadence can do to a man, I need to find a needle and a spoon. Roadies eventually herded the Iggy-dubbed "Bay Area dancers" backstage after the song ended, and we ended up back on the dance floor.

During the encore, the crowd sang along as the band struck up "Happy Birthday," and balloons bearing Iggy's image dropped from the ceiling. A fan handed him a white T-shirt inscribed "Birthday Boy Iggy," which Iggy proudly displayed to his unimpressed bandmates. He seemed thrilled by all the attention, but did not dwell too much on the special occasion. He muttered a few thanks along the way before returning to scheduled programming: stagediving, manic singing and dancing, spitting into the crowd, scampering onto the speakers, and throwing his microphone stand around the stage. The whole thing was over in 80 minutes. Iggy doubtless headed to bed with an obscure novel and a cup of tea, and I went back to my hotel room to write up my story. Missions accomplished.

I assumed his life was happier than it had been a decade earlier, when his marriage crumbled and he got dangerously introspective. The enjoyably grim spoken-word intro on his 1999 album *Avenue B* said it all, "It was in the winter of my 50th year when it hit me: I was really alone and there wasn't a hell of a lot of time left."

The only thing that prevented me from buying into the album completely was that Iggy distanced himself from the lyrics when pressed during interviews. I shared my disappointment with him during a 2001 conversation.

"It's a shame, Dean, that one does interviews at all," he said. "My great solace in that is that the nature of the medium, the CD medium, renders it more lasting than the other media! In a year the CD will still be there, albeit low on somebody's pile or dust-covered in the corner, whereas hopefully the newspaper or magazine, the publication will be shredded or decomposing somewhere, and the stuff has a chance to live. You're damn right. The interviews get in the way and I wasn't ready or willing or able to relive what went into that record in the interviews. No, way, dude! No fuckin' way!"

* * *

But a few years before that, Iggy had been very willing to relive one of the episodes that couldn't have helped his marriage to Suchi, his second wife. On a balmy Los Angeles night in 1992, Iggy and a pal were cruising the seedy warehouse district. Iggy met a shady lesbian couple on the street, did a back-alley deal with them, and returned to his car with one of the ladies. She had some methedrine, an amphetamine derivative. The next morning Iggy woke up and his female companion said to him, "Iggy, you have got a biggie!"

The incident was recounted, pretty much word for word the following year, in the song "Wild America," the first single from his album *American Caesar*.

"It's just a straight true narrative," he told me just before *American Caesar* came out. "It was influenced really by rap songs: Every time I turned on MTV I'd see some spade bragging about 'Yeah, my dick's this big' and 'Yo, I did this to this ho.' And I thought the theatricality of the presentation and the narrative quality in a lot of those songs was to be emulated if possible: 'Let me try that, I think I could do that.' So I searched my memory—'Oh yeah, there was one night last year'—and came up with that."

(Efforts to confirm the details with his driving buddy, Delicious Vinyl Records co-founder Matt Dike, both at the time and more recently, were unsuccessful.)

American Caesar marked the follow-up to the 1990 Don Was–produced comeback *Brick By Brick*, which was my tragically belated introduction to Iggy Pop. After peaking at a relatively impressive No. 90 on the U.S. pop album chart, bolstered by the radio-friendly duet on "Candy" with Kate Pierson of the B52s, *Brick* sold about a quarter of a million copies. It would be his last entry on the Billboard 200 until 2007.

I was surprised that *American Caesar* failed to chart. The grunge revolution that Iggy helped fuel more than 20 years earlier was raging. It seemed natural for him to ride that wave. But Iggy waited several months after the album's release to tour, an executive at his Virgin Records label later explained. It couldn't have had anything to do with Iggy being on a useless label.

Anyway, the executive was only half right. Iggy was also on the road before it came out. That's when I called him. He was checked in at his London hotel under the name Julius Caesar, and was watching a lady in a miniskirt wheel a pushchair through a park in South Kensington. He and his band were playing festivals as well as their own headlining shows, previewing a few songs including "Wild America" and a surprisingly well-received ballad called "Fuckin' Alone."

But he was wary of pushing unfamiliar material down fans' throats. "When guys get to be my vintage, a lot of times they just sort of descend from the heavens every three or four years when they have something new to sell, and they sort of come down and say, 'Pardon me, but I've run out of cash. Would you care to attend a concert and buy my new line of products?' So it all gets a little bit like 'Who is this fuck, anyway?'"

It's been three years since *Brick By Brick* came out. Can you summarize in 15 seconds or less what's happened between then and now in your life?

Yeah, sure. One of the years was just touring *Brick By Brick* and that was basically it. By the end of that year there was a realization, "My God, you've had a successful record!" And it also upped the success of my entire other catalog, which is all in print now.

I sorta went, "'Oh my God, I have resources." And the first thing I decided to do was I wanted a place outside America where I could base so that I wouldn't be totally subject to the American point of view and the cacophony and the bullshit: "We are the number one burger. Kiss my ass! Yo!" et cetera. So I built a house in Mexico and got established there, in a remote part of a foreign country—that took about six months—and started gardening. And while I did that, I looked at reclaiming an old way to approach my writing, which was just as low tech as possible with a very cheap acoustic guitar, a Spiro pad, and a pencil—which is how I started. And then somewhere along the line, I got caught up in the horror of tracks, and 4-tracks, and "Let's save this and let's call up Number 23 and see if I have a poem that goes with it, et cetera, et cetera, et cetera." And I started working like that far away from the clutches of MTV or anything else from the big—capital "I"—Industry. That took me midway through the second year. Then I took that stuff to New York to my home base, along with a couple of pets I'd acquired in Mexico. One of them was a puppy, a stray puppy. I raised the puppy, which was an interesting experience, learning that puppies shit and pee! And want constant attention and whine if you don't hold 'em. That was very interesting.

Iggy also assisted Balkan composer Goran Bregovic on the soundtrack for Emir Kusturica's 1993 film *Arizona Dream*. The first single, "In the Deathcar," related the quotidian experience of riding around with an underage girl "after she gives you a handjob and neither of you have anything more to say to each other," he said.

Iggy then headed to New Orleans to record the *American Caesar* tracks at Daniel Lanois' Kingsway Studio, an old three-story townhouse where he and his band also lived with their wives and girlfriends. "It was harder work. It was a lot harder than having your little setup in the hotel and your privacy and you can go home after eight hours, and go, 'I hate those fuckin' guys!' None of that."

The album alternated between rockers and ballads, spanning a "sonic emotional spectrum," per *Rolling Stone*'s rave four-star review. "Wild America," featuring an ad lib by Henry Rollins, led in to "Mixin' the Colors," a rare socio-political observation about racial tolerance. But the feel-good vibes disappeared with the quietly seething "Jealousy" and the venomous "Hate." My favorite one was the moody, acoustic guitar-driven road tune "Highway Song," with the line "I understand the circus well. I've played the clown when down he fell."

You refer to "playing the clown," with the implication that you've been entertaining us, and we've been laughing at you.

At times I've played the clown, but I think everybody has. In their most impotent moments everyone plays the clown.

Are you weary of playing the clown for the rest of your life though? There may be times when you want people to take you seriously?

I haven't played the clown in a long time. It's been a long, long time since I was in that position. I'm a respectable citizen!

Are you in danger of becoming too respectable? You almost qualify for the Rock and Roll Hall of Fame [the Stooges eventually made it in 2010 after years of rejection].

I suppose I could, but I don't expect them to come knocking my door down. I think I'm already in another kinda hall of fame. I think that's a little better. I'm happy where I am right now and I'd like to go further. As far as being respectable, I'm happy to be as respectable as is appropriate as long as I'm useful. You want to be useful, that's the main thing. And that's always been the motive force behind my self-critique of my work. I try to say, "Well, is this really useful? Or does this resemble the git I saw last week who was totally useless but nobody realized it?" Or maybe they did, or whatever.

Do you have more self-confidence now than you did before?

I have more self-confidence. I certainly have a great deal more self-confidence about, let's say, my past work. There's been a certain amount of vindication there: an album like [the Stooges' final album] *Raw Power*, that was in the 39-cent bin at [now-defunct L.A. record store] Aron's very shortly after its recording, then subsequently cost that many dollars again as a collector's item to get, and now does very steady business and is included in the various top-so-many albums of the century or universe or whatever, lists that you see. So in worldly terms there's a certain confidence that is inevitably going to come after you see your work mentioned a lot. I feel a certain quality to what I do. Whether or not that's something that any particular person would or should be interested in, is another whole question. There's certainly no reason that somebody couldn't completely ignore me and have a very good life! Without any help from my stuff whatsoever! But if they do, I'm gonna do everything in my power to get them to check it out, y'know?

There's a whole generation of kids for whom the Stooges aren't even a memory. They weren't even born. So we don't have these expectations of you cutting yourself up—
You mean you were born, like what, 1971? Or something?
Nah, 1968.
Oh, you were born though?
Barely.
Just barely. You were very young. I think in the case of that band, what happened there is that I had a girlfriend when I was in that band who I married very briefly and she always said, "Well, these guys are a bunch of bums, this band's never gonna make it, why don't you leave?" And I said, "This band'll make it or I'll die first." And basically the band made it. It just took a long time. We went into the black, as far as our record royalties, 20 years after we started. So it started in '89 really. And basically, somewhere along in the '70s people started paying attention to us. It doesn't really matter, especially in these days when everything's so fake and disembodied and de-physicalized anyway, it doesn't really matter whether we're there or not! Once the recordings are there and the pictures are there and the idea of us is there, we're just as present for you, probably more so, as we might have been for the erstwhile ragtag collection of numbed-out bikers and drifting runaway chicks, high school dropouts, drug-deluded avant-gardists, fags, hags, and derelicts that we played to.

You said a few years ago that you wanted to be like John Lee Hooker or Muddy Waters. Are you still on course for that?
I kinda feel like I'm kind of a little bit like that now. Yeah, I feel pretty good about that part. That's the part of this whole ball of shit, that's the part I feel most good about, is like I feel like I made a little musical contribution.

Not only did *American Caesar* fail to chart, but so did 1996's enjoyably sophomoric *Naughty Little Doggie*, the aforementioned *Avenue B*, and 2001's raucous *Beat 'Em Up*. But at least *American Caesar* and *Avenue B* made a *Mojo* magazine list of Iggy's best solo albums, coming in at No. 6 and No. 9, respectively.

* * *

Iggy and I reconnected by phone to discuss *Beat 'Em Up* ("lame-brained rock," per the above *Mojo* survey), and two days later he appeared on *Late Night with David Letterman*. He took to the stage of the Ed Sullivan Theater shirtless and sporting gold elbow-length gloves and a necklace crowned by a head of broccoli. He barked right in the faces of the uncomfortably bemused tourists in the front rows. The song he performed was called "Mask," which was inspired by Slipknot, the Iowa heavy metal band whose members sport grotesque masks on stage. Iggy told me how he visited them once after a show.

"They were demasked and in a change of clothes, and the sorta girl that probably 'knew' her way backstage from other experiences approached one of them with a drink in her hand. He was taller and she looked up at him and she said, 'Which mask are you?' And I just thought, 'Whoaaaaa!' And I wasn't sure what I thought. It just got me. That was like a tripwire to startin' that song."

The title track references his parents, former executive secretary Louella and schoolteacher James Osterberg Sr., in the last stanza: "Mom and Dad worked and saved, good and honest every day. For their sweat, what did they get? An old-age home and a medical debt."

They're both dead now?
No, my dad's still alive and he's recovered. But when my mom had a long illness, that led to a death and he practically killed himself trying to care for her, and then went into a tailspin and a depression after. In fact there's an article in my local news yesterday to the effect that Florida now leads the nation in murder-suicides because of old people. It's a classic setup now: old, sick lady, depressed husband, lovers all their life, and he decides the best thing to do is to kill us both.

Do you have a death fantasy? Do you wonder what your funeral would be like?
I never think about the funeral but I think a lot about my life in terms of my death. I always have since I was a kid, and it helped me

to do chancier things. I thought, Fuck, y'know? This is my life. This is a one-shot deal here. I don't wanna do what I don't wanna do. It was a great escapist tool! I don't wanna stay in school, and I feel good playing music. And everybody said, "If you play music you're throwing your life away." And I was like, Well, OK, but I'll throw it away and I'll be a scumbag, but at least I'll feel good. I think in those terms, and I think about things that you wanna do before you die and also how you feel about yourself. Yeah, it helps. So that was that.

Death is one of my favorite subjects, which is why I got off on *Avenue B*. And *Beat 'Em Up* revisited that topic with "Death Is Certain." Coincidentally, the bassist in Iggy's band was killed in a drive-by shooting just before the album came out. Lloyd "Mooseman" Roberts was best known for his work with Ice-T's speed-metal band Body Count. Iggy was proud that he had a black guy in his band. "It was not lost on me that there's a lot of racial mixing and blending, and racial-style blending is a trend in American rock," he said. "I didn't really want to turn a baseball cap backwards and pose like a black guy. So I got one.... I can't imagine a better name for somebody that does that instrument than Mooseman. That's what you want, y'know?"

But back to Iggy...

You're 54 with a physique to kill for, but how long can you keep it up for in terms of stage presentation?
I can work as long as I like, I'm confident of that. But again, more than most people care to notice, I've already changed things. My life is much less physical than it was. If you looked at my work schedule from the last year, you would have found voiceover work, acting gigs, lectures, hire-outs as a songwriter, and guest shots as a singer, with music ranging from jazz with Françoise Hardy to techno trance with Death in Vegas. So, there's more than one thing I can do. If you look at the number of actual gigs I play in a year, if you look at 1985 through 1990 and I'm doing a hundred gigs a year, now it's somewhere around 25 to 30.

* * *

Iggy was 56 when he reunited for the first time in three decades with Stooges bandmates Ron Asheton and his drummer brother Scott on a couple of tracks of his 2003 album *Skull Ring*. They recorded a Stooges album, *The Weirdness*, which ended his 17-year chart drought by lasting one week, at No. 130, in March 2007.

Later that month, I saw the Stooges for the first time when they performed for about 300 fans at a Yahoo Webcast on the 20th Century Fox lot. The nine-song set included two breaks where Iggy, the Ashetons, and bassist Mike Watt (subbing for late Stooge Dave Alexander) took chairs at the front of the stage to answer questions from the older-skewing hipster audience. "I'm starting to feel like [former *American Idol* judge] Paula Abdul sitting here," Iggy joked at one point, heavily tanned and bare-chested as usual.

Someone asked about his slim physique. He credited tai chi exercises, "but I'm not spiritual about it," he noted. "I had a benefactor, and when I hit about 45, he just went, 'You're either gonna be like the potato, or The Dude [Jeff Bridges' slacker character in *The Big Lebowski*]."

Ron Asheton recalled that he used to forage for food from a supermarket dumpster in Los Angeles after the Stooges broke up in 1974, and said the reunion was the highlight of his career. Iggy wandered into the audience at the end of the show. I shook his hand, and he said, "Thanks for coming."

It's December 2011, and 64-year-old Iggy is back at the Warfield with the Stooges. But the Ashetons are not there. Scott, 62, was ill for much of the tour and replaced by longtime Iggy drummer Larry Mullins. Ron died of an apparent heart attack in 2009, reportedly undiscovered at his Detroit home for several days. He was 60. In his place was James Williamson, also 62, who had joined the Stooges in time to record their final album, 1973's *Raw Power*. After the band broke up, Williamson worked with Iggy for a bit and then quit the business to become an electrical engineer at Sony. Stooges redux was his retirement lifestyle.

I flew up from Los Angeles a few hours before the show, bought a $50 ticket at the door, and set up base in the second row of the mosh pit. I had not worked out much during the year and was worried about jumping up on the stage. I wasn't even sure what the crowd-participation song would be. The invite went out early in the set. "Everything's cool," Iggy said. "C'mon, do what you want!" The intro to "Shake Appeal" was well underway while I was struggling to cross the no man's land between the metal barricade and the stage. A bouncer tried to throw me back into the audience but I wormed out of his grasp. The last addition to the dance lineup, I conducted a furious air bass duel with Mike Watt, and bounced around the stage feeling like Justin Bieber in my hoodie. It's all on YouTube. "We wanna thank our very generous, lovely, and well - coordinated Bay Area spazzes," Iggy said as we exited to loud applause and a doleful saxophone accompaniment.

I awoke the next day with bruised shins and sore muscles to show for my four minutes of exertion. I may not be cut out for rock stardom.

SPORTY SPICE: MY BIG SCOOP

People occasionally ask me about my scoops, the big stories I published before anyone else did. Back when I was a financial journalist, my interviews with company executives, economists, and politicians frequently moved the markets. One time the stock of a company slid after I published a bearish analysis about its prospects—and then I kicked myself for not selling my shares beforehand.

I dug for those scoops, but many are spoon-fed to favored journalists by publicists or other insiders with specific agendas or axes to grind. For example, Julian Assange handpicked a select number of publications to receive first access to Wikileaks' cache of U.S. diplomatic cables, and former government contractor Edward Snowden went to Britain's *Guardian* when he wanted to expose the extent of U.S. government spying.

Celebrity journalism, although comparatively worthless, follows similar customs. A famous couple planning to divorce will arrange through their advisers for their story to be told tastefully in *People* or *Us Weekly*, depriving a seamier rag of the opportunity to break the news with a less-favorable angle. If you have a new album to promote, like Tim McGraw did in 2012, you can get yourself on the cover of *People* by claiming you had a drinking problem.

In 2010, a publicist offered me an exclusive about the "coming out" of a lesbian Christian music singer. It wasn't as if I stumbled upon the story by myself. I just did the interview and wrote up a nice story. When former Guns N' Roses guitarist Slash decided to clear out his warehouse and auction off the contents for charity, the auction house's principals allowed me to break the news after giving me a tour of the items and putting me on the phone with him. In terms of my dreaded performance evaluation, these were viewed positively as scoops—not that my good works saved me from the axe.

With a slight tinge of embarrassment, I confess that perhaps my most important scoop involved the Spice Girls, the biggest stars on the planet for a fleeting moment. My story made the front pages of the London tabloids and I was interviewed live by a U.K. breakfast TV show. All because one of the girls told me she was leaving the band.

For the record, I don't know any Spice Girls songs. And it was about a year after Spicemania started sweeping the world that I bothered trying to learn who was who. A *Rolling Stone* cover story in 1997 piqued my interest, and the extent of my analysis was to decide that "Posh Spice," now known as Victoria Beckham, was the hottest of a lukewarm bunch.

Then in 1999 "Sporty Spice" released a solo record, which I listened to because she looked buff on the cover. Sporty, née Melanie Chisholm, a.k.a. Mel C., was the one who wore tracksuit pants. It's not a sexy look, but it's the sort of low-maintenance, loose-fitting gear I'd lazily choose if I were in the band. Her record, *Northern Star,* was among my favorite releases in a solid year that also yielded great albums by Moby, Iggy Pop, and June Carter Cash. Sporty had the good sense to recruit some A-list writers and producers, including Rick Rubin and a trio of Madonna veterans. The album, not surprisingly, sounded like a younger sibling of *Ray of Light*, Madonna's last decent record. In hindsight, there were also elements of some of Robbie Robertson's atmospheric outings, thanks to collaborator Marius De Vries' work on a couple of the former Band front man's solo records.

Northern Star boasted a harder edge than the Spice Girls. Some of the songs, predictably, were strident tunes of self-empowerment directed at errant lovers. But she also touched on themes such as neediness, insecurity, her penchant for destructive relationships, and homelessness.

I first interviewed Sporty backstage at the Mayan Theatre in October 1999, just before the album came out. Her pal, Sex Pistols guitarist Steve Jones, crashed the interview to say hi, and joined her onstage a few hours later for a pretty weak version of "Anarchy in the U.K." It was a bizarre show, grown men jostling with five-year-old girls for prominent positions in front of the stage. She focused on the new material but tossed in the Spice Girls hit "Wannabe" for old times' sake.

Her record failed to chart in the United States. It also got off to a slow start internationally, but snowballed into a substantial hit. In a testament to its legs, it produced a second No. 1 single in the U.K. almost 10 months after its release. Rubin told me that his favorite Sporty song was left off the record, "I Wonder What It Would Be Like," a straight-up bubblegum tune reminiscent of the Archies. "It's really good, though," he said. (It ended up as a B-side.)

Sporty was on a hectic worldwide tour and complained to me, "I haven't got time to shit at the moment." She was spiky-haired, wearing—shock!—tracksuit pants, and attended by a coterie of young women. That combination made me (wrongly) suspect her sexual orientation. "Believe me, I'm not celibate," she said, as I pictured backstage lesbian orgies. "The truth is I've never had a serious relationship [since becoming famous]. Young, free, and single."

We moved on to politics. One or two of the Spice Girls had identified with Margaret Thatcher and her Conservative Party. Sporty was not one of them, but confessed to a general ignorance as befitted her mere quarter-decade and the rigorous distractions of the past few years.

"Everything I know about politics is just from my upbringing. I was brought up in Liverpool, a working-class background, a very anti-Thatcher household, and that's as much as I know: Tories are baddies and Labour are goodies."

While "Ginger Spice" had once described Thatcher as "the original Spice Girl" on account of her humble upbringing, Sporty was less charitable. "It's very, very difficult for me, being somebody from Liverpool, to have any respect for Margaret Thatcher whatsoever."

Seventeen months later, in March 2001, we reconnected on the phone. In that period the Spice Girls had issued a third album. Sales paled against those of the previous blockbusters. The girls did not promote it aggressively, and were not surprised by its poor showing. Sporty, in particular, had bigger fish to fry. She called me at home at the absurdly early hour of 8 a.m. while still touring the world to promote *Northern Star* and vaguely making plans to record a second album.

Among other things, we discussed her battles with depression and eating disorders, all eagerly reported in the U.K. tabloids where she was dubbed "Sumo Spice." There had also been some speculation about her sexuality—"which has always baffled me," she said. I facetiously pointed out that her buffness automatically meant that she must be Sapphically inclined.

"The way that the press has reported on my sexuality I just think it's really rude, and it's saying stereotypically what a lesbian looks like. I am quite a muscular person naturally and then I went very heavily into training and I got quite muscular then. It's just something for them to write about it, isn't it?"

My interrogations about her personal life must have worn her down, leading to the scoop of the century. After a tawdry inquiry about whether she had had a sexual relationship with some bloke who had been mentioned in the tabloids, I moved on to an innocent question about whether the Spice Girls were getting in the way as she pursued her solo career. She answered in the past tense, indicating to me that something was amiss.

"We were such a huge phenomenon and there's not really anywhere else to go with that. It was a question of sacrificing our lives and trying to maintain the success or just being honest with ourselves. We've all been very honest and we all wanted to pursue solo careers. Really I've not been comfortable being in the Spice Girls for probably the last two years. It doesn't really feel that natural to me anymore. I've grown up. I just feel that I wanna do things my own way and not compromise. We haven't split up as a band. The third album's out there, but I think we just have different priorities now."

As far as you're concerned, you're a solo artist now?
Yeah . . . I don't intend to do any more work with the Spice Girls.
Do you feel sad? It's like the end of an era?
Not really. We've all moved on. It's time for a change. Because I've been questioning doing it for a long time, I've kind of come to terms with it now. It was very hard at first. It was a very hard decision to make, but I think I'm quite comfortable with it now.
So you consider yourself officially split?
We're still linked businesswise and we're still friends, but I don't really consider myself to work as a band anymore.
So you're no longer a Spice Girl?
I'll always be a Spice Girl!

And I proceeded to deeper topics such as whether she might consider getting a boob job in order to boost her chances of American success, and whether she had considered suicide. I can't believe she didn't hang up on me. I guess we had struck up a rapport.

After the call ended, I wrote up a story headlined "Sporty Spice pulls out of the Spice Girls," and all hell broke loose within minutes of its publication on the Reuters wire as news outlets around the world called the newsroom to confirm the story and ask if we had any more information. *The Sun* held the front page and got a denial from the group's management. Someone from the paper asked me to play the relevant portion of the recorded interview over the phone, which seemed like fact-checking overkill. The local correspondent from London's *Daily Telegraph* also called me at home, worried that Sporty had made her remarks at a news conference. He was relieved when I told him that he hadn't screwed up. And then I shifted gears to speak with some Australian punk rockers.

At the end of the day it was Sporty Spice time again. I went to a TV studio to appear live on Britain's *Good Morning Television*. I was suddenly the world expert on the Spice Girls, asked to speculate about their life and times and legacy. I bluffed my way through it. The best part was applying my own makeup beforehand.

Over the next day or two I raced around Los Angeles newsstands looking for copies of the London tabloids. I couldn't find *The Sun*, which carried the news in a late edition that didn't make the flight, but the *Mirror*, the *Daily Star*, and the *Daily Express* all carried headlines on the front page, with deeper stories inside. None of them credited Reuters or me. The *Daily Express* story, a virtual word-for-word reproduction of my story, was credited to Sally Guyoncourt; the *Daily Star* story, with a bit more analysis and background, was credited to Simon Wheeler; and the *Mirror*'s Eva Simpson had the gall to attribute Sporty's comments to a press release. Worst offense was committed by the Spice Girls' publicist, Alan Edwards, who was interviewed the next day for a dubious follow-up story written by a Reuters colleague in London. He was quoted as saying, "Mel C. has not left the Spice Girls and the Spice Girls have not split up." I believe his moniker is Bullshit Spice.

Little was heard from the Spice Girls until a reunion tour in 2007. They also showed up at the closing ceremony of the 2012 Olympics, holding microphones and moving their mouths. Sporty has enjoyed the strongest solo career of the girls. Nearing 40, she has delivered six solo albums and one daughter, found Jesus, and dabbled in prostitution. Or, more accurately, she teamed up with Andrew Lloyd Webber on a British TV talent show that sought the title character for a revival of his rock opera *Jesus Christ Superstar*, and she played Mary Magdalene in the resulting U.K. arena tour.

SOME KIND OF CONSPIRACY: THE BALLAD OF ARTIMUS PYLE

Lynyrd Skynyrd drummer Artimus Pyle survived his band's fatal plane crash, braving snakes and a shotgun blast to seek help for his injured friends. But that was a relatively minor horror. Years later he was accused of child molestation and faced life in prison.

After exhausting his life savings on attorneys, he accepted a plea deal to fend off what he considered a conspiracy by Florida officials to take down any of those long-haired redneck hell-raisers from one of America's biggest rock bands. But by that time he had quit the reconfigured lineup, backstabbed at every turn by the guys who might have died if not for his heroism. Artimus was beside himself with rage when I spoke with him in 1997 for a story marking the 20th anniversary of the crash. "They're a bunch of punks," he said.

The two key targets of his venom were guitarist Gary Rossington, the band's nominal leader, and Johnny Van Zant, who stepped in as the singer after his elder brother Ronnie died in the crash. Artimus had worshiped Ronnie, the tough-as-nails front man who co-founded an early version of Lynyrd Skynyrd with high school buddies Rossington and guitarist Allen Collins in the mid-'60s. The lineup eventually solidified around a third guitarist, Ed King, bassist Leon Wilkeson, pianist Billy Powell, and drummer Bob Burns.

Ronnie didn't take shit from anyone. He may have been short of stature, but his fist always connected when a wayward member fell out of line. The only person Ronnie did not mess with was Artimus, who was the oldest person in the band and also the most worldly. The two of them bunked together and developed the closest bond among any of the bandmates. To this day Artimus' autographs always include an "R.V.Z." signoff.

Artimus' reverence did not extend to Johnny. "He's never done a thing for that band except go out there and sing the words that his brother wrote, and he gets paid real good money to do it. And he sings flat and he sings sharp. He's got no stage presence, and the guy is a puppet." And Rossington? "He acts like the leader and he walks around like Elvis and thinks everyone should get down and praise him."

I hadn't expected such a tirade when I called Artimus at his home in Florida. Rossington had told me about Artimus a few months earlier after I innocently asked why Artimus was no longer in the band. "He just has a lot of personal problems, really," Rossington said. "He was in jail. I don't even know what for. . . . He just has a lot of problems, and he didn't fit in anymore."

I researched those personal problems. Artimus was arrested in 1992, accused of sexually abusing his former girlfriend's eldest daughter. The girlfriend, Angela de Smit, had two younger daughters with Artimus. Those girls were also dragged into the mess, with consequences that last to this day. The paternity of the first daughter is unknown.

I assumed this was why he was no longer in Skynyrd. But it was much more complicated than that. Every band has intense domestic politics—creative, personal, and financial disputes amplified by drugs, alcohol, managers, attorneys, wives and girlfriends. That's an understatement when applied to the seven members of Skynyrd, who courted death and destruction at every turn while churning out unofficial national anthems like "Sweet Home Alabama" and the 15-minute-or-so guitar extravaganza "Free Bird."

Artimus—born Thomas Delmer Pyle in Kentucky in 1948—served in the U.S. Marines from 1967 to 1971, working as an aviation electronics technician. He rose to the rank of sergeant and was inevitably nicknamed "Gomer." The "Artimus" moniker came later when he was studying at a technical college. His imaginative classmates managed to draw a connection between his baby-face looks and Artemis, the Greek goddess whose diverse portfolio includes virginity.

After doing session work for Charlie Daniels, Artimus joined Lynyrd Skynyrd in 1974 when an exhausted Burns quit. By that stage, Skynyrd had released two albums and hit the top 10 with "Sweet Home Alabama." Thanks to their incessant touring and incendiary three-guitar frontal assault, the good ol' boys from the wrong side of the tracks in Jacksonville were huge rock stars. With Artimus on board, the band recorded three additional studio albums and the double live set *One More From the Road*. While Artimus was relatively clean-living—he used to take showers upside-down to restore his inner balance—the same couldn't be said for his bandmates. "Whiskey bottles, brand-new car, oak tree you're in my way," Ronnie Van Zant sang in "That Smell," a cautionary tale inspired by one of Rossington's car wrecks.

That song came from Skynyrd's last album, *Street Survivors*, which saw the band energized by a hot new guitarist from Oklahoma named Steve Gaines. The album, released on Oct. 17—three days before the plane crash—featured a cover photo of the road warriors in a lineup. Gaines is engulfed in flames. Artimus, sporting cut-off jean shorts, knee-high socks, and a blue "Vegetarian" T-shirt, looks like an overgrown schoolboy with his arms stiffly at his side. His crotch appears to be on fire.

The first leg of the *Street Survivors* tour was a four-month jaunt scheduled to end with some R&R in Hawaii. The band flew in relative style on a private plane leased for the first 11 shows. It later emerged that the 30-year-old Corvair had been deemed unsafe by the Aerosmith camp. As a qualified pilot whose father died in an air crash, Artimus was aware of the plane's shortcomings. On one flight he saw a 10-foot burst of flame shoot out from the right engine for about five minutes. Four gigs into the tour, others were becoming nervous. Several people, including backing singer Cassie Gaines, Steve's older sister, booked commercial flights to get from Greenville, SC, to Baton Rouge, where a gig was scheduled for the next day, Oct. 21. But they canceled their plans when Van Zant chose to board the Corvair. It took off about 4 p.m. local time with 24 passengers on board. Flight time was two hours, 45 minutes.

Artimus, as usual, was sitting in the cockpit, occupying a jump seat between the captain, Walter McCreary, and first officer, William J. Gray Jr., waiting to relieve either of them during a bathroom visit. As the plane began its initial descent, the right engine cut out. Walter McCreary radioed Houston Air Traffic Control advising that he was low on fuel and seeking clearance to make a landing—"posthaste please"—at McComb, MS, about 70 miles northeast of Baton Rouge. Artimus walked through the three-compartment cabin in what he called the "stewardess role" to tell everyone to extinguish their cigarettes and buckle up.

Not long after Artimus had returned to the cockpit, the left engine died. The terrified McCreary told him to take a seat in the cabin and brace for a crash. Artimus sat behind Cassie Gaines as the plane silently spiraled in from 6,000 feet at about 250 miles per hour, and brushed the tops of trees before crashing in heavily wooded terrain about 10 miles short of the airport. He watched as the left wing was torn off and the fuselage crumpled. "It sounded like a thousand people with baseball bats on the fuselage going crazy," Artimus said. Since there was no fuel—investigators recovered just one quart from both engines—there was no fire.

Artimus never lost consciousness. He kicked his way out of the wreckage, stumbled across the dead pilots, and administered basic first aid to a few people. "As a combat-trained Marine, I knew the only thing that was going to help my friends was help. I yelled for everybody to hold their wounds." And he set off, trailed by two roadies.

"First I had to navigate the swamp. A couple of snakes came up to me while I was up to my neck in the deep, black water. I looked at one of them and said, 'Look, I just survived a plane crash. If you mess with me, I'm gonna bite your head off.' It swam away.

"Then I got to a freshly plowed field, and struggled to keep my balance while navigating the narrow furrows. I had to roll over some barbed wire fences because I couldn't really jump or hold the wire. My chest was cracked, the sternum cracked from just below my throat to the top of my belly button. I was spitting up blood, not even sure whether I would drop dead at any moment. Every step of the way, all I could think about was my friends—Gary, Leon, Billy, Allen—are losin' blood.

"I could hear music coming from a field and I saw a farmhouse. I made for that light. I came in to the barnyard of the guy's farmhouse. Thinking some prisoners had escaped, he came out with a shotgun, leveled it over my head, pulled off a round, caught me in the left-shoulder padding of my jacket, spun me around. I yelled 'Plane crash!' as loud as I could, and fell to the ground. Johnnie Mote ran over to me, and said, 'Man, I'm sorry. Are you OK? Is that what that was? A plane crash?'"

Artimus staggered into the house, made a beeline for the telephone, and called his wife back home in South Carolina. He quickly told her there had been a crash, there were fatalities, but he was all right. Then he hung up.

"Then all these emergency vehicles started pulling up, and they all yelled, 'Where is this?' And Johnny Mote put me in his pickup truck and we drove through fields and fence lines with about 30 or 40 cars behind us with help for my friends. We came to the corner of the swamp in the woods where I'd come out.... The last thing I saw was hundreds of men going into the woods to rescue my friends..."

Three of the fatalities were in the forward compartment: Ronnie Van Zant, Steve Gaines, and assistant tour manager Dean Kilpatrick. Van Zant was 29. He had once confided to Artimus that he would "die in battle" and not live to see 30. "He knew his destiny," said Artimus, who believed he died from a single blow to the head, probably from an unsecured television set. As for 28-year-old Steve Gaines, "Gary Rossington could not shine Steve Gaines' shoes,"

Artimus said. "He was a beautiful person, man. The potential was there for a Lennon-McCartney of Southern rock." Indeed, Gaines wrote half the songs on *Street Survivors,* including a pair with Van Zant. Kilpatrick "lived, ate, and breathed Lynyrd Skynyrd, man, believe me."

Cassie Gaines, in the center compartment with Artimus, was crushed to death. With a degree in physical education and a stint on Broadway in the original production of *Hair,* she was "a role model for women," Artimus said. To the great anguish of the Gaines family, Billy Powell recalled years later in an episode of VH1's *Behind the Music* series that Cassie's throat was slit from ear to ear, and she expired in Artimus' arms after pleading that she didn't want to die. Total fiction. Powell withdrew the allegation at a band meeting after the episode aired and went on as if nothing had happened.

Among the survivors, Gary Rossington had been sitting opposite Steve Gaines. His arms and pelvis were broken. His right leg was severed below the knee and had to be re-attached. A steel rod inside his left forearm connects his wrist and elbow. Leon Wilkeson, at one stage in danger of having his arms amputated, ended up with a left wrist that did not bend. The neck of his bass guitar had to be turned toward the ground so that he could move his fingers along the strings. Powell's nose was almost ripped off. Allen Collins, who had been on a couch with Van Zant and Kilpatrick, suffered spinal injuries.

And Artimus? He had survivor's guilt. "Everyone for years had [credited me for] saving everyone's life that could be saved. I couldn't hear it very well, because I didn't have a chance to save everyone's life. So I felt like I had let them down."

The crash report from the National Transportation Safety Board pointed the finger at the crew for "inattention to fuel supply" as well as "inadequate flight planning." Lawsuits inevitably followed, but the fine print in the lease agreement, signed by the band's tour manager, indicated that the lessee (i.e., the band) was to be the operator and thereby have "paramount and complete responsibility for the supervision and direction of the flight crew." The plane's Texas-based owners were clearly wary of liability issues, especially with a band as notorious as Lynyrd Skynyrd. Another clause in the agreement read: "Lessee shall hold lessor harmless in any event that drugs or narcotics of any kind should be brought aboard this aircraft for any purpose."

With two members dead, and the others facing lengthy recoveries, the survivors agreed to discontinue the Lynyrd Skynyrd name. In 1979 they reunited as the Rossington-Collins Band, with Rossington's future wife Dale Krantz on vocals. Artimus was not on board. He crashed his motorbike after a drunken driver swerved in front of him and shattered his leg. To this day he is in constant pain from steel grinding against bone, and must wear a built-up boot. He formed The Artimus Pyle Band, which released two albums on MCA Records and still plays gigs.

A year after the demise of Rossington-Collins in 1982, Allen Collins—just as unimaginative as the others when it came to naming bands—formed the short-lived Allen Collins Band with Powell and Wilkeson. Collins was in bad shape. He never got over the crash and dulled the pain with drugs and alcohol. His wife died in 1980 from complications of a miscarriage. In 1986 he was paralyzed from the waist down after he drunkenly crashed his car and killed his girlfriend. As part of his plea agreement, he was occasionally wheeled out on stage to warn the kids about drunk driving. He succumbed to pneumonia in 1990, aged 37.

The Lynyrd Skynyrd name was resurrected in 1987 for a tribute tour, with Johnny Van Zant in the fold. Ed King, who had quit in 1975, replaced Collins. Artimus recorded one studio album with them before leaving in 1991, frustrated by his bandmates' addictions. He signed a big legal document after they assured him they would take care of him, and later realized he had given up all his merchandising rights. King lasted until he collapsed on tour in 1995. His heart had been weakened by a virus, and doctors said only 10 to 20 percent of the organ was working. The plan was to undergo a transplant and then rejoin the band. But that never happened, and he later sued for royalties. King finally got his transplant in 2012.

* * *

Things got really bad for Artimus, who was 45 when the molestation allegations surfaced in 1992. "All of a sudden, I'm being charged with something I didn't do, thrown in jail, and my band and everybody else turns their back on me. It cost me $500,000, everything I'd ever worked for in my life. I went through 12 bloodsucking weasel attorneys. I went before the court 60 times, was never allowed to open my mouth."

A year after the arrest, Artimus agreed to plead guilty to attempted battery and lewd and lascivious assault. He received eight years' probation. Why cop a plea if he was innocent?

"A week before I went to trial, the state prosecutor came to my attorneys and said, 'It doesn't matter whether he's innocent or guilty, we're going to take him down and make an example out of him in Jacksonville because he's from Lynyrd Skynyrd.'

"My attorneys said, 'The fix is in. You're going to jail for the rest of your life on capital sexual battery if you don't make a plea bargain. And besides, if we do go to trial, we need another $100,000.'

"I said, 'Boys, I don't have $100,000. I've given you $385,000 to date. That's all I've got.' I plea-bargained. I didn't go to trial. The fix was in. They were going to take me down, whether I was innocent or guilty. That's what they told me.

"Everyone in town plus everyone in Skynyrd knew I was innocent, yet they didn't lift a finger to help me . . . I looked to my band to stand behind me, and they're so yakked out on cocaine and alcohol they can't even talk, and they leave me to face life in prison by myself. If they'd stood up for me as a band like I stood up for them when they were dying in that plane crash, and they were bleeding to death and I walked out and saved their lives . . . They'll trade their friends in on a gram of cocaine.

"I got eight years' probation, two years of psychosexual counseling. Because the whole thing was a fleece job with their hand in my pocket, I went to three years and five months of psychosexual pervert school. I sat in a room with 18 guys that did stuff to their children. I heard stories that men on death row don't hear. . . . It twisted me, and this is the kind of stuff that I faced by myself because Gary Rossington is a punk."

Not surprisingly, the prosecutor had a different view of events. For starters, both assistant State Attorneys James Kowalski Jr. and Laura Havey-Baer claimed to be Skynyrd fans. "No one at the office, as far as I know, had any issues with Skynyrd at all, and no one on the prosecution team was asked to do anything differently because of Mr. Pyle's background," Kowalski, now a personal-injury lawyer in Jacksonville, wrote in an email in 2011.

"Prosecuting anyone of notoriety or any media-covered case puts enormous pressure on the state to get it right. I handled many high profile cases during my career at the [State Attorney's Office], and I was very aware that we had to be cautious in cases that got a lot of media attention, because of the damage we could do. . . . In sex crimes, in particular, we were always cautious in every case, because we usually had young victims and the crimes were so egregious. The worst thing imaginable for a prosecutor is to convict an innocent person, and I tried to make sure before the cases were filed and throughout the prosecution that I had more than enough evidence to convict.

"In this case, the kids were consistent in their statements, and the other evidence backed them. That being said, by the end of the case, the children had been removed, Mr. Pyle had spent a significant amount of time in jail . . . and he ended up on probation to make sure he was monitored so the opportunity would not present itself again. He had very aggressive defense counsel, who explored every option in the case." (Artimus denied the girls made any incriminating statements.)

In 1995 while Artimus was trying to get his life back on track, the ex-girlfriend hauled him into court again, this time for a child-support case that reopened all the sordid details. Angela de Smit was seeking financial aid for the couple's two daughters, who were aged 7 and 6. According to the final judgment, both girls suffered from post-traumatic stress disorder and they exhibited behavior consistent with that of sexual-abuse victims.

The judge also described as "inappropriate" Artimus' behavior when he participated in what must have been a hellish experience for all concerned, a "supervised therapeutic confrontational meeting" with the three girls and their therapist the previous year. Artimus' own expert witness, who charged him $40,000 for her services, admitted that Artimus "attempted to control the meeting, make demands off the subject, argue and defend himself, validate his own feelings instead of the children's, disregard the children's statements, blame others, and manipulate and bribe the children."

The judge ordered him to have no contact at all with the girls. But Artimus did catch a break. Under child-support guidelines, he owed $1,400 a month. But his legal troubles had wiped him out financially and he also owed about $73,000 in federal back taxes. So the judge cited "extraordinary financial difficulties" in reducing the monthly payout to $900. His current earnings were negligible, and his gross royalties from Lynyrd Skynyrd album sales were $59,000 in 1995. He really needed to get his old job back.

Sure enough, in early 1997 Rossington asked Artimus to rejoin Skynyrd for their next album, which was to be named *Twenty*. "In front of 20 witnesses, Gary came down, hugged me, kissed me right in the mouth, and said, 'Artimus, I love you, brother. I want you back in the band. Get in shape.' I said, 'Gary, I'm in shape. Whenever you're ready. Just call me.' Eight months went by and those punks never called.

"They hired some session drummer from Nashville, gave him my job that was something I worked for, and never even called me, and finished the album before I even knew what had happened. Not one of them called me. They've hurt me several times over the years, but that hurt pretty bad. Gary Rossington, Billy Powell, Leon Wilkeson, all of them have said for years that I saved their lives in the plane crash, there would be no band if it wasn't for me, they loved me, I was their brother. And then they do this to me. It hurt me very much."

Around this time, a drunken Wilkeson jammed with Artimus at a club gig, and told everyone that Lynyrd Skynyrd would not exist without Artimus. But that was the extent of his public support for

Artimus. "Billy Powell and Leon Wilkeson are both as spineless as they come," Artimus said. "I love these guys. These guys are like my brothers, but they've got the cocaine and alcohol problem."

His relationship with Rossington was even more complex. "In Hamburg, Germany, in 1976, Ronnie Van Zant got drunk on Jack Daniel's and gored the back of Gary's hands. Gary was afraid to go to a doctor in Europe to get his hands fixed, and I basically did surgery on Gary's hands and took the stitches out, and nursed him back to health because I loved the man." When I relayed Rossington's comment that Artimus had a "lot of problems," it set him off.

"It's very easy for him, because he's surrounded by a bunch of bloodsucking weasel managers and lawyers and a bunch of people that will kiss his ass and a bunch of people that will listen to his wife rant and rave like a maniac. That's his pat answer to say that I've got problems. I don't have problems. They've got problems.

"If that punk was sitting here in front of me right now, he would run the other way because he knows better. Gary and Leon and Billy and every one of them and Johnny included and whatever else scabs that they hire for that band, they all know what they've been doing.

"We live with that plane crash every single day. It's a part of our lives. It's something you don't get away from. You learn to deal with it, or you learn to jump in a bag of cocaine and jump in a bottle. And that's what they do. On any given day, you might find them straight, but most of the time. . ."

Artimus recalled that when he and the former bandmates attended the premiere of the Skynyrd concert documentary *Freebird* a year earlier in Cleveland, in 1996, he saw the band's management shake bags of coke in front of them, and herd them back into the tour bus. Artimus was left to greet the 1,500 fans standing out in the cold.

"I watch these guys go out, make money, using the name, wallowing in their false glory, going all over the world. . . . If anybody wants to see Lynyrd Skynyrd, see the movie [*Freebird*]. There's only one man that is Lynyrd Skynyrd and that is Ronnie Van Zant. I was in his band and I am proud to have been in Ronnie Van Zant's band.

He is the band. People with character and integrity like Steve Gaines and Allen Collins and Cassie Gaines and Ronnie Van Zant and Artimus Pyle, you won't find any one of them in that band now, but they're milking the name."

As of 2013 Rossington was the only member of the pre-crash lineup still in the band, meaning it was in technical violation of a 1987 consent decree that gave de facto control of the band to Ronnie's widow, Judy Van Zant. After Lynyrd Skynyrd reunited in 1987, a decade after everyone had agreed to bury the name, she sued. The consent decree declared that the band had to include Rossington and at least two of four designated members from the pre-crash era: Wilkeson, Powell, Pyle, and King. But the rule has been in abeyance since 2001 when Wilkeson died in a hotel room. He was 49, a victim of too much drinking.

I've met or interviewed Lynyrd Skynyrd on numerous occasions. Rossington introduced me to one of his daughters backstage. I even interviewed Leonard Skinner, the high school teacher whose name was co-opted for the band's name by his rebellious students. It was never a struggle to find a fresh angle, because their life is such a soap opera. After writing features tied in with the *Freebird* documentary and the 20th anniversary of the crash, I chatted with Johnny van Zant before a show in Southern California in 1999.

Not without some discomfort, as we sat in a hotel coffee shop, I relayed some of Artimus' choice comments about Johnny. He, in turn, recalled that he had begged Artimus not to quit the band. "He just had a total mental breakdown and walked away from this thing. . . . I can remember he hit his hand, me sitting there holding this guy's hand. He broke his damned hand and denied that he'd flipped out. I tried to be his friend and every damned thing, and he goes around and calls me a spoiled shit and living off my brother. You know what? Fuck him," Johnny said with a laugh. "There's no reason for him to act that way towards me. I pulled for Artimus more than anybody in this band, and for him to say one bad thing about me, I think's total bullshit." (Artimus denied the broken-hand incident happened.)

I then had the difficult task of interviewing most of the band less than a month after Wilkeson's death in 2001. They're scary-looking guys at the best of times, and I was sequestered in a bland conference room at the Universal Hilton in Los Angeles, me on one side of a big table facing Rossington, Van Zant, Powell, and post-crash guitarists Rickey Medlocke and Hughie Thomasson.

I noted that the band had to deal with four estates—Van Zant, Gaines, Collins, and now Wilkeson—further complicating their lives. But Rossington shrugged it off. "They get their money, we do our thing," he said, claiming that they had long ago made peace with Judy Van Zant and her ally Teresa Gaines Rapp, Steve's widow. "Who wants to fight, y'know?"

So, I asked, Judy allows the band to tour even though they are violating the consent decree? That was a sore subject.

"I don't think she 'allows' any damn thing," her former brother-in-law said. "If she didn't like it, we would do it anyway."

Added Powell, "We've even told her that: Go ahead and sue us."

"Judy ain't 'letting' us do shit," Rossington said. "We're playing our music like we've always done. We're playing the States like we've always done."

"The bottom line of all this," Medlocke said, "him [Rossington], Allen, and Ronnie started the band. That's the bottom line. And if this guy can't do what he wants with this band, then fuck everybody."

Powell, for good measure, summed up the Lynyrd Skynyrd ethos, an ethos that we should all try to apply to our lives (up to a point, at least), "We do what the hell we want to do."

Powell was especially shaken by Wilkeson's death. They had been friends since third grade, and managed to get kicked out of both the Cub Scouts and the Boy Scouts together. "Our motto was that we would be hoods until the day we die," he said.

Wilkeson was in bad shape, though. The plane crash, the drinking, the hepatitis B—his body just wore out on him. His wife couldn't have helped matters by getting knocked up by another man in 1996. His worried bandmates did pack him off to rehab, but Wilkeson's hard-won sobriety fell by the wayside as so-called fans and friends gravitated to his hotel room to drink and do drugs. Two weeks before he died, Wilkeson was sentenced to a year's probation for drunk driving.

"No matter how bad all his fans were Leon would still take them under his wing, and take 'em into his room and let 'em sleep on the floor—people that we wouldn't trust with five cents," Powell said. "He just loved people. He had to be surrounded by people all the time."

Added Rossington, "We're not blaming the fans, or anything. That's just the way he was. If somebody wanted to talk all night, he'd talk to 'em all night, or watch movies all night with them."

"It's kind of put a lightbulb up here a little bit," Powell added, pointing to his head. "'Man, you are 49, too.' And I've had drinking problems and I'm still not totally over it. As far as hard drugs, I'm totally over it. I just think, 'Wow! This is like a wake-up.' I don't have hepatitis B, my liver's still in real good shape, but that doesn't mean nothing. I have lost sleep over it, to tell you the truth. I've woken up in a cold sweat, man, with nightmares, with Leon talking to me."

I was supposed to interview Powell in 2003 to discuss a new Skynyrd album, but he failed to call at the scheduled time and I never got another chance. He died of a suspected heart attack in early 2009, aged 56. A melodic keyboardist in a loud rock band with three guitarists might just as well not bother showing up for work. But Powell's exquisite solos and honky-tonk stylings were never far from the action on such songs as "Working for MCA," "Free Bird," and the bluesy "Ain't No Good Life."

The only composition on which he received a songwriting credit was "Whiskey Rock-A-Roller." It appears on the band's third album *Nuthin' Fancy*, whose back cover photo showed Powell flipping the bird to the camera. Powell was aghast when he saw that picture, wondering, "Oh no! What's my granny gonna say?"

He got religion after the crash, but that did not stop him from beating up his wife in 1996 as their 13-year-old daughter watched. He was sentenced to 30 days in county jail.

Death also stalked the post-crash members of the band. Thomasson died of a heart attack in 2007, and Wilkeson's replacement succumbed to cancer in 2009, three months after Powell died.

***

Artimus is still going strong, touring with his band and sharing custody of his son with his estranged second wife. But he was back in court in August 2009, two years after being arrested for allegedly failing to register as a sex offender and lying on a driver's license application. The charges stemmed from a paperwork snafu by Florida bureaucrats. They lost the change-of-address form he had mailed them.

The publicity from the arrest reopened all the old wounds. Bookings for his band dried up, his mother died from the stress, Artimus spent his last $75,000 on attorneys, and he sold his drum kit to comedian Artie Lange for $5,000. He was offered a plea deal, but Artimus desperately wanted his day in court. He underwent a five-day jury trial in St. Augustine convinced of his innocence yet braced for the worst.

"I took the stand in my own defense," he told me in 2012. "I didn't pander to any of the jury members. I sat at military attention for five days behind my desk. I didn't turn around yahooing with the people in the peanut gallery. I didn't whisper and write frantic notes like I'm my own attorney. I looked at the judge and the prosecutors in the eye when they spoke to me. The jury came back, so emphatic. They said it so emphatically. They said, 'We find Mr. Pyle not guilty on all charges.' The jury foreman, I'll never forget it, she goes, 'So say we all.' So emphatically."

After the verdict was delivered, Artimus happily signed autographs for court staff. Among his jubilant supporters was his younger daughter Kelly. She told a newspaper that she never believed Artimus sexually assaulted her or any other child. She was immediately disowned by her mother. Artimus is not in contact with the other two girls, Kelly's sister Misty or their half-sister Shannon.

I called Artimus in 2012 because I had so many questions about his initial case. For starters, I wanted to know more about his alleged admission to therapists that he committed sexual acts "in the presence" of Kelly. Artimus explained that he and Angela had sex while Kelly—who was two at the time—slept in a crib nearby.

"Angela was very sensual," Artimus said. "She gave no regard whatsoever to children when she wanted to have sex." (De Smit married her new boyfriend in 1998. Two years later he pleaded no contest to domestic battery and she was given a permanent restraining order against him. They are still married. She did not respond to a letter seeking comment.)

"They tried to focus in on Kelly and Misty because they were two and three and four years old during that time," Artimus added. "They tried to get these little babies to say something against me. They never said anything against me. . . . [The police] initially asked me, 'Do you change your children's diapers?' And I said, 'Of course I do. I'm a good parent. You've gotta clean 'em. You've gotta splash 'em out . . . so they don't get a rash. But certainly nothing inappropriate. Only a father changing their child's diaper. What are you saying?' And they're going, 'So you admit that you did touch your children?' I said, 'Yes. I touched them. How do you change a poop diaper when the mother's nowhere to be found, and not touch them? But nothing inappropriate.'"

And if Artimus were such a monster, I wondered, why did officials let him within a hundred miles of the supposedly traumatized girls in order to convene that disastrous "supervised therapeutic confrontational meeting"? Did they ignore the girls' best interests in hopes that Artimus would explode on cue?

"They made a deal for me to go back and see the children. Who would do that with a guy that they say sexually molested the children?" Artimus said. "There were eight women in that room—guardian ad litem, victim's advocate, attorneys, and Angela. And those children, when they saw me, ran over and sat down beside me on the couch, said, 'Hi, Daddy!' They told me that I was allowed to say, 'Hello, Kelly,' 'Hello, Shannon,' and 'Hello, Misty.' Kelly heard my voice—she's three years old—and she goes, 'You are my daddy!' And a big smile came on her face. 'Where have you been?' And Shannon and Misty both chimed in and said, 'Where have you been, Daddy? . . . I can count to 10 . . . I can say my ABCs.' The children were warming up to me. All eight of these women stood up and said, 'This meeting is over!' We were five minutes into it. They saw that the children loved me and were not afraid of me, because they had no reason to be."

As for Artimus, he cannot attend events at his son's school or watch him play baseball at the local park. It's an uphill and costly battle, but he wants to get the molestation convictions overturned and get removed from the sex offender registry.

"I am going to clear my name. I'm never gonna give up. I'm gonna play drums till I'm one hundred years old. Then I'm gonna switch to stand-up comedy. I've got a lot of material."

MICHAEL NESMITH: MYSTERY MONKEE

The Monkees vied with the Beatles for my first rock 'n' roll affections, although both groups were long gone by the time I got hysterical over "I'm a Believer" and "Twist and Shout" as an eight-year-old.

That was in the mid-'70s, when former Monkee Michael Nesmith was coincidentally all over my local radio station with his easy-listening solo tune "Rio." When he released "Cruisin' (Lucy and Ramona and Sunset Sam)" three years later, my playmates and I ogled the roller-skating gals in the weird video clip, and giggled as he sang "gay." For some reason, Nesmith was big in New Zealand and Australia—where he cracked the top 10 on multiple occasions—but nowhere else. America largely ignored his solo endeavors, perhaps because of the phony stigma attached to his old made-for-TV band.

I never gave it too much thought. The Monkees were an audio experience since I didn't catch old episodes of their screwball sitcom on New Zealand's sole television channel. Great songs aside, they were also more of a gateway to other bands and songwriters, an occasional guilty piece of nostalgia.

Fast-forward to late 1994. I had been in America for two years, and the Monkees' nine albums were about to be reissued with bonus tracks by Rhino Records. The archival specialist was also working on the home-video release of their psychedelic feature film *Head* and all 58 episodes of *The Monkees* TV show. I thought it would be a great story and arranged to interview Nesmith since he seemed like the most interesting Monkee. Besides being an early practitioner of country rock, and therefore somewhat to blame for the Eagles, he helped pave the way for MTV—which might also count as a strike against him.

I had met Nesmith's former bandmate, Peter Tork, at a random music-industry luncheon a year or so earlier and we'd gotten into a heated political argument. Tork was a socialist and I wasn't. When I told Nesmith about the encounter, he recalled that they used to while away the time on set—possibly dressed as French Legionnaires? Or as matadors? Or in nightdresses?—engaging in philosophical debates about the notion of individualism, pitting avowed free-marketer Ayn Rand against Catholic theologian Thomas Aquinas.

"Peter is much more of the mind that your individualism should be dedicated to the whole of society, and I'm much more of the mind of the rugged individualist who follows his own conscience independent of the conventions of the times," Nesmith said. "Peter is at heart an academic. He's always been a standard East Coast kinda liberal upper-class college-educated person."

Tork was the first to leave the Monkees, at the end of 1968, and Nesmith followed a year later. That left Davy Jones and Micky Dolenz to carry on the name for one final album before calling it a day in 1970. The band—mostly sans Nesmith—reunited in various permutations throughout the years.

At the time of our interview, Nesmith hadn't played onstage with the Monkees since a guest appearance in 1989. He wasn't opposed to a reunion, though he didn't need the money. His mother invented Liquid Paper and sold her company to Gillette for about $47.5 million in cash (that's $134 million in 2013 money) just before she died in 1980. Nesmith was her only child.

Rather, he was busy with his own ventures. He told me how he had formed his own production company in 1974, Pacific Arts, as a vehicle for his prolific solo recordings. Besides his hour-long "video-record" *Elephant Parts*, the inaugural winner of the Grammy category for Video of the Year in 1982, Pacific Arts produced cult films such as *Tapeheads* and *Repo Men*. It also distributed home videos of popular public-television shows like *Masterpiece Theatre* and Ken Burns' *Civil War* documentary series. He told me he was working on an adaptation of *A Hitchhiker's Guide to the Galaxy* with the book's author, Douglas Adams, and was hoping to direct a film based on his own script about a woman's relationship with her dead father. Pacific Arts employed about two dozen people and enjoyed high profit margins on annual revenues of less than $10 million, he said. Nesmith planned to take it public in a couple of years.

That's what he said. In fact, his company was collapsing and he faced personal ruin. Pacific Arts suffered severe cash flow problems because of hefty start-up costs and high royalties it had promised to the Public Broadcasting Service and several major independent producers, including Burns and Children's Television Workshop. They terminated their deals with Pacific Arts in late 1993, and sued for about $5 million in unpaid royalties and fees in the hope that Nesmith would be forced to live up to a personal guarantee. But PBS had played dirty along the way. Nesmith countersued the government-subsidized broadcaster, claiming fraud and negligence. The consolidated cases went to trial in early 1999, and Nesmith took the stand to plead poverty. A jury awarded him almost $47 million, although the amount was later reduced in a confidential settlement.

For all his business worries—which somehow completely escaped me at the time—Nesmith looked completely at ease during our chat. I interrupted a romantic breakfast with his future third wife, Victoria, when I was shown into his West Los Angeles office. He was 51, bearded, and just as sophisticated and urbane as I had imagined. He was also cool enough to refer to himself by his nickname, Nez, when he paged an underling.

We talked at length initially about the Council of Ideas, a powwow of pointy-heads that he hosted every two years at his Santa Fe ranch. Beginning in 1990, Nesmith had gathered a handful of eminences to identify a thorny problem of global significance and propose some solutions. The whole thing was funded by the Gihon Foundation, which his mother set up in 1977. (As of 2013, Gihon's new focus seemed to be on producing live performances for free consumption by the public.) The *Wall Street Journal* had published a big front-page column about it a few months before we spoke, and Nesmith was relieved that the writer hadn't trivialized the council's work by focusing on his pop-star infamy.

Nesmith and his mother, a divorcée who worked as a bank secretary in Dallas while perfecting her correction fluid on the side, had been very close, speaking to each other several times a day every day, the *Journal* said. "I was very grateful for my mother," he told me. "She was a very strong and very intelligent woman. I'm an egalitarian and the notion of women being repressed is abhorrent to me, so we connected very strongly when the women's liberation movement hit in the early '70s."

As for the Monkees, he hadn't spoken about the group in many years, "not due to any reluctance on my part, but because there was nothing to talk about." But he was thrilled with the reissue program, perhaps hoping for a favorable reevaluation from critics and music fans. The Monkees got a bad rap at the time when—shock!—it emerged that they didn't play the instruments on their early records. They were actors in a TV show, after all.

"People either get it, or they don't. And if they don't get it, then they don't get it. I can't explain it to 'em. If somebody comes up and says, 'Well, the Monkees weren't a real rock 'n' roll band,' it's the same as coming up to me and telling me that Roseanne's not really a Midwestern housewife, or Tim Allen doesn't have a home improvement show. What do you say to people like that?" he asked with a laugh. "Certainly nothing to defend yourself against. You look at the poor sap and you say, 'By golly, I think you've uncovered something.' It's not exactly something that's rich with insight!"

The Monkees were conceived by producers Bert Schneider and Bob Rafelson, who envisaged a show about an American version of the Beatles. It would be zany and improvisational, inspired by *A Hard Day's Night* and the Marx Brothers. The producers placed an ad in 1965 seeking four beatnik types, and held extensive auditions and rehearsals. Manchester-born Jones, who had Broadway experience, was the first to be cast. Los Angeles native Dolenz got the gig after his status as a former child star earned him a private audition. Tork, a folkie from Washington, DC, found out about the Monkees gig from his pal Stephen Stills, with whom he had moved in the same New York music circles.

Nesmith served in the U.S. Air Force for two years before deciding to become a folk singer. At the age of 21, with teenaged wife and infant son in tow, he moved from Texas to Los Angeles. He performed under the name Michael Blessing after going through the telephone book and finding no suitable last names in the "A" section. In 1965 he wrote "Different Drum," which became Linda Ronstadt's first big hit two years later. During the Monkees casting process, the producers referred to Nesmith as "wool hat," a nod to his trademark headgear.

The foursome got along fairly well, despite their different backgrounds. "This was finding three brothers I never had," Jones once said. The show's pilot tested disastrously, and the producers recut it to show actual audition footage that established their characters. Jones was the short, cute one; Dolenz was the funny one; Tork was the dummy; and Nesmith was the droll straight man. The action revolved around fun-loving, long-haired pals who lived in a house in Malibu, and underwent madcap adventures in their quest to come up with the rent. There was a lot of sped-up action, usually set to the song the band was plugging that week.

Music impresario Don Kirshner was hired to pick the songs for each episode and compile the albums with tunes from current and future A-list composers such as Neil Sedaka, Jeff Barry, Gerry Goffin and Carole King, Barry Mann, and Cynthia Weil. The Monkees' first single, "Last Train to Clarksville," written by Tommy Boyce and

Bobby Hart, was released a month before the show premiered in the fall of 1966. It reached No. 1. They topped the album chart for 30 consecutive weeks in 1966–67 with their self-titled debut and its follow-up, *More of the Monkees*. For seven of those weeks the Monkees also ruled the singles chart with their best-known hit, the Neil Diamond–written "I'm a Believer."

Ratings for *The Monkees* were never great, but the show was almost an afterthought to the records and merchandise. The obligatory touring was accompanied by *Tiger Beat*–driven hysteria, though the kiddies' enthusiasm dimmed considerably when a relatively unknown Jimi Hendrix opened a handful of shows. Nesmith, now a respectable businessman, was cagey when I asked my standard question about rock-star hijinks. Sadly, I was unaware that both his wife and another woman were carrying his sons by early 1968.

"There was excess if you work at Denny's. There was not excess in terms of the way the Who lived," he said carefully. "When we were in England and met all the extant rock 'n' roll people at the time, no we didn't keep pace with them! . . . It is a life of Lear jets and limousines. But in terms of the debauchery that I read about from time to time, that wasn't going on around us." The adventures evidently tended to revolve around mob scenes—they were almost torn apart by crazed fans in Cincinnati once!—rather than underage groupies and massive amounts of drugs. "It was just hard work. That's what I remember about it mostly. I've had much more exotic adventures since the Monkees . . . for sure."

Behind the scenes, things weren't going too well. The Monkees hated the hastily compiled second album—not to mention the J.C. Penney fashions they were modeling on the cover—having been led to believe they would get more musical input. Studio musicians, including Glen Campbell, played on the first two albums, with the stars simply overdubbing their vocals. Sadly, the names of the performers on "I'm a Believer" have been lost to history.

Nesmith, who was allocated some of his own compositions, led a battle for control of the group's destiny. He was offended on two counts: that studio musicians were not being credited, and that everyone inferred that the Monkees did the playing. He delivered an ultimatum to Kirshner. "It's real simple," he told Kirshner. "Number one: We'll continue on. The music says 'the soundtrack' [to the TV show]. That's fine, just put the people who played on it. Number two: If you're interested in implying that we are a band, well, we could probably play as a band so we will. Or, number three: I quit. So you decide between one of those two, or I'm outta here." And then he smashed his fist into the wall for good measure.

Nesmith also called a news conference to reveal the truth. The Monkees were quickly labeled "a disgrace to the pop world." It didn't matter that everyone from Frank Sinatra to the Beach Boys and the Mamas and the Papas had recorded with studio musicians, or that Motown had never bothered crediting its musicians. The Monkees had done a great job convincing everyone that they were a real, self-contained band.

"The Monkees were confusing, in a way, to a lot of people because it was a television show about a make-believe band and just of its time. And when the first records came out, they were just simply soundtracks to that television show. Nobody thought too much about the music as anything other than the adjunct," Nesmith said.

"A mighty struggle ensued. The producers of the show took my side, which was to say you can't just continue to imply that the Monkees are anything other than a make-believe television show. We're happy to let them play, or we're happy to let the music stand on its own. But you can't go into the gray area in between. Don Kirshner just wanted . . . to pretend that he was the creator, that he put together a band called the Monkees, which of course was just madness. Not only had he not done that, there was no band called the Monkees—it was a television show.

"So Bert and Bob turned to us and said, 'Well then, just take the music over. You guys gotta go play it.'" And Kirshner was fired. (Both he and Schneider died in 2011.)

Sales for the Monkees' third album, *Headquarters*, duly plummeted. It spent one week at No. 1 in June 1967, and the next 11 weeks playing second fiddle to *Sgt. Pepper's Lonely Hearts Club Band*. But the Monkees were justly proud of it. They wrote half the songs, and played all the instruments. It was their only true group effort. The band ended the year on a strong note, with "Daydream Believer" and *Pisces, Aquarius, Capricorn and Jones Ltd.* topping the singles and album charts, respectively, throughout December.

The final original episode of *The Monkees* aired in March 1968. The following month, *The Birds, the Bees & the Monkees* ended their string of No. 1 albums, peaking at No. 3. By that stage, Schneider and Rafelson had moved on to movies with Jack Nicholson. The trio had just made *Five Easy Pieces* and were about to start work on *Easy Rider*. They teamed with the Monkees for the darkly surreal 90-minute feature *Head*, in which the boys tried to escape their prefabricated image. It flopped but is considered a cult classic today. The soundtrack album yielded the memorable Goffin/King psychedelic tune "Porpoise Song," which was resurrected years later in *Vanilla Sky* and an episode of *Mad Men*. Reduced to a threesome by 1969, the Monkees released two albums, toured North America and Mexico, and appeared on the TV variety shows of Johnny Cash and Glen Campbell. Nesmith's swan song was a December show in Salt Lake City. Three days later, he was in a Hollywood recording studio working on his own material.

"The Monkees was not really a creative forum for me, as anybody who looks at the stuff I've done since then can see," he said.

Nesmith had mixed opinions on the Monkees' output. He was fond of "Last Train to Clarksville," "Daydream Believer," and "Porpoise Song," marginally liked "I'm a Believer," and disliked both "A Little Bit Me, A Little Bit You" and "Valleri." He was proud of his own compositions, spanning "Papa Gene's Blues" in 1966 to the countrified "Listen to the Band" three years later.

When I interviewed Nesmith, he had just released his 12th solo album. *The Garden* was a multimedia project that involved listening to the seven largely instrumental tracks while reading a seven-chapter novella illustrated with seven Claude Monet paintings. It was nominated for a New Age Grammy.

Gardening was one of Nesmith's passions. His 12-acre ranch in Santa Fe was fed by a huge underground aquifer. "I have this notion that if I can turn it into Monet's garden in New Mexico, I will. I've got to do xeriscape [landscaping by minimizing water use], because all those fabulous flowers that he had [at his home in northern France] I can't grow there. That's where I spend my time, working on that. It's really coming up beautifully. I've got huge cottonwoods and willows on the property in the middle of the desert. I live in a place where nature conspires to make it work."

The Garden was a sequel of sorts to a similar 1973 album called *The Prison*. I didn't ask if he was equally passionate about the penal system. Sadly, I didn't inquire too much about his solo output at all, since the emphasis was on the Monkees reissues. I did note that while the Monkees were getting the reissue treatment a lot of his solo stuff was unavailable. He jumped out of his seat and called an executive into the office. The man confirmed that just six albums were currently in print. Nesmith then gave me his copy of *The Newer Stuff*, a compilation that was out of print at the time, and the conversation moved on.

None of Nesmith's albums—delivered in what he called "my soft Southern twang"—set the American pop charts on fire. But the early ones are touchstones in country rock, the cult genre that was more or less invented by Gram Parsons in 1967. In mid-1968, Nesmith flew to Nashville to record a handful of banjo- and fiddle-infused songs that ended up on the Monkees' albums the following year. He modestly described as "utter balderdash" suggestions that he was also a pioneer, saying plenty of more-talented musicians were fusing country and rock at that time. Maybe, but people like Neil Young, Linda Ronstadt, and Bernie Leadon weren't teen idols with six-album deals at RCA Records.

Magnetic South, the first of three albums credited to Michael Nesmith & the First National Band, peaked at a career-best No. 143 in 1970 on the strength of "Joanne," his yodeling ballad about unrequited love (No. 21 in the U.S., but No. 3 in Australia and No. 1 in New Zealand). The follow-up *Loose Salute*, also released that year, included a thrilling cover of the Patsy Cline standard "I Fall to Pieces." All the RCA albums, ending with 1973's *Pretty Much Your Standard Ranch Stash*, showcased the steel guitar of Orville "Red" Rhodes, the only other constant in the First National Band.

By the mid-'70s, when I boarded the Nesmith express, he had fulfilled his obligation to the vexed folks at RCA. Now an indie artist running his own label, he was venturing into pop and, more importantly, into videos. His promotional video for "Rio" found a warm reception when sent to foreign broadcasters, helping the dreamy travelogue reach No. 4 in both Australia and New Zealand and No. 28 in the U.K. It failed to chart in America where there were few network platforms for airing videos. So Nesmith decided to produce a music-video show for local audiences. *Popclips*—the street name for these videos—showcased diverse acts, including Queen, Devo, Alice Cooper, Carly Simon, and, ahem, himself. (Through his lawyer, Nesmith in 2013 denied a Wikipedia claim that *Popclips* was inspired by a New Zealand music-video program called *Radio with Pictures*.)

Nesmith sought to syndicate *Popclips* as a five-day-a-week, half-hour program. But his efforts went nowhere until he learned that a nascent joint venture between Warner Bros. and American Express was in the market for cheap, trailblazing cable television programming. The executives got excited when he played them the "Rio" clip and the *Popclips* pilot, and they commissioned additional episodes. They tested the clips in Columbus, OH, on the fledgling Nickelodeon kids' channel, "and the needle just went off the meter," Nesmith said. The partners decided to launch a nationwide 24-hour music channel and asked him to run it for them.

"I was at a crossroads as I'd just finished *Elephant Parts* as a longform video and wanted to stay much more in the software side of it. I didn't want to get in the business side of it. I said, 'No, I don't want to run a network or a television station, but I could consult and you could buy the idea from me.' So we worked out a deal where they bought the idea from me [for undisclosed terms] . . . and I took my money and went home."

MTV is now one of the biggest brands on the planet, but Nesmith did not consider his deal to be a modern version of selling Manhattan for $24. MTV got off to a wobbly start and encountered a lot of resistance from fuddy-dud advertisers and cable operators. Many millions of dollars were spent keeping it afloat. "I did very well on it. I was very happy with the money that I got for it at the time and I'm very happy with the money that I got for it now. . . . Would MTV have existed if I hadn't brought that to them? I doubt it. But is the MTV that you see on the air, the MTV that I brought them?" He shook his head (and no, he did not watch it).

Nesmith kept in touch with his bandmates to varying degrees. He had just sung harmonies for a Tork album, and he frequently had lunch with Dolenz. He saw Jones less than the others. "I think he wanted to be more successful than he was," Nesmith said of Jones, choosing his words very carefully, "and maybe still doesn't understand why it wasn't, that there was more to it in his mind that never was realized. The conversations that I've had with Davy have expressed his frustrations: 'This could be so much bigger . . . It could be so much better . . . We could be doing so much more with this than is actually happening.' I've always sensed a level of frustration, and of course my response is, 'It was what it was, and we've done everything we can do.'"

I went into the interview having read Dolenz's 1993 memoir, *I'm a Believer*, in which he claimed that Nesmith and Tork couldn't be "two more incompatible characters," had "always been adversarial, if not downright combative," had fought for creative control, and that Tork's departure "was probably the happiest day of Mike's life."

"Peter and I got along fine," Nesmith countered. "Either he misspoke or you misread it [I paraphrased the gist to him]. You are right in saying that Peter and I had completely different musical sensibilities. But then so did Micky and I, and so did Davy and I. We were not uniform in our musical tastes at all, but this was not the cause of battles. There was nothing to fight over. When we started playing together as a band, there was a pretty equal contribution to it.

"As a matter of fact, some of Peter's music is the music that I like the best, that the band's done. It would be a mistake to say it was an acrimonious, bitter, difficult environment. In fact it just had the normal pressures and normal vicissitudes of any other show, and the relationships were professional. The confusion, I think, comes when you think, 'Well, you guys were organically formed buddies and the pressures of success tore you apart.' We'd never laid eyes on each other until we walked on the set. It was just a professional alliance that grew up, stayed together happily and well for a couple or three years, and just dissipated."

Dolenz also wrote that his initial impressions of Nesmith hadn't really changed much over the years, and they included "somewhat insecure, and definitely a control freak."

"Well, I'm assuming that these are observations that he made during the time of the show," Nesmith responded. "I don't know whether that's an accurate assessment of the way I felt about myself. I certainly was insecure during those times. I didn't have a great deal of confidence in myself in that environment, certainly not the confidence Micky does. As a matter of fact I flew a lot by his light. His confidence was very inspiring to me during those times. So yeah, I would say I was insecure.

"I don't know about being a control freak. I'm not a control freak and I think at the time if he [Micky] would characterize me as a control freak it would probably mean wanting to get a better sense of my own destiny in that kind of environment. I did feel a little bit pushed along by the events rather than having any sense of the events coming from who I was. When you feel like that, you do feel out of control. But it doesn't mean you're feeling out of control because you're a control freak. You're feeling like you're out of control because you don't understand the logic of events, and clearly I didn't. David and Micky did. They had a great sense of it because they were pros. They knew how it worked."

I didn't want to keep Nesmith on the defense over some ancient history, and was happy to tell him that Dolenz also considered him to be funny, smart, generous, and cool.

Is it fair to say, I asked, that the Monkees were a footnote in your life?

"Well, it's fair to say my life didn't peak when I was 26," he said with a laugh. "'Footnote' is perhaps a little less than I would give it. It was a good time and it was a big time. It was the best of times and worst of times . . .I wouldn't want to go back there. I'm very happy with what I'm doing right now, which is not to say that I wouldn't enjoy going on the road with the guys and playing."

Aha. Nesmith was unable to participate in their hugely successful 1986 reunion because he was producing a movie at the time. But he did come out for the two-song encore at one show in Los Angeles. Similarly, he made a special appearance during the second half of the L.A. stop on their less-successful 1989 tour. He was open to the possibility of a full reunion, subject to scheduling and quality control. He liked what Jones and Dolenz had done in the past, touring with a backup band. "I don't think I would like to go out and just the four of us play. It was like a garage band. We were pretty earnest, but at the end of the day it was clumsy."

And he sighed when I asked if they would write and perform new material. "The four of us acting as a band is like getting . . . a great tennis star and a great golf star and a good baseball player and a good basketball player and say, 'Let's all get together and form a football team because you're all good athletes.' The logic is screwy. Maybe it'll work, but just because you're all good athletes doesn't mean you're gonna make a good football team. That's kinda the way we are. It's very hard for us to make music. We'd have to create a musical engine of some kind—find writers and find producers and players and that whole thing. There's no reason to do that."

Ignoring screwy logic, the foursome reunited in 1996 for their first album together since 1968. "That's the ultimate goal, isn't it?" Jones said at the time. "The four of us together. Nobody died in this band." They wrote and played on all the songs of their album, *Justus*. But it became the first Monkees album to fail to make the U.S. chart.

In November, with *Justus* headed straight to the bargain bins, the Monkees played an eight-song showcase at a private event for industry types and lucky fans. The gig, at the now-defunct Billboard Live club in Los Angeles, garnered little press attention. I didn't write about it because there was a company clampdown on overtime. I simply noted in my diary that there was an abundance of fine women and food. They played just two oldies, "(I'm Not Your) Steppin' Stone" and "Pleasant Valley Sunday." Nesmith, dressed as if he had come straight from an office job, sang lead on one of the new songs and retreated to the shadows for the rest of the show, perhaps more clued in to the absurdity of the whole enterprise than his bandmates were. Still, he hung around long enough for a monthlong tour of the U.K. in March 1997. The reviews were brutal. A dispirited Nesmith backed out of a proposed American leg, and barely communicated with his bandmates for 15 years. Jones was furious with Nesmith and smeared him in interviews.

Early in 2011, the sleuths at London's *Daily Mirror* tracked Nesmith to his new base in the coastal California resort town of Carmel. The report claimed that he enjoyed an anonymous existence getting discounted haircuts, a benefit sure to stop now that his cover had been blown. In February 2012 Jones died of a heart attack. He was 66. His bandmates, seemingly unaware that it was no longer 1967, said they did not want to create a media circus by attending the funeral.

Nesmith, however, set a new standard in eloquent tributes with a 242-word elegy. But it wasn't sound bite–friendly, and my former colleagues at Reuters reduced it to "David's spirit and soul live well in my heart." Hopefully this portion gives a better picture:

"While it is jarring, and sometimes seems unjust, or strange, this transition we call dying and death is a constant in the mortal experience that we know almost nothing about. I am of the mind that it is a transition and I carry with me a certainty of the continuity of existence. While I don't exactly know what happens in these times, there is an ongoing sense of life that reaches in my mind out far beyond the near horizons of mortality and into the reaches of infinity.

That David has stepped beyond my view causes me the sadness that it does many of you. I will miss him, but I won't abandon him to mortality. I will think of him as existing within the animating life that [ensures] existence. I will think of him and his family with that gentle regard in spite of all the contrary appearances on the mortal plane.

David's spirit and soul live well in my heart, among all the lovely people, who remember with me the good times, and the healing times, that were created for so many, including us.

I have fond memories. I wish him safe travels."

Jessica Nesmith told a local cable-access TV show that her father viewed Jones' death as "the end of his youth," and it paved the way for reconciliation with Tork and Dolenz. By November, the trio was on the road for Nesmith's first American tour with the Monkees since 1969. "Getting together with old friends and acquaintances can be very stimulating and fun and even inspiring to me," Nesmith told *Rolling Stone* before the 12-date trek began. "We did some good work together and I am always interested in the right time and the right place to reconnect and play."

It's a pity that it took a death to get Nesmith back on board, unless Jones was the obstacle removed?

Boomer fans—accompanied by children and grandchildren—were beside themselves as the latest incarnation of the Monkees rolled through about 30 songs and paid tribute along the way to their fallen front man. Amid generally favorable reviews, the *Los Angeles Times* said Nesmith seemed indifferent and "chagrined." But he returned for a second leg in the summer of 2013, and booked a couple of brief solo tours in his downtime. His alleged grumpiness could have been a piece of brilliant acting. He was on a TV show once.

PERMISSION CREDITS

L.A. My Kinda Place By Barry White © Seven Songs (BMI) All Rights Administered by Warner-Tamerlane Publishing Corp. All Rights Reserved.

Far-Side Banks of Jordan Words and Music by Terry Smith © 1975 (Renewed) Warner-Tamerlane Publishing Corp. All Rights Reserved.

Cop Killer Written by Ernest Cunnigan and Tracy Marrow © 1992 Polygram International Publishing, Inc. (ASCAP), Ernkneesea Music (ASCAP)/Reach Music Publishing Inc. (ASCAP) and Rhyme Syndicate Music (ASCAP). Used by Permission. All Rights Reserved.

Theme from *Shaft* Words and Music by Isaac Hayes Copyright © 1971 Irving Music, Inc. Copyright Renewed. All Rights Reserved. Used by Permission. Reprinted by Permission of Hal Leonard Corporation.

Michael Nesmith's Facebook Tribute to Davy Jones Reprinted by kind permission of Michael Nesmith.

ACKNOWLEDGMENTS AND SOURCING

Strange Days was edited by Kelly Luce (http://www.kellyluce.com) and Alison Dotson (http://www.alisondotson.com), and now makes more sense. I did overrule them on a few points and take complete responsibility for the final version. The cover photo was taken by Sonja Quintero (https://www.etsy.com/shop/squintphotography). The book was designed by Nils Davey at Binary & the Brain (http://www.binaryandthebrain.com) and Indie Designz.

I'm not a heavy reader, but four books started me on my journey: *Nowhere to Run: The Story of Soul Music*, by Gerri Hirshey; *In the Country of Country: People and Places in American Music*, by Nicholas Dawidoff; *Stories Done: Writings on the 1960s and Its Discontents* by Mikal Gilmore; and *In Conversation: Encounters with 39 Great Writers*, by Ben Naparstek.

Following is what I hope is a fairly complete list of sources for this book.

AT HOME WITH JOHNNY AND JUNE CARTER CASH
- INTERVIEWS

    John Carter Cash, Johnny Cash; June Carter Cash; Jack Clement; Chris Cornell; Kris Kristofferson; Julian Raymond; Rick Rubin;

- BOOKS

    Cash, John Carter. *Anchored in Love: The Life and Legacy of June Carter Cash*. Nashville: Thomas Nelson, 2007.

    Davis, Hank. *Anita Carter: Appalachian Angel* liner notes.

Germany: Bear Family Records, 2004.

Dawidoff, Nicholas. *In the Country of Country: People and Places in American Music*. New York: Pantheon Books, 1997.

Zwonitzer, Mark, with Charles Hirshberg. *Will You Miss Me When I'm Gone? The Carter Family & Their Legacy in American Music*. New York: Simon & Schuster, 2002.

- ARTICLES

    Brinkley, Douglas. "Bob Dylan's America." *Rolling Stone*, May 14, 2009

    McCall, Michael. "Raw Beauty: June Carter Cash Steps Out on Her Own for the First Time in 25 Years." *Nashville Scene*, May 20, 1999.

    Washburn, Jim. "Johnny Cash Speaks with Candor about Friends, Family, Pain and Pleasure in His Life." *Los Angeles Times*, August 7, 1992.

IN DEFENSE OF MIKE LOVE
- INTERVIEW

    Mike Love

- BOOKS

    Dannen, Fredric. *Hit Men*. New York: Vintage Books, 1991.

    Wilson, Brian, with Todd Gold. *Wouldn't It Be Nice: My Own Story*. New York: HarperCollins, 1991.

- ARTICLES

    Bates, James. "No Harmony in Beach Boy Suit between Cousins Love and Wilson." *Los Angeles Times*, October 4, 1994.

    Becklund, Laurie, and Chuck Philips. "Sexual Harassment Claims Confront Music Industry." *Los Angeles Times*,

November 3, 1991.

Caro, Mark. "25 Years After Brian Left, Beach Boys Still in Limbo." *Chicago Tribune*, August 9, 1992.

Morris, Chris. "Jury Rules for Love in Suit over Beach Boys Credits." *Billboard*, December 24, 1994.

Yearbook, *Rolling Stone*, 1988.

- ONLINE

    http://www.onamrecords.com

DAVID BOWIE: THE GOLDEN YEARS
- INTERVIEWS

    Carlos Alomar; David Bowie; Gail Ann Dorsey.

- ARTICLES

    "Bowie's Minders Upset Fans at Airport Welcome." *Auckland Star*, November 27, 1987.

    Deevoy, Adrian. "Boys Keep Swinging." *Q*, June 1989.

    Goodman, Dean. "A Guitarist in Fashion." *New Zealand Herald*, December 4, 1987.

    Murray, Charles Shaar. "And the Singer's Called Dave. . . ." *Q*, October 1991.

    "Savage Sues David Bowie, BMG for Breach of Contract." *Billboard*, January 13, 1996.

    "Savage Suit against David Bowie Dismissed." *Billboard*, August 2, 1997.

- ONLINE

    http://www.bowiedownunder.com;
    http://www.bowiewonderworld.com.

- **OTHER**

    David R. Jones Insurance Trust, 1980; "David Bowie—Five Years." *BBC*, 2013.

STEVE CROPPER: SOUL SIDEMAN
- **INTERVIEWS**

    Steve Cropper; Barbara Jackson; Booker T. Jones.

- **BOOKS**

    Bowman, Rob. *Soulsville USA: The Story of Stax Records*. London: Books with Attitude, 1997.

    Guralnick, Peter. *Sweet Soul Music: Rhythm and Blues and the Southern Dream of Freedom*. New York: Harper & Row, 1986.

GARTH BROOKS, CHRIS GAINES, & THE AIRHEADED REPORTER
- **INTERVIEW**

    Garth Brooks.

- **BOOK**

    Cox, Patsi Bale. *The Garth Factor: The Career behind Country's Big Boom*. New York: Center Street, 2009.

- **ARTICLES**

    "Brooks' Set as Fictitious Pop Star Due from Capitol." *Billboard*, July 31, 1999.

    "Chris Gaines Album by Garth Brooks Sells Well, but Not as Well as Earlier Efforts." *Billboard*, October 16, 1999.

- **ONLINE**

    http://www.planetgarth.com.

Acknowledgments and Sourcing | 287

GUNS N' ROSES: IN BED WITH STEVEN ADLER
- INTERVIEW

    Steven Adler.

- BOOKS

    Adler, Steven, with Lawrence J. Spagnola. *My Appetite for Destruction: Sex & Drugs & Guns N' Roses*. New York: HarperCollins, 2010.

    McKagan, Duff, with Tim Mohr. *It's So Easy ... And Other Lies*. New York: Touchstone, 2011.

    Slash, with Anthony Bozza. *Slash*. New York: HarperCollins, 2007.

ICE-T FOUGHT THE LAW
- INTERVIEW

    Ice-T.

- BOOK

    Ice-T, and Heidi Siegmund. *The Ice Opinion*. New York: St. Martin's Press, 1994.

- ARTICLES

    Goldstein, Scott "At Least 20 Wrote No-Show Tickets." *Dallas Morning News*, October 27, 2009.

    Light, Alan. "The Rolling Stone Interview." *Rolling Stone*, August 20, 1992.

    "New Zealand Police Seek to Ban Ice-T Concert." *Reuters*, July 21, 1992.

- OTHER

    http://www.therecoveringpolitician.com/contributors/jeffs/jeff-smith-sexliesandprison.

PHIL COLLINS: NO MORE MR. NICE GUY
- INTERVIEW
    Phil Collins.

- ARTICLES
    Hedegaard, Erik. "Phil Collins' Last Stand." *Rolling Stone*, November 25, 2010.

    Smith, Giles. "Why Phil Collins Never Clocks Off." *Q*, March 1990.

QUEEN: THE SHOW MUST GO ON
- INTERVIEW
    Roger Taylor.

- ARTICLE
    "You Were Wonderful, My Dears!" *Q*, June 1992.

GENE SIMMONS: KISS MY ASS
- INTERVIEWS
    Gene Simmons; Paul Stanley.

- ARTICLE
    Snow, Mat. "Who You Calling Gay?" *Q*, June 1992.

STRANGE DAYS DOG THE DOORS
- INTERVIEWS
    Ray Manzarek; John Densmore.

- ARTICLES
    Densmore, John. "Riders on the Storm." *The Nation*, July 8, 2002.

"Former Doors Drummer Wins Suit against Bandmates." *Reuters*, July 22, 2005.

Lewis, Randy. "The New Doors Documentary Offers a Primer on the Group, but Little Insight into the Band's Enduring Popularity." *Los Angeles Times*, April 9, 2010.

Nichols, Natalie. "Resurrected Doors, Seeds Find the Past Closed in Separate Shows." *Los Angeles Times*, February 10, 2003.

- ONLINE
  http://www.doors.com.

AEROSMITH: WINGS CLIPPED
- INTERVIEWS

  Tim Collins; Keith Garde; Tom Hamilton; Joey Kramer; Joe Perry; Steven Tyler; Brad Whitford.

- BOOKS

  Kramer, Joey, with William Patrick and Keith Garde. *Hit Hard: A Story of Hitting Rock Bottom at the Top*. New York: HarperCollins, 2009.

  Tyler, Steven, with David Dalton. *Does the Noise in My Head Bother You?* New York: HarperCollins, 2011.

- ARTICLES

  Edgers, Geoff. "A Classic? Dream On. Steven Tyler's Memoir Tells the Tired Story of Just Another Rock Star Behaving Badly." *Boston Globe*, May 3, 2011.

  Kalodner, John David. "Aerosmith Can't Get off the Ground and Speedwagon Stalls." *Philadelphia Inquirer*, October 7, 1975.

Morse, Steve, and Jim Sullivan. "Aerosmith Fires Longtime Manager." *Boston Globe*, August 1, 1996.

Stern, Perry. "Lust for Life." *Music Express*, 1989.

RAY CHARLES: BEST FUNERAL EVER
- INTERVIEWS

    Joe Adams; Valerie Ervin.

- BOOK

    Robinson, Jr., Ray Charles, and Mary Jane Ross. *You Don't Know Me: Reflections of My Father, Ray Charles*. New York: Crown, 2010.

- ARTICLES

    Hiltzik, Michael. "Ray Charles' Children Battle over His Legacy." *Los Angeles Times*, April 20, 2008.

    Klinger, Rafe. "Ray Charles' Brave Last Days." *Globe*, May 10, 2004.

ISAAC HAYES: BALD AND BEAUTIFUL
- INTERVIEW

    Isaac Hayes.

- BOOKS

    Bowman, Rob. *Soulsville USA: The Story of Stax Records*. London: Books with Attitude, 1997.

    O'Neil, Thomas. *The Grammys*. New York: Perigree, 1999.

INXS: FLESH AND BLOOD
- INTERVIEWS

Garry Beers; Andrew Farriss; Jon Farriss; Michael Hutchence; Kirk Pengilly.

- BOOK

    INXS, and Anthony Bozza. *Story to Story: The Official Autobiography*. New York: Atria Books, 2005.

- ARTICLES

    "Geldof's Hatred for Hutchence." *Daily Mail*, 2001.

    "Michael Hutchence Planned to Leave Paula Yates before Death, Kirk Pengilly Says." *Sydney Morning Herald*, February 24, 2014.

- ONLINE

    http://www.inxsweb.com; http://www.aria.com.au.

BILLY IDOL: INTERNET ICON
- INTERVIEW

    Billy Idol.

PUTTING THE "SEX" IN SEX PISTOLS
- INTERVIEWS

    Steve Jones; Glen Matlock.

JOHN CALE, DOUG YULE: VELVETS UNDERGROUND
- INTERVIEWS

    John Cale; Doug Yule.

- BOOK

    Reed, Lou. *Between Thought and Expression: Selected Lyrics of Lou Reed*. New York: Hyperion, 1991.

- ONLINE
    http://www.dougyule.com.

- OTHER
    The Violin Maker, a film by Greg Brotherton and Frenetic Productions.

DANCING WITH IGGY POP
- INTERVIEW
    Iggy Pop.

SPORTY SPICE: MY BIG SCOOP
- INTERVIEWS
    Melanie Chisholm; Rick Rubin.

LYNYRD SKYNYRD: THE BALLAD OF ARTIMUS PYLE
- INTERVIEWS
    Rickey Medlocke; Billy Powell; Artimus Pyle; Gary Rossington; Johnny Van Zant; Judy Van Zant.

- BOOKS
    Ballinger, Lee. *Lynyrd Skynyrd: An Oral History*. New York: Spike/Avon, 1999.

    Odom, Gene, with Frank Dorman. *Lynyrd Skynyrd: Remembering the Free Birds of Southern Rock*. New York: Broadway Books, 2002.

- ARTICLE
    St. Prior, Richard. "Jury Clears Former Lynyrd Skynyrd Drummer Artimus Pyle of Charges." *St. Augustine Record*, August 29, 2009.

MICHAEL NESMITH: MYSTERY MONKEE

- **OTHER**

  Court documents, Duval County, Florida.

- **INTERVIEW**

  Michael Nesmith.

- **BOOK**

  Dolenz, Micky, and Mark Bego. *I'm a Believer: My Life of Monkees, Music, and Madness*. New York: Hyperion, 1993.

- **ARTICLES**

  Anson, Robert Sam. "Birth of an MTV Nation." *Vanity Fair*, November 2000.

  "Burns Sues Pacific Arts for Back Royalties on Videos." *Billboard*, October 22, 1994.

  "PBS Ordered to Pay Michael Nesmith Nearly $47 Million for Broken Contract." *Billboard*, February 27, 1999.

  Wold, Robert. "PBS and Nesmith Settle Home Video Dispute—but They're Mum about Price." *Current*, July 19, 1999.

  Wood, Mikael. "The Monkees: Nothing to Believe in at the Greek Theatre." *Los Angeles Times*, November 11, 2012.

- **ONLINE**

  http://www.monkees.net;

  http://www.monkeesconcerts.com.

- **OTHER**

  "Hey Hey We're the Monkees." *Disney Channel*, 1997.

  Ken Kleinberg, Kleinberg Lange Cuddy & Klein LLP.

  Phil Matcham, Recorded Music NZ.

Sandoval, Andrew. Rhino Records' Monkees CD reissue liner notes, 1995.

Tara Thomas, Australian Recording Industry Association.

"The Blairing Out with Eric Blair Show." Interview with Jessica Nesmith, 2012.

"The Michael Nesmith Radio Special," 1980.

www.ingramcontent.com/pod-product-compliance
Lightning Source LLC
Chambersburg PA
CBHW022059090426
42743CB00008B/654